A BLUEPRINT FOR CHURCH RENEWAL

John Wesley's Relevance
in the
Twenty-First Century

Blaine Taylor

JOHN WESLEY: A BLUEPRINT FOR CHURCH RENEWAL
By Blaine Taylor

Printing and assembly by Crouse Printing, Champaign, Illinois. Special appreciation is expressed to David and Shirley Crouse, Steve Askins, Sonnie Schrock, Aimee Ward, David McDaniel, Ralph Crabtree, Ed Anderson and Nan Craig.

ISBN 0-914527-19-3

ii

TABLE OF CONTENTS

PREFACE

Is it possible for any institutional church to be faithful to the Gospel? Will the Christian church ever again be an important influence for good in the world or in American life? Its activities are no longer news for any of the media and its leadership appears to be of accidental importance in contemporary events. Christian thought appears to have less and less influence in the academic community where relatively few take the claims of Christ seriously. Indifferent to both theological claims and the institutional church, most of the world's people, including many Americans, do not accept Christianity as the major force in the decision-making areas of life.

Instead, it is commonplace, even for church members, to treat matters of faith as relevant to only a small area of life. This book is written with the conviction that the thought of John Wesley, who did renew the Christian church in the eighteenth century, is relevant today. It is written for laity and clergy who wish spiritual and ethical renewal within both church and society. It is ecumenical in scope because the Wesleyan inheritance is relevant for all churches, catholic, orthodox, and reformed.

The doctrine of the separation of church and state, originally intended to protect the government from being under the domination of the institutional church and to protect the religious liberties of individuals and groups of believers, is now used for a different purpose. In the minds of many, the areas of "real life" should be kept free from religious "prejudice." While most people would grant that religious teachings are important for personal morals and the development of individual values, more and more individuals "turn-off" any suggestion that ethical standards based on Christianity should influence matters of society, government, politics, economic justice, world peace, and life-style.

Sociologists claim that the influence of the institutional church in both the lives of its members and in the life of the wider community has been eroding for many years. Even the leaders of the institutional church lack confidence in the influence of their own church. They seem to be in the midst of an "identity crisis", both in terms of their church and themselves. For instance, in 1979 the United Methodist Church undertook the Delphi project which sought to determine the attitudes of its leaders. The General Council on Ministry reported that church leaders themselves felt that their own church was "unlikely to develop, even by the year 2000, the sense of direction and identity needed to enable it to marshal its resources and move with vigor toward fulfilling its mission in the years ahead." Further, the leadership felt that "the denomination lacked the will or the resolve to take the steps necessary to prepare itself for what it saw in the future."[1]

The erosion in influence and direction has been accompanied by a downturn in membership and participation. In 1769 for every one thousand colonialists in what was soon to become the United States there was but one Methodist. During the next one hundred years Methodism grew two thousandfold and by 1869, of every twenty Americans, one was a Methodist.[2] In 1864 President Abraham Lincoln wrote: "It may fairly be said that the Methodist Episcopal Church, not less devoted than the rest, is by its greater numbers, the most important of all."[3]

For the next eighty years after 1869 the United Methodist Church grew at a slow pace reaching its high point after a "Crusade for Christ", inaugurated in 1944, brought more than a million new members into the church. At the close of the crusade one in every fourteen Americans was a Methodist.[4]

In the middle of the 1980's, despite a major merger between the Methodist Church and the Evangelical United Brethren Church in 1968 which increased the total membership substantially, the new United Methodist Church could claim only one in twenty-three Americans as members. A good case can be made that the true "health" of the United Methodist Church is a good deal worse than these statistics indicate because the average church member during the 1940's was far more likely to center his or her life in the church and be more active in the mission of the church than is the case today.

I use the United Methodist Church as a primary example because it is the church which grew out of Wesley's activity. What applies to the United Methodist Church, however, also applies to most other major denominations.

When reminded that faithfulness to the Gospel, not church growth, is the point of church life, most people readily agree. Yet, after a while that emphasis can fall into a form of sophisticated rationalization. Can any claim be made that the institutional church has failed to grow because it has been more faithful to the gospel? Has it, in fact, demanded too much material sacrifice and spiritual discipline from its members? Has any institutional church dismissed any significant number of members on theological or ethical grounds? Is the institutional church in America losing membership in an attempt to become a remnant of God's people, formed by

Christ into a loving, caring community, sacrificing its physical growth out of faithfulness to the Gospel?

I see churches and individuals, including my church and myself, quietly laying aside spiritual disciplines to take up quite selfish concerns and causes. Those of us who are ordained ministers have talked a great deal about mission, ministry and various social concerns while maintaining for ourselves relatively affluent middle-class lives of upward mobility. There is an even greater contrast with the past when we consider the lifestyle of the average clergyperson of 1934 and compare it to that of most ordained ministers today. Few, I think, would claim that the clergy lifestyle of today is more faithful to the Gospel. An equally great fifty year contrast could be made in the lifestyle of institutional churches at the local, regional, national, and international levels. Any study made of the executives' salaries and benefits, administrative expenses, travel and entertainment expenses, standards of luxury in office and meeting places, and standards of institutional and personal sacrifice would not be apt to show improved faithfulness to the Gospel.

It may be that the failure of churches to grow reflects most clearly a lack of spiritual discipline within ourselves and in the institutions we represent. Have we been too full of our own visions and too sure of our own righteousness? Have we been overimpressed by our own wisdom and by the sounds of our own voices? Have we been afraid to admit that we share an awesome responsibility for the problems of our society? Have we in the church been preoccupied with the trivial and the insignificant?

This book is written for those who share the inevitable frustration of trying to be faithful to the Gospel amid the pressures of a secular world and an immoral society. We speak of peace and there is no peace. We feel self-righteous as we lift up the hurt souls of people, even though more millions are hurt every year. We hear of the hungry and of the economically deprived while eating banquets in luxurious hotels. We delight with our self-image as we speak of racism, agism, sexism and the other just causes which we embrace, often without much personal cost. Most of all, many of us come to our decisions according to our own opinions and not within the discipline of a community of faith.

No one expects much from the Christian church these days. For many it has become a comfortable club to which they belong. There a person can look after personal needs, expect the joys of polite society, and bask in the good feeling that comes from a few good deeds.

In a parallel time of history, when the church was weak and in retreat, John Wesley was able to furnish spiritual disciplines that refreshed and reformed both the church and the society. Reaching back into the depth of the Gospel, claiming the full inheritance of the ecumenical church, including the Patristic fathers, the Reformation, and the Catholic and Orthodox traditions, and making radical claims on individual lives and institutions, Wesley was able to accomplish revival and renewal. He did so primarily through four disciplines, which form the major sections of this book.

(1) DISCIPLINES OF SPIRITUAL FORMATION

(2) DISCIPLINES OF LAY MINISTRY

(3) DISCIPLINES OF ORDAINED MINISTRY

(4) DISCIPLINES OF THE CHRISTIAN CHURCH

These disciplines were built exclusively on faithfulness to the Gospel and resulted in both church growth and in significant works of grace, justice and love within the eighteenth century world. As the most effective practical theologian in history, Wesley was able to help people live lives of grace and service. His theology has been largely ignored in our contemporary world. This book makes the claim that his disciplines have a unique relevance for a civilization shaped by the celebration of the trivial, of the technological wonders of scientific advance, and of a general skepticism about all claims of truth and meaning.

When we mention discipline, most of us think in terms of punishment for misbehavior. In contrast, Wesley's approach was positive. He thought of discipline as that method which allowed a Christian to structure life according to the blessings and opportunities that come from Christ.

Contemporary Americans who are so in tune with the therapeutic value of diets, jogging, exercise and yoga have not yet invested similar discipline in the realm of the spirit. The root of the word "discipline" caomes from "to yoke, harness, use, set to work, and concentrate the mind." Coming from the same family as words meaning "to learn", "to train", and "to teach,"[5] discipline brings the skills that enable successful performance. Only a disciplined dancer can experience all that dancing can be. Only the disciplined musician can create fully satisfying music. Only a disciplined student can learn a foreign language. Only a disciplined Christian can receive all the spiritual strength Christ has to give.

Wesley helped an entire people to understand Jesus's words: "He that loseth (or abandoneth) his life for me . . . shall find it." Wesley knew that an uncontrolled life is an unhappy life. For him sanctification was the "path of righteousness" in which God gained control of a wayward soul. John Wesley saw discipline as that which enabled a life full of purpose and joy.

It is my prayer that this book can help the reader recapture and communicate Wesley's spirit of vitality, enthusiasm, wonder, and joy. On several theological and practical issues I believe he was wrong and is best safely ignored at those points. On other issues he stated orthodox opinions which have been much better presented by others in the history of Christian thought. However, he addresses the great questions that should be addressed by the church in every period of history. If the Gospel and the early church are relevant, Wesley is relevant.

I am very thankful and indebted for the advice and help of the following colleagues who have read the manuscript and made many suggestions: Stephen Mott, Michael Curry, Betty Sweet, George Bashore, Florence Freeman, Rossing Smith, Bob Sweet, Bruce Fisher, Sue Mauck, and Steve Clapp.

Dr. Henry Lambdin, a great spirit in United Methodism, suggested in his classes on preaching that a pastor should preach his or her first sermon in a new parish on I Corinthians 2:1-5:

> "When I came to you, brethren, I did not come proclaiming to you the testimony of God in lofty words or wisdom. For I decided to know nothing among you except Jesus Christ and Him crucified. And I was with you in weakness and in much fear and trembling; and my speech and my message were not in plausible words of wisdom, but in demonstration of the Spirit and power, that your faith might not rest in the wisdom of men but in the power of God."

It is in that spirit that this book is offered. I believe this to be a decisive moment for the Christian church in the United States, a moment that will be missed if it fails to respond to the historic disciplines of the faith. Thus, believing that John Wesley offers us a much needed perspective on the gospel, a perspective of faith and practicality for today's faithful, let us begin an adventure into one man's thought, long since past, but perhaps capable of launching us into an improved new future.

INTRODUCTION

John Wesley was interested in the simplest, most practical things in life. He was afraid of death, fearful of failure in his chosen profession, insecure, and timid as an ordained minister in the years before his Aldersgate experience, and perfectly willing to drive others to accomplish goals he had not yet attained himself. He also possessed qualities that seem inappropriate in a spiritual leader: an authoritarian style, the urge to confront others, an intense devotion to the "work ethic," and a tendency to make outrageous demands on his associates. At the same time he had a willingness to innovate, break rules, and strike off alone if such was necessary for growth in ministry and mission.

He was a militant Arminian, rejecting predestination and election, while holding that salvation was by grace through faith alone. Against Calvin he insisted on free will as the necessary corollary to conversion and the process of sanctification. In an age of bitterly partisan theology he was remarkably ecumenical, finding truth in Roman Catholic tradition, Puritan piety, Lutheran exegesis, and Anglican ecclesiology. He was amazingly eclectic, finding help from literally hundreds of different sources.

It is amazing how many different scholars have seen aspects of their own traditions in him. Roman Catholic theologians Maximin Piette and John Todd claim Wesley in the mainstream of their church while Philip Watson and Franz Hildebrand found that he had "the essential spirit" of Martin Luther. George Croft Cell even presents Wesley as an orthodox Calvinist. Mystics, Pietists, Puritans, Evangelicals, Liberals, and Fundamentalists have all seen Wesley as one of their own. This astounding range of theological interpretation came about essentially because Wesley insisted on taking his theological roots from the Bible and on modeling his societies on the experience of the early church. Since this foundation is the common inheritance shared by almost all Christians it is not surprising that many feel an identity with him. However, in great contrast to most other church leaders, both in his time and since, Wesley's searching spiritualism and faith gave birth to a rigorous, academic zeal which opened for him new understandings of the Biblical message and its implications for the world. He turned not only back to the Bible but out into the world.

How could it be that a person of such a strong will and with so many controversial opinions, would produce so much spiritual fruit? At his death he left behind more than 130,000 who called

1

themselves Methodists, a figure which within another century would grow to make his creation one of the largest denominations in Protestantism. Historians Lecky and Vulliamy claimed that, as the "most influential man of his time", he saved his country from violent revolution. In addition Wesley was a major figure in the establishment of the first charitable hospitals and public schools for the poor, relief programs for sailors, miners, the aged and the abandoned, public health clinics, orphanages, a rehabilitation program for alcoholics, and a home for unwed mothers. He helped to organize missionary activity in other nations at a time when most other Protestant churches, influenced by the distortions of Calvinistic theology, did not.

We can understand the phenomena which was John Wesley only if we take him on his own terms. His interpretation and commentary has never been definitive. Instead, Wesley enables us to address with more clarity and illumination than any other theologian the simpler questions that are closer to the human heart, the Christian life and the local church. He was a pastor and he attempted to answer pastoral questions. He had several habits that eventually became unconscious rules in all he did:

---

(1) All his work pointed first to Jesus Christ. He judged everything he and others did by a simple standard: Did the action help carry out the saving work of Jesus Christ?

(2) All his work was directly dependent on the covenant community which is the Christian Church. He looked at all acts of ministry with the single question: How do they enable the church to carry out its great commission, ministry, and mission?

(3) All his work depended upon Biblical foundations first, and then on the experience of the Christian church. He checked his disciplines by means of reason and his personal experience.

(4) All his work was founded on acts of daily devotion, corporate worship, and the study of scripture. As a witness who described God's action as he personally observed it, Wesley found that acts of redemption, reconciliation, confession, conversion, and sanctification were part of his daily experience.

(5) All his work showed him to be a deeply caring, loving person behind the ordered, methodical exterior. He was a person who reached out to everyone in human need.

Frank Baker suggests the Wesley's thinking can be summarized in a "nutshell": "Theology without experience is empty; experience without theology is blind."[1] Albert Outler described him as a "folk theologian": an eclectic who had mastered the secret of simple profundity and the common touch."[2]

Using John Wesley as its prototype, this book attempts to formulate positive proposals for church renewal. Attempts at renewal are never dependent on denominational labels, congregational size or location, or even the availability of strong leadership and financial power. Instead, as Wesley's experience demonstrates, it is more a matter of the determined faith and obedience of those who embark on the challenging journey of renewal.

Obviously any mandate for renewal implies a recovery of that Spirit the church had when it was new. The early church was a community in which the Holy Spirit shaped both message and purpose while providing power for discipleship. Each succeeding generation has subtly and often unconsciously reshaped the image of the church, making renewal the raw material of church history. With the Reformation, and again in Vatican II, an entire section of Christendom began to understand that renewal is both a continuing responsibility of the faithful and a necessary prerequisite for Christian service in each generation. For those who hope for renewal today, Wesley is a most significant figure. The condition of the secular world and the problems of the contemporary church are remarkably similar to what they were in Wesley's time. His experience, fears, and even his limitations, are relevant today.

Wesley's own mission, self-consciously conceived, was the formation of a witnessing, serving community similar to that found in the primitive church. During his lifetime, the French Revolution, the American Revolution, and the Industrial Revolution took place. A brief overview of his world shows essential similarity between it and the twentieth century:

(1) Society was in a state of social, economic, and political change. Great writers offered evidence of moral and spiritual erosion. Fielding, Swift, Lecky, Trevelyan, DeFoe, Pope, Steele, Addison, Johnson, Butler, Sterne, and Walpole gave testimony to enormous social, economic and moral change. The ethical norms which furnished roots for the previous generations were challenged and the morality of the people, especially in the more privileged classes, underwent marked erosion. The accepted economic order was under serious question. Contemporary commentators spoke of a difference in values (a gap) between the young and the old.

(2) The church as a living and vital force in the life of the community and as a power to shape the lives of its members had been losing ground for more than a century. Wesley spoke of "a lifeless, formal religion", which ignored the needs of the community in a futile effort to serve itself. Few people of intelligence had any interest in it.

(3) Many theologians of his day seemed to offer three equally unexciting alternatives: an anthropocentric rationalism which attempted to eliminate the need for revelation by falling back upon the quality of the human mind; a dogmatic Calvinism shaped by Puritan experience; and a radical skepticism which made no positive statement.

(4) Wesley's nation was the most powerful in the world, but it faced long-range, serious challenges. Already it was deeply involved in many adventures thousands of miles from the kingdom.

(5) Education was seen as the way of competitive advancement, and science was accepted as an alternative to religion. Spiritual power was seemingly unavailable and often unwanted. Wesley wrote: "God is not in all our thoughts. We leave him to manage his own affairs, to sit quietly, as we imagine, in heaven and leave us on earth to manage ours; so that we have no more of the fear of God before our eyes, than of the love of God in our hearts."[3]

(6) The period was one of prosperity and consistent progress for the privileged, while minorities of all sorts were degraded and forgotten. Over ninety percent of the people had no vote or voice in the national government. Out of a population of eight million only one hundred and sixty thousand were electors. The great cities of the poor, like Manchester or Birmingham had not a single representative in Parliament, while tiny boroughs where the nobility lived had representation.[4] The fruits of the Industrial Revolution were obvious. "The factory system was the 'new money-making, death-dealing Moloch' to whom the poor people . . . were thrown. A new moneyed class arose, imbued with a greedy materialism which swept away most if not all of the old restraints. The suffering and misery of the poorer classes, herded into the factory towns, caused them to seek temporary release in the new, cheap 'tipples,' such as rum and gin. Every sixtieth house in London was a saloon, and drunkenness became so universal throughout the whole land that the very nature of the people was changed. Crime was rampant among all classes. And, so common was murder and robbery that no one thought of stirring out of his house at night without arms."[5]

William Hogarth, a powerful etcher and painter, gave a vivid picture of the English society. "Two hundred offenses were punishable by death, and a popular pastime was that of watching public hangings and whippings."[6]

(7) All political and social institutions were under fire and all tradition suspect.

(8) It was an age of exploration and discovery.

Into such a world, intent to "redeem the time" and find new life in Christ, came John Wesley. His conviction that everything necessary for the renewal of the church had already been revealed by God was considered naive. He called the people back to the Bible and urged them to go out into the world. While others could not assimilate enough of the world into the church, Wesley set his sights on the experience and the spirit of the primitive church. His methodism tested all spiritual disciplines by immediate experience, Bible study, social action, reason, and prayer. Religion was taken out of its institutional framework and made part of life.

His was not a simplistic faith, but one grounded in the best tools of Biblical research available. He studied the early fathers, scholastic philosophy, and loved the great Catholic devotional classics of the Middle Ages. Although he did not read Luther extensively, Aldersgate was only one example of the power of the Reformation in his life. While one of a few theologians to follow Arminius, he gave Calvin a fair hearing. There was an affinity between Wesley and the Puritan divines, especially in ethics and pastoral care. His indebtedness to Richard Baxter, Jeremy Taylor, and William Law is both acknowledged and easily recognized. The outstanding scholar Martin Schmidt sees Wesley as an ecumenical theologian who belongs to the entire church. *The Cambridge Modern History*, after listing the great men of the eighteenth century, adds, "But more important than any of these in universality of influence and range of achievement were John Wesley and the religious revival to which he gave his name and his life."

In contrast to theology in the modern mood, which is usually critical, Wesley's is always "positive," made up of essentially plain statements, drawn from the Bible and from tradition, in order to serve "practically" the needs of the world parish and each individual. His theology is practical in the sense that it is pastoral. He dealt with questions that came out of ordinary experience and he concentrated on essentials. He wrote to Samuel Furley in September of 1762: "I have entirely lost my taste for controversy. I have lost my readiness in disputing . . . All I can do now . . . is not to enter into . . . controversy . . . but simply to declare my judgment, and to explain myself as clearly as I can."[7] He continued: "If I find other persons of equal sagacity with myself, of equal natural and acquired abilities, apprehend it not, I immediately suspect my own judgment; and the more so because I remember I have been many times full as sure as I am now, and yet afterwards I found myself mistaken."[8]

Wesley recognized the difference between the preacher and the professional theologian and teacher. He saw them as separate callings which, while each being dependent on the other, have different roles to play in God's service. The theologian has the responsibility of clearly expressing the fundamental groundwork and articles of faith; the pastor-preacher the responsibility of communicating that faith and applying it in the world. Wesley, while competent in the first area, was a genius in the second.[9]

As he grew older, Wesley progressively found an ever diminishing number of problems to be "theologically important."[10] His thought "ripened usually under the pressure of events." It was Jeremy Taylor who recommended that men should not "make more necessities than God made, which indeed are not many."[11] John Wesley opposed the schismatic tendencies so prevalent in his day. When he opened the "new Chapel" in City Road, London, he proclaimed, without exaggeration: "Methodism, so called, is the old religion, the religion of the Bible, the religion of the primitive Church, the religion of the Church of England."

Franz Hildebrandt claims that Wesley's role may be summarized in a single scriptural sentence, Romans 14:17: **"The Kingdom of God is not meat and drink; but righteousness, and peace, and joy in the Holy Ghost."** He continued, "The historic purpose of Methodism was a plain reduction to fundamentals, a recall of a materialist and secularized generation to the essence of scriptural Christianity, a recall of the church from her peripheral preoccupation with 'meat and drink' to the heart of the Gospel, and a new definition of the cardinal terms in the Pauline vocabulary: righteousness, and peace and joy in the Holy Ghost."[12]

Wesley found renewal because he discovered "a unique theological heritage in which faith and good works stand in their right order, in which grace and the means of grace are rightly appreciated".[13] This book is presented in an effort to help Christians of today avail themselves of Wesley's spiritual power. The Wesleyan heritage is of great value to every denomination for it is our common inheritance.

SECTION I
DISCIPLINES OF SPIRITUAL FORMATION

In the fall of 1982 I had the awesome experience of spending a month in the People's Republic of China. For a good part of the previous two years I had studied the art, culture, history, philosophy and religion of China in preparation for the trip. Our small group went to nine different cities staying in each from three to five days. Each morning at five o'clock I would jog for an hour, meditate on my experiences of the previous day, and try to absorb as much as possible of the life around me. The whole community was exploding with life early in the morning. Many people were already at work or playing games with cards or dice. All were in the streets and many stopped what they were doing to stare at the jogging American!

China is as magnificent and as mysterious as I had imagined. I learned more than my mind could hold and viewed objects of art that exposed standards of craftsmanship and creativity that I envied. The fantastic beauty of the physical landscape, the flowers, the rivers, and the mountains was much finer than photographs had indicated. Yet, the outstanding experience I had on the trip had to do more with my own ignorance than with anything I observed in China. I spoke only a few words of Chinese. This simple fact caused an overwhelming change in my life during the trip. For thirty days I was taken completely out of my natural living patterns. I didn't watch a single television show, listen to the radio, read a newspaper or a magazine, hear a record, play with a computer, or listen to a tape recorder. I went only to one movie (in Chinese) and I found that there was little night life in China for a person who did not drink. After all, if most people get up at four-thirty in the morning, they have to go to bed early at night.

I carried nine paperbacks with me. I came to the last one within six days. That book, *The Spiritual Exercises of St. Ignatious.* Slowly I became aware of how subtly my life had been trivialized. So many of the things that had occupied my time were suddenly not there. In my emptiness I discovered how much I was formed by the accidental input of my society. So many of the irreplacable hours of my life had been utterly wasted. Not only did the lost time lack "redeeming value" for me, but the experiences had been so bland that I couldn't account for the time at all. When Saint Ignatious would allude to stewardship, I was conscious of what a poor steward I had been. As a Christian minister I had been somewhat protected from the pressures of "real life." I had disciplines of study, prayer and meditation each day, and was involved in a daily round of trying to help people. At least I didn't wear a radio receiver in my ear as I jogged, go to cocktail parties or night clubs, or watch soap operas and play video games. However, my self-righteousness soon vanished as I considered how many thousands of hours I had spent playing and watching different sports and shopping for things I didn't need. It was obvious that my life was slipping through my fingers.

St. Ignatius developed his "spiritual exercises" for the purpose of clearing the self of all "inordinate attachments." This emptying of the soul was the necessary first step in his view to seeking and finding the presence of God. When Wesley advised confession as the fundamental "spiritual guide."[1] he recognized the necessity of a rhythm of salvation. For God's grace to enter there must be room cleared in the soul.[2] Confession and forgiveness are the two sides of a new beginning of what he called "sanctification," a lifetime process of spiritual formation.

My great discovery in China was of my own need for spiritual formation. Just before I left for China I had attended an "event" for clergy aimed at "spiritual formation." I came home skeptical that the new call for clerical spirituality would be yet another exercise which would drive deeper the growing gap between pastors and laypersons.

Often laity have a better opportunity to escape the secularization of the spirit for they are not "professionally" involved in spiritual formation. Ordained ministers usually approach the tools of spiritual formation asking ourselves how we can "use" them in our congregations to help others. **Our intentions are well-meaning, but as soon as we clericalize spiritual formation, we corrupt the possibility that the spirit might become alive in us, that Christ might form us as persons and mold us into the community of believers which is the church. Spiritual formation is any process which helps to open us to the forming and molding of our own spirits by Christ.** We all come to Christ in mutual nakedness, vulnerability, and sin, not according to any function we might perform. I am nervous of any spiritual discipline that radically separates clergy and laity. We need each other too much.

Wesley offered four warnings about the dangers of spiritual formation that are especially appropriate as we enter the twenty-first century:

(1) Spiritual formation in isolation can produce pathological religion. Spiritual disciplines themselves can be used as an escape both from the pressures of life and from a life of discipleship.[3]

Wesley insisted that all his followers enter corporate disciplines of spiritual formation in cells, bands, and classes to assure that spiritual formation would lead them into relationships of love and involvement instead of pathological escape.

(2) **Wesley also insisted that all people in spiritual formation work out their spiritual experience** in an ethical life of service. This is frequently not the case. Often people who feel they "have a strong sense of personal relationship with Jesus" take little or no interest in the work of Christ in the world.[4] Wesley eventually broke with the Moravians because he believed that faith without works is dead. Any attempt to form spiritual life while neglecting moral and ethical responsibility was, in his view, clearly foreign both to the Gospel and Christian experience.

(3) **Wesley believed that there must be spiritual direction by another in all attempts at spiritual formation.** Every class, band, cell and society had a spiritual director and Wesley took on that role himself at the conference level. Following the teachings of the saints of the early church and the teaching of his contemporaries such as Jeremy Taylor, Wesley believed that spiritual formation was nearly impossible without a person having a spiritual director. His disciplines provided such direction for several generations in the spirit of the Episcopal Charge Taylor gave in 1661: "Let every minister teach his people the use, practice, methods and benefits of meditation or mental prayer . . . Let every minister exhort his people to a frequent confession of their sins, and a declaration of the state of their souls; to an enquiry concerning all parts of their duty; for by preaching and catechizing and private intercourse, all the needs of souls can best be served; but by preaching alone they cannot."[5]

(4) As we will see with abundant detail later, **Wesley was very concerned that spiritual formation might lead to constant theological and dogmatic disputes.** He spent much time answering the attacks of Calvinists. And in his view his long discussions with the Moravians were needless.

Wesley had no easy suggestions of piety because, for him, spiritual formation always followed a conversion and took the form of an ongoing, never finished, process of sanctification. He did suggest, as we shall see, a good many spiritual disciplines which most of us will find very difficult. For Wesley conversion was via justification by grace through faith alone. It was not the result of a good work or a correct theology. He believed that each person is free to reject prevenient grace (the power from God which enabled sanctification). Sanctification is the process by which God enables a person to seek spiritual perfection. The word comes from the Hebrew root which means setting a person apart from ordinary secular life for a special spiritual purpose or function. It is not a constant, static state. **Individuals are always in the condition of becoming better or worse spiritually, nearer to or farther away from "perfection." Wesley believed that everyone, whether they wanted to be or not, or whether they knew it or not, was constantly being spiritually formed.** To be converted meant to intentionally accept a new direction in life by opening oneself to the power of the Holy Spirit. Once in the process of sanctification, on the road to perfection, the individual might reject the process entirely or continue in it for the rest of his or her life.

Wesley taught that this process takes place on several levels:

---

(1) Within the individual heart and soul

(2) Within the intimacy of small groups (family, cells, bands, clubs, societies, etc.)

(3) Within the community formed by Christ and called the church (including connectional conferences and corporate worship)

(4) Within the whole world created by the soverign God (the world parish, the ecumenical church, and every human being)

For Wesley spiritual formation presupposed renewal in many areas, including a wholly new view of the world. When Jon Sobrino writes that the phrase "the kingdom of God" is a "utopian symbol" which applies to three centers of life: "the heart of the human person, in societal relationships and in the cosmos at large",[6] his language and spirit are Wesleyan. Wesley also believed that "the final goal is one of universal reconciliation. People must work for that end, and the morality of specific actions depends on whether they do or do not point in that desired direction."[7] Of course, Sobrino sees both the Kingdom and theological methodology in a radically different manner from Wesley.

Wesley consistently presented disciplines of spiritual formation with both a devotional and a moral content, and with both a personal and a corporate dimension. The individual is transformed, both spiritually and morally. And, this transformation leads inevitably to fundamental change in society as well. As Jean Luis Segundo reminds us the resurrection of Christ "means that he is also present today in the midst of all societies."[8]

For Wesley, the basic resource for spiritual formation was the Bible. "God Himself has condescended to teach the way; for this very end He came from heaven. He had written it down in a book! I have it; here is knowledge enough for me. Let me be homo unius libri (a man of one book). Here I am, far from the busy ways of man. I sit down alone; only God is here. In His presence I open, I read His book; for this end, to find the way to heaven."[9]

Of course, Wesley's view of this book is quite different from that which is common today. We live in a subjective world. When we approach the Bible we bring our opinions with us: Do we agree with this passage or not? Has this any relevance for my life? We are only too willing to strain the scriptures through the filter of our own experience and our own wisdom. Unconsciously, we censor out that which we don't wish to hear or that which is not easy to understand. In an exceptionally fine book of modern Biblical scholarship, LANGUAGE, HERMENEUTIC AND THE WORD OF GOD, Robert Funk writes in the spirit, if not in the methodology of Wesley: "The word of God, like a great work of art, is not on trial. The work of art exists in its own right, to be viewed and contemplated, received or dismissed, but not reconstructed. The text, too, although shaped by human hands, stands there to be read and pondered, but not manipulated."[10]

It was also Wesley's stated intention to stand aside as much as possible to allow God to speak to his hearers through the medium of the scriptural text. His intention to live with the text until it disappeared within his own spirit was his method of spiritual formation. Just as he pointed to Christ as the test of every doctrine and as the basis for theology, Wesley believed that the Bible was the only trustworthy guide to spiritual formation because "all Scripture is God-breathed and is useful for teaching, rebuking, correcting and training in righteousness, so that the man of God may be thoroughly equipped for every good work." (2 Timothy 3:16-17)

We turn now to discuss the disciplines of spiritual formation on the three levels found in Wesley's thought:

(1) SPIRITUAL DISCIPLINES FOR INDIVIDUALS

(2) SPIRITUAL DISCIPLINES FOR SMALL GROUPS

(3) SPIRITUAL DISCIPLINES FOR CHURCHES

CHAPTER I
SPIRITUAL DISCIPLINES FOR INDIVIDUALS

In 1725, at the same time that he began his lifetime practice of frequent communion (averaging every three days), Wesley recorded, "I began to aim at, and pray for, inward holiness."[1] In a letter to William Law he describes his faith up to that time as "a speculative notional shadow, which lives in the head, not in the heart."[2] This supports the confession recorded in his JOURNAL on the voyage home from America: "I have a fair summer religion; I can talk well, nay, and believe myself, while no danger is near; but let death look me in the face, and my spirit is troubled. Nor can I say, to die is gain. . . . I show my faith by my works, by staking my all upon it. I would do so again and again a thousand times."[3]

Before his conversion experience at Aldersgate, he had used spiritual resources, especially prayer, in a vain attempt to manage the external world. After that "assurance experience" his spiritual life was radically different, no longer informed primarily by hopes concentrated on himself or by fears of either death or punishment. His spiritual struggle and eventual resolution became something of a model for those who followed him. Both Phillip Otterbein and Martin Boehm had similar spiritual experiences.[4]

From Aldersgate onward Wesley encouraged disciplines of spiritual formation.[5] After conversion he checked for changes in attitude, life-style, values, purpose and in the content of faith. He taught that:

Spiritual Disciplines Cause Changes In Attitudes

Wesley began by pointing all his followers, lay and clergy alike, back to the Bible, both Old and New Testaments, to the experience of the primitive church, the teachings of the Patristic fathers, and to the great devotional works of the Middle Ages and the Puritan period. He taught them to wait in silence: "Stand in awe, and sin not: commune with your own heart upon your bed, and be still" (Psalm 4:4). Soon the silence would be pregnant with the presence of God.

Spiritual Disciplines Cause Changes in Lifestyle

The urge to find spiritual power and inner security without any major shift in lifestyle was as prevalent in the eighteenth century as it is today. Almost everyone would like to discover spiritual disciplines which would bring them answers to their problems and a meaning in life without demanding that they give up a comfortable lifestyle.

Wesley's practice was as radical as his teaching. His spiritual teachers allowed little compromise. William Law taught self-denial as the initial ingredient of a spiritual life. Jeremy Taylor demanded that there be no holding back of self—only the dedication of all of life to God, with no reservations, could result in goodness. Thomas Kempis dealt in motivation by analyzing the obedience that was centered in the heart.[6]

It was Wesley's own ironical experience that such self-denial brought a happiness found in no other way. Life took on the excitement of challenge and every moment was creative when used in God's service. He wrote, "True religion . . . implies happiness as well as holiness." This happiness is based on a security which allows risks and adventurous living. It gives "a peace that banishes all doubt and all painful uncertainty."[7] Once a person realized that he or she was "a child of God," everything else in life was possible.

Albert Outler summarizes Wesley's own experience with a changed lifestyle. He was "convinced and consistent all his life. All his emphases on duty and discipline are auxiliary to his main concern for human happiness, (blessedness, etc.). He believed (with Aquinas, Erasmus, and Richard Lucas before him) that all our truly human aspirations are oriented toward happiness. The best end which any creature can pursue is happiness in God. The human tragedy, therefore, is that persons seek happiness (as they must) in false values that leave them unhappy, and in earthly quests that leave them frustrated if unattained or unsatisfied even when attained."[8]

The result of total commitment is acceptance and love—love of self, of God, and of others. A spiritually formed person feels needed, involved in life's crucial acts of love, secure and at peace. "The fruit of the Spirit is love, joy and peace." (Galatians 5:22) "To set the mind on the Spirit is life and peace." (Romans 8:6)

Lifestyle questions are important because they remind us that the gifts of the Spirit are given not only to effect security and happiness, but primarily to enable the recipient of those gifts to share in God's work in this world. Spirit disciplines make clear that spiritual gifts are given for the blessings they bring to life. Indeed, these gifts when discovered within the community of the church confer onto each individual believer his or her unique identity.

Spiritual disciplines empty the self so the radiant spirit of God can enter in. Once the Spirit begins forming the person, works of sacrificial, caring love are the fruits. Wesley would have joined the

13

Moravians if he could have accepted the spiritual blessings of God without the lifestyle of servanthood. He agreed with them that works were worthless to attain salvation, but insisted that they were the necessary results of the grace which made salvation possible. Gerald Craig suggests, "The Moravians had shown Wesley the true nature of saving faith. He was astonished that they seemed so blind to its necessary implications. Their Lutheran background made them recoil from anything suggestive of good works. Wesley believed that they were making the religious life a flight from responsibility."[9]

If the desire for spiritual strength is not born out of concern for God's will, and a commitment to love and serve people, that strength will die. Spiritual strength increases to the extent God is in charge of a person's life and decreases in direct proportion if the person takes charge of his or her own life. Obedience becomes the key to both happiness and spiritual strength. Individuals become spiritually formed as their lives imitate the earthly ministry of Christ.[10]

Spiritual Disciplines Cause Changes In Values

As spiritual formation takes place within an individual, his or her moral conscience is progressively developed. Wesley believed that prevenient grace restored human freedom and allowed the power to act "righteously." The "natural man" was put aside as the spiritual was formed. Wesley explicitly denied the reality of any spiritual life without the evidence of good works.

Wesley's entire plan of spiritual formation—gathering the faithful into bands, cells, societies, and conferences—grew out of his conviction that there could be no isolated, solitary Christian. Those left exclusively to their own spiritual resources would soon be too full of their own needs, their own visions, and their own desires. A person, according to Wesley, could not be formed spiritually apart from the corporate community of the church. The spiritual disciplines that one received in the church could be enhanced and expanded by private devotional disciplines. But, they could never be enhanced and expanded by private devotional disciplines alone. Spiritual formation for Wesley was not a monastic retreat of withdrawal from the pressures of the world, but the forming of an inner spiritual strength which enabled the values of love and justice to be sustained in the world. Those that chronicled the history of Wesleyan peoples traced a constant rhythm of spiritual formation and development directly resulting in a sharpening of ethical and moral values.

Spiritual Disciplines Cause Changes in Purpose
and the Content of Faith

Wesley called that process, where spiritual disciplines and disciplined ethical living came together, sanctification. That theological word describes the true purpose, or goal, of human life. Built on justification, which opens the way to conversion, sanctification is the process of spiritual formation. Wesley wrote, "Justification is not the being made actually just and righteous. This is sanctification, but, nevertheless is a distinct gift of God, and of a totally different nature. The one (justification) implies what God does for us through his Son; the other (sanctification) what he works in us by his Spirit."[11]

This work of the Spirit heals the flawed condition of humanity. Justification brings forgiveness. Sanctification as that process of formation which brings people spiritually alive, brings the assurance that God accepts the believer as a parent accepts a child. Spiritual disciplines enable the believer to live according to God's purpose and reveals the content of the Gospel faith.

Wesley taught that the spiritual discipline of prayer had transformed his life. He considered prayer as the single most important spiritual discipline for the renewal of the church. On this subject his words leap across two centuries with power and relevance. In A PLAIN ACCOUNT OF CHRISTIAN PERFECTION, he states, "Prayer especially is wanting."[12] He found that a failure to pray resulted in a "wilderness state" for "the want thereof cannot be supplied by any other ordinance whatever."[13] "Prayer is certainly the grand means of staying near to God; and all others are helpful to only so far as they are mixed with or prepare for this."[14]

Wesley regularly spent two hours daily in prayer beginning at four in the morning. John Fletcher wrote, "He thought prayer to be more his business than anything else, and I have seen him come out of his closet with a serenity of face next to shining."[15]

Wesley's first publication, in 1733, was a collection of FORMS OF PRAYER FOR EVERY DAY IN THE WEEK.[16] His JOURNAL has a page by page record of prayers, recording surprising results: "The smith had so effectually lamed one of my horses, that many told me he would never be able to travel more. I thought, 'Even this may be made a matter of prayer' and set out cheerfully. The horse instead of growing worse and worse, went better and better and . . . brought me safe to Derby."[17]

Wesley's own prayers enabled him to renew his own discipleship. This prayer for Sunday evening is instructive: "Deliver me, O God, from a slothful mind, from all lukewarmness, and all dejection of Spirit. I know these cannot but deaden my love to thee; mercifully free my heart from them, and give me a lively, zealous, active, and cheerful spirit; that I may vigorously perform whatever thou commandest, thankfully suffer whatever thou choosest for me, and be ever ardent to obey in all this thy holy love."[18]

The societies of early Methodism were built on prayer. It is possible to claim that coming together for prayer began all Methodist work: "In November, 1738," wrote Wesley, "two or three persons, who desired to flee the wrath to come, and then seven or eight more came to me in London and desired me to advise and pray with them. I said, if you will meet on Thursday night, I will help you as well as I can." This was not only the beginning "of the Methodist society" but "the beginning of prayer meetings."[19]

Class meetings escaped from being superficial because of prayer. People were able to empathize and honestly communicate in such a context. There are many examples. When Elizabeth Ritcie was appointed class leader, her friend Agnes Bulmer wrote, "She entered on her charge, impressed with its importance, and deeply sensible of her incompetency to fulfill its duties without much Divine assistance. There lay the secret of all successful class-leading. The men and women who undertook the task went from their knees to each class-meeting. Through the week they had prayed for each member daily, and they came to them fresh from the presence of God." Agnes goes on to describe "habits of reflective and consistent piety" which were coupled with "fervent zeal and charity that could expand itself beyond the circle of its own immediate interests to sympathize with others in their difficulties, cares and sorrows."[20]

In the WESLEYAN BOOK OF DISCIPLINE for 1797, Sec. 29, Article 32, is recorded the judgment that "Prayer meetings have been found exceedingly useful, therefore let us appoint them wherever we can make it convenient." Wesley's writings are filled with references to the power of prayer: "Perhaps no sin of omission more frequently occasions this than the neglect of private prayers; the want whereof cannot be supplied by any other ordinance whatever. Nothing can be more plain, than that the life of God in the soul does not continue, much less increase, unless we use all opportunities of communion with God, and pouring out our hearts before Him. If, therefore, we are negligent of this . . . that life will surely decay. And, if we long or frequently intermit them, it will gradually die away."[21]

"My dear child," he wrote in the preface of CHILDREN'S PRAYERS, "a lover of your soul has here drawn up a few prayers, in

16

order to assist you in that great duty. Be sure that you do not omit, at least morning and evening, to present yourself upon your knees before God. You have mercies to pray for, and blessings to praise God for. But take care that you do not mock God, drawing near with your lips, while your heart is far from him."[22]

He suggests that Christians begin each day with the following prayer: "Give us, O Father (for we claim nothing of right, but only of Thy free mercy), this day (for we take no thought for the morrow) our daily bread—all things needful for our souls and bodies; not only (the meat that perisheth) but the sacramental bread, and Thy grace, the food "which endureth to everlasting Life."[23]

Prayer is also a channel which allows a Christian to be effective in the area of social concerns. The practice of prayer makes one aware of need and, at the same time, brings insight and courage. Wesley's JOURNAL is filled with examples of how prayer brought renewal in individual lives and into his societies' lives. Methodists were to pray this prayer in family groups every Thursday: "We desire likewise, O God, the good of the whole world. Pity the follies of mankind; deliver them from their miseries, and forgive thou all their sins. Hear the groans of every part of the creation, that is yet 'subject to bondage,' and bring them all 'into the glorious liberty of the sons of God.' Hear the daily prayers of the Catholic church. Free her from all foul and dividing errors; let the truth as it is in Jesus prevail, and 'seek peace and ensure it.' Make thy ministers the messengers of peace, and dispose all who are called Christians to keep 'the unity of the bond of peace.' "[24]

It may seem unsophisticated to send a prayer from a spiritual leader to each local congregation to be prayed on a specific day, but what might be the result of millions of Christians praying together each day in the same way? A special prayer for each day, as fine as this example, might spiritually form a new type of lay and ordained ministry.

Early Methodists found the power for renewal in corporate worship. Wherever Wesley found trouble in a class or meeting, he looked first for a lack of sufficient prayer. "At eight the society met as usual. I could not but observe: 1. That the room was not half full which used, until very lately, to be crowded within and without. 2. That not one person who came in used any prayer at all; but every one immediately sat down, and began either talking to his neighbor or looking about to see who was there. 3. That when I began to pray there appeared a general surprise, not one offering to kneel down, and those who stood choosing the most easy, indolent posture which they conveniently could."[25]

When prayer was accented the result was the opposite. In Davyhulme "two young men, Matthew Mayer of Portwood Hall and John Morris of Manchester established a weekly prayer meeting in the village, with the immediate result that sixty persons were awakened and added to the Society in a few weeks."

Prayer became a constant and natural companion, the source of life's vitality and power. Time and again Wesley's prayers at corporate worship had more impact than his preaching. Once Dr. Wilson said to him, "My wife was so delighted with your prayer that she had been looking for it in the Prayerbook, but cannot find it. I wish you would point it out to me."

"My dear brother," Wesley responded, "that prayer came down from heaven, and I sent it up there again."[26]

Thus, the entire development of early Methodism depended on the spiritual discipline of prayer. In communion with God both society and its members found renewal. In his careful study of early Methodist people, Leslie F. Church concludes: "The development of Methodism depended finally on . . . private devotional life . . . All that was best in its ecclesiastical polity and in its social expression of the Gospel, came from their individual and corporate experience, and this was largely determined by their disciplined lives. They did not depend for their spiritual power on public services, whether held in church hours or at four o'clock in the morning. Had they not known the reality of personal communion with God, Methodism would have ceased to be—in spite of all its statesmen and its carefully developed polity."[27]

Evelyn Underhill, the fine scholar who specialized in worship, prayer, and mysticism, had a vision of ministry which was typical of the vocation shared by early Methodists, both lay and ordained ministers: "His business is to lead men out toward eternity; and how can he do this unless it is a country in which he is at home? He is required to represent the peace of God in a troubled society; but that is impossible if he has not the habit of reporting to those deeps of the spirit where His Presence dwells."[28]

For Wesley the irreplacable means of individual spiritual formation was the discipline of prayer: "You want to be justified freely from all things, through the redemption which is in Jesus Christ. It might be of use if you should read over the first volume of Sermons seriously and with prayer. Indeed, nothing will avail without prayer. Pray, whether you can or not. When you are cheerful, and when you are heavy, still pray; pray with many or with few words, or with none at all; you will surely find an answer of peace."[29]

CHAPTER 2
SPIRITUAL DISCIPLINES FOR SMALL GROUPS

In practical application of spiritual disciplines to small groups Wesley's innovations were startingly new. He did many things that very few had ever tried before:

(1) **Wesley insisted that Spiritual Formation was to be accomplished in the real world.** Previously, most people who sought to be spiritually formed withdrew from the world to go off by themselves as hermits or chose a lifetime of monastic retreat. In contrast, Wesley insisted that his spiritual children meet frequently and regularly in small groups. All were living active secular lives and their spiritual disciplines reflected their day-to-day needs and experience. In addition, they acted out the "priesthood of all believers" in their ministries to one another. Wesley believed spiritual formation must be shared or be still born. He sent people out into the world as disciples to share the fruits of their spiritual disciplines with others.

(2) **He insisted that spiritual formation was a corporate, not an individual process.** Previously, most people who sought to be spiritually formed became totally introspective, withdrawing deeply within themselves in complete silence. Most of those in monastic communities took vows of silence and were involved in a minimum of social interaction. In contrast, Wesley pushed all those who looked to him for spiritual formation into cells, bands, classes and societies which met together several times weekly. Confrontation, confession, challenge, common accountability, and the intentional focusing of concern on other persons and their needs was standard Wesleyan practice.

(3) **Wesley insisted that spiritual formation was not an end in itself, but the means of discipleship.** Previously, most people who sought to be spiritually formed were entering a process which was an end in itself. The goal was the spiritual peace and power of the individual. The motivation was personal salvation. Only the spiritual disciplines themselves (prayer, begging, crusades, etc.) sometimes involved other people. In contrast, the process of spiritual formation for Wesley was sanctification and entrance onto the path to perfection. This goal is only possible through corporate, spiritual disciplines of ethical and moral obedience. The purpose of spiritual formation was worked out in the real world in a struggle for peace

and justice and through the caring, sharing love of other human beings. This is exactly what Wesley meant by spiritual fruits. The Holy Spirit is the only power that can form the Kingdom of God.

(4) Wesley insisted that spiritual formation must be accomplished by all God's people together. Previously, most people who sought to be spiritually formed entered a world of absolute division between lay and clergy persons. To be spiritually formed was a full-time church occupation. Even those not ordained usually withdrew as brothers or sisters from the world and gave all their time to the process. In contrast, Wesley took seriously the Reformation doctrine of the priesthood of all believers, in practical terms, as no one had done in the past. His itinerant clergy (the great majority in his lifetime were lay persons according to the standards of every church then in the world) were involved primarily in common ministries with laity. The Holy Spirit made no division between clergy and lay.

(5) Wesley insisted that spiritual formation depended on a commitment to Jesus Christ alone, not on any particular dogma or doctrine. Previously, most people who sought to be spiritually formed were accepted only by those with whom they shared a fairly rigid doctrinal and dogmatic orthodoxy. In contrast, Wesley accepted a wide variety of philosophic and theological opinions as long as the individual accepted Jesus Christ as Savior and Lord and was willing to commit himself or herself radically to the service of God. "If your heart is with Christ, give me your hand."

(6) Wesley insisted that spiritual formation took place in inclusive groups. Previously, all people who sought to be formed spiritually were either alone or grouped together in narrow, homogeneous orders. Always before Wesley, it was thought that people had to be placed with those who were as much like themselves as possible, to be molded together, with all idiosyncrasies eliminated. Wesley, for the first time in recorded history, involved great numbers of heterogeneous people in groups of spiritual formation. Women, as well as men, were included in places of leadership. The poor were together with the rich, the nobility with the commoner, the old with the young, the weak with the strong, the excriminal with the aristocrat, the uneducated with the Oxford don, the black with the white, the Roman Catholic with the Moravian, the Anglican with the Calvinist. No innovation in the history of the church had more to teach God's people about spiritual formation. The Holy Spirit brings people together and never separates them from one another.

He knew that every person is too full of his or her own soul and thus needs time to listen to, and be involved in, the needs of others. **He had had the experience of being in a small group, in his own family, where he had been spiritually formed by his mother.** Since he was the fifteenth child, John Wesley was in a group from the day he was born. Susanna Wesley's stewardship made that group one of the most rigorous and effective spiritual formation experiences in history.

Early training with the disciplines of private and public prayer, worship, Bible study, Christian education, confession and forgiveness, and a shared environment of Christian love gave him his image of life and ministry. Although he made some changes, many of his basic innovations came out of this initial grouping and his mother's prevailing spirit. That group was certainly heterogeneous, including old and young, educated and uneducated, weak and strong, male and female. There were even differences in politics and theology, as the opinions of his mother and his father, Samuel, demonstrate.

Others were often included in the family group. Susanna at one time had Sunday classes and worship services for over two hundred people. All her children were involved in the life of the parish church.

As soon as they left home the Wesleys, who did not know what it was to exist in solitude, began joining and forming groups. Charles formed the holy club at Oxford which John eventually joined and dominated. This was the beginning of a long lists of cells, bands, societies, Bible study and prayer groups, clubs and conferences, all designed primarily for spiritual formation.

Two hundred years after Wesley, most churches and evangelists still have not learned the basic lessons he taught. They still give their primary attention to advance work (publicity, advertising, and an organization which, while having great sophistication in stimulating and planning for a great "event," usually leaves the community as soon as the event is over). Wesley, who gave equal attention to building a community of believers and to pastoral care, understood that evangelism must be the work of the whole church, not just of charismatic individuals. He spent a lifetime forming people into lives of spiritual growth and corporate service as he insisted that every person relate first to a society and then to the institutional church.

His model, as in all things, was from the Bible and the early church. He studied what Christ did with His disciples and what the early church did with its new members. In those days, as soon as a person was convinced of the truth of Christ they were joined together as catechumens apart from the great congregation. Here they were given spiritual instruction and advised to watch over each other. In his study of the Eastern fathers' teaching on perfection, Wesley found that they would rebuke, instruct, exhort, and pray with and for each other. He discovered that the primary purpose of these groups of catechumens was discipline. Mutual confession based on James 5:16 was a common practice. "Whosoever loves discipline loves knowledge, but he who hates reproof is stupid." (Proverbs 12:1)

Later developments were just an expansion of this basic foundation. The primary purposes of all his groups were spiritual formation and spiritual discipline. Here was the place of mutual Bible study, prayer, confession, spiritual introspection, worship, affirmation, and support. Those who were too full of themselves were forced to relate to the needs of others. Those who had fallen back into sin could confess and, after suitable penance, receive forgiveness. They could embrace and touch one another in common need. They acted out the Protestant principle of the priesthood of all, believing each brother and sister became priests for others. They corporately built their faith and spiritual lives and corporately determined (with some rather specific suggestions from Wesley) how to better act out their spiritual lives in the community and the world.

The best contemporary image to help us understand what went on in Wesley's societies is ALCOHOLICS ANONYMOUS. In a sense each of his societies were made up of "Sinner's Anonymous." Just as alcoholics have a weekly need to confess, "I am an alcoholic," and keep up that regular confession for years after they have stopped drinking—in fact, for the rest of their lives, so members of Wesleyan societies confessed, "I am a sinner!" They realized that they were apart from the grace of God and needed his love and the love of other people to survive. A corporate structure and absolute mutual interdependence was fundamental to Christianity itself. Christians realized that they could not maintain their spiritual lives without being constantly under God's grace and care and without sharing his work of love in the world.

On a Barbara Walter's special, Daniel Travanti, the star of the television program, HILL STREET BLUES, testified with great emotion, that ALCOHOLICS ANONYMOUS had saved his life. He recited before millions of people on commercial television, the twelve steps that had made such a difference for him:

(1) We admitted we were powerless over alcohol—that our lives had become unmanageable.

(2) We came to believe that a Power greater than ourselves could restore us to sanity.

(3) We made a decision to turn our will and our lives over to the care of God as we understood Him.

(4) We made a searching and fearless moral inventory of ourselves.

(5) We admitted to God, to ourselves, and to another human being the exact nature of our wrongs.

(6) We were entirely ready to have God remove all these defects of character.

(7) We humbly asked Him to remove our shortcomings.

(8) We made a list of all persons we had harmed, and became willing to make amends to them all.

(9) We made direct amends to such people wherever possible, except when to do so would injure them or others.

(10) We continued to take personal inventory and when we were wrong promptly admitted it.

(11) We sought through prayer and meditation to improve our conscious contact with God as we understood him, praying only for knowledge of His will for us and the power to carry that out.

(12) We, having had a spiritual awakening as the result of these steps, tried to carry this message to alcoholics, and to practice these principles in all our efforts.[1]

Travanti spoke of his personal commitment to these principles and of his utter dependence upon the power and grace of God to keep that commitment. He pointed out that Alcoholics Anonymous had given him resources for life. He claimed the steps had formed him as a person and involved him in helping others. As a member of Alcoholics Anaonymous one is responsible for and dependent upon others. Members can call one another at any time for aid and each member must respond when called. Travanti stated that in Alcoholics Anonymous members have unlimited liability for one another. They care so much for each other that no inconvenience or selfish need should interfere.

To understand what Wesley's societies of spiritual formation were about, project the absolute commitment which members of

Alcoholics Anonymous take upon themselves concerning alcohol to every area of life, however large or small. Once a person accepts a Christian vocation—a call from Jesus Christ—everything is under a similar mandate. Wesley made certain that everyone understood that his call had nothing to do with clergy or lay divisions. He believed that everyone had a call from Christ to a Christian vocation—the living of life according to God's will. What a person did to earn a living was irrelevant. Each person had a spiritual vocation—work to do—in his or her own life and in the world, for Christ.

Once this fact was understood, the society became the key place where a person could find all that was crucial: faith, values, moral standards, missional opportunities and responsibilities, relationships of love, a purpose in life, and communion with God.

As the societies grew, and as personal intercommunication became ever more specific, Wesley found it necessary to subdivide the members into cells, bands and classes to provide what he called the means of even "closer union."

"The chief rules of these bands, that is, little companies (as that old English word signifies) run thus, 'In order to confess our faults one to another, and pray with one another that we may be healed, we intend: (1) To meet once a week, at the least; (2) To come punctually at the hour appointed; (3) To begin with singing or prayer; (4) To speak each of us in order, freely and plainly, the true state of our soul, with the faults we have committed in thought, word or deed, and the temptations we have felt since our last meeting; and, (3) To desire some person among us (thence called a Leader) to speak his own state first, and then to ask the rest, in order, as many and as searching questions as may be, concerning their state, sins and lives.' "[2]

Soon Wesley had to go even farther and provide a more intimate cell group which he called the select society. This included separate groups for penitents and for those who were making "marked progress toward inward and outward holiness." In the 1744 Conference Minutes, Wesley wrote that these classes "consist of awakened persons. Part of those who are supposed to have remission of sins are more closely united in the bands. Those in the bands, who seem to walk in the light of God, compose the Select Societies. Those of them who have made shipwreck of the faith meet apart as penitents." Wesley laid down three rules beyond the band rules for the Select Societies: "(1) Let nothing spoken in this Society be spoken again; no, not even to the members of it; (2) Every member agrees absolutely to submit to his Minister in all indifferent things; and, (3) Every member, till we can have all things common, will bring once a week, bona fide all he can spare towards a common stock." The reference to "all things common" suggests that at this stage Wesley had the ideal of a true community of goods among those who were closest to attaining the life of the Kingdom of God.[3]

In addition, he gave these important instructions to the leaders: "In meeting classes let them diligently inquire how every soul prospers; not only how each person observes the outward rules, but also how they grow in the knowledge and love of God." It was also suggested that the classes should be made "lively and profitable to those who meet."[4] The band and class members, in addition to twice weekly meetings, met four times a year for love feasts, a tradition Wesley borrowed from the Moravians. Only those who made progress were allowed into these groups of spiritual formation and only those who remained true to their ideals maintained membership.

It is important to note at the close of this chapter some of the specific ministries of these small groups:

(1) They were the center for devotional life, Bible study, and prayer. They kept spiritual diaries (occasionally in cipher) and spent at least some time in silent meditation after Bible study. They often fasted, observed all feasts and activities of the parish church, and received the sacrament often. Prayers of intercession for the entire ministry of church, conference, and society were offered daily. They became centers for the singing of hymns and for joyful celebration in worship.

(2) They were the center of pastoral care. They listened to one another, reviewing all the pressures and tribulations of the immediate past often having been confronted with intolerance and physical danger. They shared bereavement and grief, failure and success, sickness and health, problems of sex, marriage and parenting, the agony of poverty and economic injustices and, even, in some places, political oppression.

(3) They were centers of Christian service and moral reform. Often they cared for the poor, the orphans, and the sick. They visited in prisons and worked for reform. They cared for children. They educated and helped poor scholars to the university. They created health clinics and hospitals and were the reserve from which missionaries were sent and pastors called. Although they did not attack the systemic causes of injustice and oppression within their society, they did far more than any other political or religious group of those times.

CHAPTER 3
SPIRITUAL DISCIPLINES FOR CHURCHES

Wesley formed conferences to order, inspire, and encourage his societies while he gave his lifetime loyalty to the Anglican church. However, a church was formed in the United States, based on his principles. Thus, we can speak of his spiritual disciplines for the church.

He saw the church from three perspectives:

> (1) A community called by God for spirit-building
>
> (2) A community called by God to provide love and care for one another
>
> (3) A community called by God to share Christ's mission and love by service to the world

First, Wesley saw the church as a community called by God for spirit-building. It is amazing how little time he spent at church meetings and in conferences on matters of institutional or custodial care. For the most part he made those decisions quickly by himself without feeling the need for much consultation. The time was spent primarily on spiritual questions, theological clarification, and on a prayerful evaluation of the effectiveness of their common ministry.

The very first Methodist Conference, convened in London on June 25, 1744, was called by Wesley to answer the question, "What may we reasonably believe to be God's design in raising up the preachers called Methodists?" In a sense this was his all-encompassing question every year. In the first conference a group of ten (six clergymen of the Church of England and four laypreachers) considered many possibilities. On the fourth day they recorded their agreement that they had discovered the divine purpose. It is important to note that they had not entered into a democratic process seeking a common opinion, but into a process of spiritual formation seeking the will of God. They believed Methodism had been called "to reform the nation, more particularly the church; and to spread scriptural holiness over the land."

At the famous Christmas Conference held in Baltimore exactly forty years later, at which the Methodist Episcopal Church in the United States was organized, the same question was asked and a similar answer recorded.[1] Wesley himself, many years after the fact, described the beginning: "Two young men, reading the Bible, saw they could not be saved without holiness, followed after it, and incited others to do so. In 1737 they saw holiness comes by faith. They saw likewsie, that men are justified before they are sanctified; but still holiness was their point. God thrust them out, utterly against their will, to raise a holy people."[2]

That quest for holiness left its mark on every church meeting held during Wesley's lifetime. His church conference was the place where basic spiritual questions were asked and the societies were called to account according to the content of scripture and the activity of the Holy Spirit. Questions were asked about the work of the society (church) locally, nationally, and around the world.

Also, questions were regularly asked concerning the spiritual health of those in ministry—the preachers, the assistants, the class leaders, the lay speakers, and the members of the societies. **A careful reading of the early minutes is impressive because it shows how little time was then spent on nonspiritual, nonmissional concerns or on administrative and institutional matters that now dominate most church meetings.** The church conference was the time of spiritual formation for the society, for the people of Christ, living in community together. How was it possible that so little time was spent on custodial care of the institution, on finance, and on pragmatic matters? The reasons are obvious:

(1) Those conferences dealt primarily with volunteers. There was no superstructure to maintain or full-time administrators to support. No member who led local societies, bands, cells, or groups was paid.

(2) Full-time ministers (of which there were very few if that term implies individuals who receive all of their income from funds of the church) were so dedicated that they willingly accepted a very frugal lifestyle. Their demands were so modest that each of them raised far more income for the conference than was needed to support them. This continued to be true for almost a hundred years after the beginning of the first Methodist societies.

(3) Many pastors were involved in "tent-making" ministries. Although they were called to ministry, they earned their living expenses elsewhere. Wesley himself was the classic example. Throughout his life, he always contributed more to his conferences and societies than he took from them. From the days when he supported himself with an income as an Oxford fellow through all of his

ministry, when he made, for the time, a fabulous income by means of his publications, Wesley was self-supporting.

(4) The attitude of the church conference, as displayed so clearly in the questions it asked of itself, and in those posed by the founder, was always looking outward, away from itself. It pointed either back to the health and needs of the local societies and their members, or outward to the needs of the people of the world who were hurting in pain or thirsting for the good news of the Gospel.

(5) There existed a willingness at every level to maintain the disciplines of spiritual formation. It was the spiritual discipline of these early churches and societies which fascinates us. This. discipline kept the attention of the church and its units on spiritual life and its fruits. A contemporary theologian writes, "Church discipline is to be understood in this way: The church sees to it that the power proceeding from the Word and sacrament actually becomes effective in the members of the church. It cannot simply look on, when Word and sacrament exists without evidence of the life which should proceed from them. It cannot tolerate that individuals who are members of the community drop out of the living relation to the community."[3]

Both Wesley and Asbury often expelled members for a lack of spiritual or moral discipline as their journals reflect. Wesley recorded, "Finding there had been no discipline here for some time, I determined to begin at the foundation, and settle everything. So, I first visited and regulated the classes, then restored the bands, which had been totally neglected, and then gave directions for meeting the leaders both of bands and classes."[4]

Asbury's witness is very similar. "I heard that many were offended at my shutting them out of the society meeting as they had been greatly indulged before. But this does not trouble me. While I stay, the rules must be attended to, and I cannot suffer myself to be guided by half-hearted Methodists."[5]

From the beginning Wesley was willing to let everyone have his or her say. This rule was laid down as a principle. "Question: How can we effectively provide that everyone may speak freely whatever is in his heart? Answer: By taking care to check no one, either by word or look, even though he should say what was quite wrong. Question: How shall we provide that every point may be fully and thoroughly settled? Answer: Let us beware of making haste or showing any impatience, whether of delay or of contradiction."[6]

The Church Seen As the Community Called by God
to Provide Love and Care For One Another

How is the membership of the church formed and shaped by the Holy Spirit into a community of faithful people who will love and care for one another? In Wesley's thought "Christianity is essentially a social religion, to turn it into a solitary religion is indeed to destroy it." The few essentials he demanded of his followers had little to do with "negatives" or "in bare harmlessness of any kind; not merely in externals, in doing good, or using the means of grace, in works of piety (so called) or of charity." Instead, he called for "the mind that was in Christ"; the image of God stamped upon the heart, inward righteous, attended with the peace of God and 'joy in the Holy Spirit." The only way to enter such a community is through "repentance toward God and faith in our Lord Jesus Christ."[7]

The church as a community of love is formed by Christ. Wesley understood that redemption had a "here and now" effect on the believer. It was "not only the means of our obtaining the favor of God, but of our continuing therein."[8] Redemption never comes to human life in isolation.[9] Justification, as he defined it, is "another word for pardon, is the forgiveness of all our sins; and, what is necessarily implied therein, our acceptance with God."[10]

Leslie Church in his fine series on the early Methodist people gives many examples of the quality of the community. "Wesley's . . . ideal Methodist . . . (has) a quality which we would describe as Neighborliness . . . this commandment is written in his heart . . . 'That he who loveth God, love his brother also.' And he accordingly loves his neighbor as himself . . . That a man is not personally known to him, is no bar to his love; no, nor that he is known to be such as he approves not, that he repays hatred for his goodwill. For he 'loves his enemies'; yea, and the enemies of God, 'The evil and the unthankful.' "[11]

Wesley saw his societies as vehicles of happiness: "You seem to apprehend that I believe religion to be inconsistent with cheerfulness and with a sociable, friendly temper. So far from it, that I am convinced as true religion or holiness cannot be without cheerfulness, so steady cheerfulness, on the other hand, cannot be without holiness or true religion. And I am equally convinced that true religion has nothing sour, austere, unsociable, unfriendly in it; but on the contrary, implies the most winning sweetness, the most amiable softness and gentleness. Are you for having as much cheerfulness as you can? So am I. Do you endeavor to keep alive your taste for all the truly innocent pleasures of life? So do I likewise. Do you refuse no pleasure but what is a hinderance to some greater good or has a tendency to some evil? It is my very rule; and I know no other by which a sincere, reasonable Christian can be guided."[12]

Contemporary culture often defines pleasure and goodness as opposites when in reality they are most often bound together. Wesley's followers sometimes misunderstood his teaching. His personal copy of Shakespeare's plays, fully annotated by his own hand, was destroyed after his death by one of his own preachers, so that evidence of such frivolity would never be discovered.

Community is a condition of happiness that creates an environment in which individuals are not threatened by one another. Love can never be judgmental. Community brings one close to holiness, and with holiness, humility, for the nearer one gets to holiness, the more acute the realization of how far one still has to go. Secure in status under the forgiveness of God, no member of the community needs to drag another down or strive for personal superiority. The community of the church should be the most open society in the world. Only when it loses its openness does it lose the environment of happiness.

This is what Martin Luther meant when he talked about the "bondage of the will." As people are fully free only as they are bound in the love of Christ, so they can be fully happy only in a community of love. But, ruptures in the community continually occur. Wesley was called to give pastoral care in situations of fracture: "(1) Let all the people sacredly abstain from backbiting, talebearing, evilspeaking; (2) Let all our preachers abstain from returning railing for railing, either in public or private, as well as from disputing (3) Let them preach not controversy, but plain, practical . . . religion."[13]

It was his experience that "if patience, contentedness and resignation are the properties of zeal, then murmuring, fretfulness, discontent, impatience are wholly inconsistent with it."[14] Convinced that negativism of spirit never furthered his cause and that judgmental behavior always hindered the community, Wesley believed that many of the reformers had gone far astray in their lack of love and understanding. **His strong stand against the persecution of Quakers, Roman Catholics, and free churches reflects his willingness to help all in need, irrespective of social position, religious loyalty or attitude towards him.**[15]

A judgmental attitude, the disease of Pharisees, is the mortal enemy of the Christian community. Wesley taught that Christians had no time to stand in judgment as they sought sanctification. The cancer of judgmentalism centers attention upon self and results in the disruption of spiritual progress. Well over a hundred times in his writings Wesley prescribed tolerance: "There is no station in life, nor any period of time, from the hour of our first repenting and believing the gospel, until we are made perfect in love, wherein this caution is not needful for every child of God. For occasions of judging can never be wanting; and the temptations to it are innumerable; many whereof are so artfully disguised, that we fall into the sin before we suspect any danger. And unspeakable are the mischiefs produced hereby—always to him that judges another, thus wounding his own soul, and exposing himself to the righteous judgment of God; and frequently to those who are judged."[16]

Spiritual truth is preserved and shared in the community: "The profound and progressive spiritual experience of the first Methodist was better understood and more wisely directed because it was shared. The dangers which always beset the path of the solitary mystic were avoided and mistakes corrected by the fellowship they enjoyed together." In contrast to judgmentalism, it was the quality of "yieldingness," a readiness to submit to others, to give up our own will, which, according to Wesley, built up the community.[17]

A nurturing process was developed for all ages, adults as well as children. Growing in the faith became the great responsibility of the community. Wesley not only prescribed a loving community, but also desperately needed it himself. Living without the security of warm, personal, family relationships in his adult life, without personal confidants who were equals in training and charismatic quality, Wesley had to have such a community. Here, able to find "a select company to whom I might unbosom myself on all occasions without reserve, and whom I could propose to all their brethren as a pattern of love, of holiness and good works,"[18] he was able to express his fears, hopes and anxieties.

Often the members would study a great devotional classic together. The first such group, organized by Wesley in Savannah, developed a pattern which would serve throughout his ministry. Showing Moravian influence, the meeting started with evening prayers, as found in the Book of Common Prayer. Following some singing the group turned to Law's CHRISTIAN PERFECTION and used this as a study document and as a resource to open up personal concerns. Each person spoke of his or her fears and anxieties and was subject to the comments and suggestions of the others. All were expected to take part in the introspective examination. The meetings were closed by prayers oriented to the discussion.[19]

Christian education was another responsibility of the community. Living in a day when public schools were unknown, Wesley was forced to provide his people with fundamental skills before group study was possible. He taught his followers how to read and develop the habit of reading. In consequence he spent a large portion of his long life reading, writing, editing, and selling books. He was faced with mass illiteracy. Today, there is a similar illiteracy concerning the content of the Bible, of theology, and of Christian ethics.

It is precisely this intimate experience of a loving community which is lacking in the contemporary church, in church conferences, and between church members. Renewal would follow the building of such a community.

The Church Seen As a Community Called by God to Share Christ's Mission and Love by Service to the World

Following the military analogy, Wesley gave his societies a discipline only possible within small groups as parts of a larger church. While no modern denomination could take on such spiritual discipline as a way of life without losing the majority of its members, it would be possible for a group or a society within a denomination (or denominations, as the Emmaus movement so well demonstrates) to leaven the whole body. This discipline assumed acceptance of the qualities of stewardship, mission, and social action described in detail later in this book. The essential purpose of the chkrch was to share Christ's mission and love by al action described in detail later in this book. The essential purpose of the church was to share Christ's mission and love by service to the world. Wesley said, "The world is my parish," not "The parish is my world."

An annual conference at every level of the church was an important innovation which gave a practical forum through which the mission to the world might be carried on. It evaluated the ministry of the past year and planned for future service. Wesley had each conference examine THE SPIRITUAL HEALTH of each parish and the FRUITS OF EACH MEMBER over the past year. Emphasis was put on the quality of the witness and on fidelity to the Biblical word. All else was of secondary importance. **The minutes of these early conferences show how insignificant, relatively speaking, were procedural or methodological questions.** Wesley described a local meeting in the JOURNAL. "I inquired into the state of the society. Most pompous accounts had been sent me, from time to time, of the great numbers that were added to it; so that I confidently expected to find therein six or seven hundred members. And how is the real fact? I left three hundred and ninety-four members, and I doubt if there are now three hundred and ninety-six! Let this be a warning to us all how we give in to that hateful custom of painting things beyond life. Let us make a conscience of magnifying or exaggerating anything. Let us rather speak under than above the truth. We, of all men, should be punctual in all we say, that none of our words may fall to the ground."[20]

Wesley had little to do with our contemporary custom of emphasizing ecclesiastical statistics and of self-congratulation at annual meetings. He not only thoroughly investigated the spiritual health of the church society by questions and answers at the meeting and by observation of general conditions, but also he would personally visit the members "to determine whether he ought to continue to carry names upon the lists where no fruit of righteous living was manifest." He was altogether open in declaring results that must have been disheartening. Ardent as was his devotion to the preaching of what he called Christian perfection, he admitted time and again that the results were so meager as to cause him to ask whether the preachers should cease preaching upon this theme.[21]

Wesley's rules for such conferences are especially relevant: "(1) While we are in Conference, let us have an especial care to set God always before us; (2) In the intermediate hours let us visit NONE but the sick, and spend all our time that remains in retirement; and (3) Let us then give ourselves to prayer for one another, and for the blessings of God on this our labor."[22]

The annual church conference was the practical means through which business might be considered in the immediate presence of God. Wesley created an environment of "peace and love," searching constantly for God's will through prayer and communal study of scripture. He used no political techniques and made no effort to ingratiate himself or his point of view. Nor did he soften the prophetic voice of his message or compromise his principles under threat of dissention. Not one to panic in time of crisis, Wesley openly avoided democratic procedures and militantly demanded obedience from his followers. His example reveals little about the efficiencies of church government, but much about the power of the spirit to shape the church in mission.

The itinerant ministry, when pastors were responsible for up to thirty churches and changed circuits annually, was another of Wesley's innovations. It is now largely forgotten but was of immense value, enabling service and effectiveness in mission. It prevented secular motivations from being uppermost in most preacher's minds, moving them on before they became wedded to physical comforts, the more wealthy parishioners, or any identification of self with "the success of my church." This system gave all

33

churches an opportunity to share both inspired leadership and the burden of weaker pastors. None was favored by circumstance or by location. Lay ministers were forced to take up every aspect of ministry, and did well. It became possible to serve communities who did not have located churches or mission stations. All were under continuing supervision and their work could be fairly evaluated. Personality counted for less; discipline, dedication, and sacrificial service for more.

The arguments for a located ministry were understood by Wesley for he lived in a world where all other ministries were located. And the arguments, when evaluated in the perspective of mission, were unimpressive to him. Wesley recognized that location gave great selfish advantage to the minister—but he had established a called ministry where no person was ever forced to enter or to continue in the calling. He wrote, "It is a shame for any Methodist preacher to confine himself to one place. We are debtors to tell the world. We are called to warn everyone, to exhort everyone, if by any means we may save some."[23]

Another of Wesley's great advances, an indispensable companion of an itinerant ministry, was his insistence upon the integrity and the freedom of every pulpit. Whenever a church, or a chapel, was constructed he insisted that the property be vested in the national church conference. It was not placed under the control of local trustees. The usual form among the dissenting churches would have been fatal to the general scheme of Methodism because "wherever the trustees exert the power of placing and displacing preachers, there itinerant preaching is no more. When they have found a preacher they like, then the rotation is at an end; at least until they are tired of him, and turn him out. While he stays, the bridle is in his mouth. He would dare not speak the full and the whole truth; since, if he displeases the trustees, he would be liable to lose his bread; nor would he dare expel a trustee, though ever so ungodly, from the Society. The power of the trustees is greater than any patron, or of the King himself, who could put in a preacher, but could not put him out."[24]

I have learned from my own mistakes that although Wesley's practice sounds good in theory, it often will not translate effectively into the modern world. There are many benefits to long term pastorates in society today. Real progress might be made if local churches did not pay their ordained ministers directly; but instead, supported the national or regional church which would appoint or assign ministers according to the missional needs of the local situation. Ability to pay would then become less important than missional potential and the specific needs of a local church. Strong churches would have the privilege of helping weaker ones and the weaker ones would have the leadership necessary to become strong.

A two year attempt to organize a large New England Church along the lines of the class societies of Wesley proved to be a failure. The parish was divided into over one hundred geographic sections. Groups of fifteen to twenty were formed, to meet together weekly for Bible study, prayer, and discussion of mission. Group members were chosen with care, all ages represented with a diversity of interest, style, and spiritual experience in each group. Each class elected a leader. They were trained over a six month period in the Wesleyan heritage and modern group methods. The plan was for the elected leaders of each group to become the governing board of the church. All questions of mission to come before the church were to be discussed in the classes first. The class was to initiate all plans for ministry, pastoral care, and mission. At the end of a year all but two groups had stopped regular meetings and the plans for a new Wesleyan church government never materialized. It was primarily because the plan was imposed from above before a felt spiritual need was realized and because spiritual preparation had been inadequate. The trustees and the boards had approved tce plan but the spiritual disciplines that could have reparation had been inadequate. The trustees and the boards had approved the plan but the spiritual disciplines that could have resulted in commitment had not been accomplished.

Wesley had four prophetic disciplines which few religious leaders had previously emphasized:

(1) His disciplines of spiritual formation led him to apply the doctrine of stewardship to the resources of his community, his society, and himself. This was the beginning in Christian thought of modern ethical thinking about economic justice and freedom from economic oppression.

(2) His disciplines of spiritual formation led him to challenge himself, all his followers, and his societies to take upon themselves disciplines of self-sacrifice. He connected the Reformation emphasis on justification by grace through faith with the Roman Catholic emphasis on works.

(3) His disciplines of spiritual formation led him to emphasize the essential oneness of the human family and the responsibility of all peoples for one another. To consider the world as a parish, all people equal before God, and Christians responsible for the needs

and security of non-Christians was radical thought in the eighteenth century. His tolerance and willingness to cooperate in good work and missions with other Christian and non-Christian groups were equally creative.

(4) His doctrine of sanctification which required Christians to "be fully conformed to the will of God, as recorded in His written word" meant that disciplines of spiritual formation and Christian ethics and morals would be forever united.

Ecumenical Concerns of a Spiritually Formed Community

John Wesley has been called "the ecumenical theologian" because he had little concern for what we now call denominations. It is not possible to claim, however, that he has had any great influence on the ecumenical movement. His importance for the international missionary movement, the World and National Councils of Churches, and Vatican II has been, in microcosm, somewhat similar to the influence of Christian heritage upon western civilization—always present but not very determinative or definitive in the structuring of goals, values and programs.

It is interesting that some of the best works on Wesley in this century have been written by those who are now, or were at the time, non-Methodists. Roman Catholics, Lutherans, Baptists, Presbyterians, Reformed theologians, and Anglican scholars all have had much to say about Wesley. All of them see the essentials of their own heritage in his thought and all pronounce him an ecumenical figure of the first order.

The Belgian, Franciscan priest, Dr. Maximin Piette, in his extensive study interprets Wesley as a reactionary, Catholic force in the face of the continental reformation. Wesley's conception of the corporate life, emphasis on the sacraments, return to the patristic church, acceptance of order and discipline are presented as continuations of Roman Catholic influence. More recently, Father John Todd places Wesley in the Catholic mainstream. Writing within the Methodist movement, Dr. J. Ernest Rattenbury shares this judgment, "In some ways the Protestant Reformation in its natural protest against the ecclesiastical abuses of the sixteenth century may have gone too far in the direction of individualism, and a Wesley was needed to restore the balance. His religious method, inside and outside of Methodism, has shaped modern Protestantism more definitely than any other thing."[25]

Ironically, the former Lutheran, Franz Hildebrant, finds Wesley in the Lutheran tradition and Wesley's thought to include the essence of the Reformation. Hildebrandt and his students present him as a leading force and full participant in the current revival of Reformation studies.

Wesley, rooted in Biblical and patristic thought, exalted a theology which was naturally both Catholic and Reformed. He was willing to give up the identity of his societies to form a more inclusive spiritual community. Openly associating himself with tolerance in an age of persecution, Wesley wrote, "With persecution I have nothing to do. . . . Let there be as boundless a freedom in religion as any may conceive."[26] While admiring Calvin, he condemned his intolerant spirit and his persecution of Servetus.[27]

His guide for the societies (his church)—back to the Bible, out to the world—would make an excellent common theme for ecumenical activities. Combining a deep love for his own tradition and heritage with a commitment to scripture as the source of truth for others, he warned: "(we must learn) that a catholic spirit is not speculative latitudinarianism. It is not an indifference to all opinions; this is the spawn of hell . . . A man of truly catholic spirit . . . is fixed as the sun in his judgment concerning the main branches of Christian doctrine. It is true, he is always ready to hear and weigh whatsoever can be offered against his principles: but as this does not show any wavering in his own mind, so neither does it occasion any. He does not halt between two opinions, nor vainly endeavour to blend them into one."[28]

On the level of the local congregation, Wesley had practical advice:
(1) Loyalties are often focused on the wrong things. Wedded to buildings, tradition, circumstance, and competitive expansion, church members are sometimes caught up in idolatry.[29]
(2) By returning to the example of the primitive church Wesley was able to forgo much of the divisive tradition of Christianity. For him such tradition ceased to matter—his evangelical revival was interdenominational in every sense. All were welcome into his societies. He advised Christians to do together everything that they could. This included sharing common facilities, social programs, youth activities, social service, prayer and study experiences, evangelical outreach, and missionary activity. He found a new inclusiveness for Christian organization.
(3) Wesley believed that "the deepest and bitterest cause of division in the Church" and the "hardest to be healed" is "the human element." People became separated not "by an honest difference of opinion but also by suspicion, and even hatred. (They) can easily mistake sinful pride, prejudice, and self-will for zeal for the truth of God."[30]

He kept two general principles in mind: openness in non-essentials and abiding loyalty to the one great essential—the confession of Jesus Christ as Lord. Probably the most famous of all Wesley quotations has been misused so often as to destroy its point. The famous reference which concludes "if your heart is as my heart, give me your hand," is often used to show that Wesley was not interested in theological truth. Nothing could be more false. Open in what he considered opinions or unessentials, Wesley held steadfast to his basic beliefs and principles throughout his lifetime. A serious person, he did not take himself as seriously as do many of today's denominational leaders. His sense of humor concerning himself allowed freedom in dealings with others. Wesley's own attitude is summarized in one of his sermons: "I dare not, therefore, presume to impose my mode of worship on any other. I believe it is truly primitive and apostolic; but my belief is no rule for another. I ask not, therefore of him with whom I would unite in love: Are you of my church, of my congregation? Do you receive the same form of church government, and allow the same church officers with me? Do you join in the same form of prayer wherein I worship God? I inquire not. Do you receive the supper of the Lord in the same posture and manner that I do? Not whether, in the administration of baptism, you agree with me (concerning) those to whom it should be administered."[31]

No Protestant leader of his stature before the present century demonstrated a more compassionate attitude toward the Roman Catholic Church. Wesley saw the church as Catholic and Reformed, fully appreciating the rich Roman tradition. He believed Roman Catholics to be in full communion with Christ. This truism, so universally granted today, was universally condemned in his. Protestant and Catholic alike looked upon the other as pagan and demonic. Although bred in a century of persecution, Wesley had nothing to do with such activity, accepting Catholic practice when it did not compromise his essentials. In 1749 he defended the use of the mixed chalice and prayer for the dead. He wrote that he honored the "Blessed Virgin as the mother of the Holy Jesus, and as a person of eminent piety," although he "dared" not worship her.[32]

His attitude toward Roman Catholics in regard to persecution was far ahead of his time: "Would I, then, wish the Roman Catholics to be persecuted? I never said or hinted any such thing. I abhor the thought; it is foreign to all I have preached and wrote for these fifty years. But I would wish the Romanists in England . . . to be treated with the same leniency that they have been these sixty years; to be allowed both civil and religious liberty, but not permitted to undermine ours. I wish them to stand just as they did before the late Act was passed; not to be persecuted or hurt themselves, but gently restrained from hurting their neighbors."[33]

In direct communication with Roman Catholics, Wesley showed his pastoral spirit when he wrote: "I think you deserve the tenderest regard I can show, were it only because the same God hath raised you and me from the dust of the earth, and has made us both capable of loving and enjoying him to eternity; were it only because the Son of God has brought you and me with his own blood. How much more if you are a person fearing God (as without question many of you are) . . ."[34]

"Let us resolve, first, not to hurt each other, to do nothing unkind or unfriendly to each other, nothing which we would not have done to ourselves. Rather let us endeavor after every instance of a kind, friendly, and Christian behavior toward each other. Let us resolve, secondly, God being our helper, to speak nothing harsh or unkind of each other. The sure way to avoid this is to say all the good we can, both of and to one another. In all our conversations either with or concerning each other, to use only the language of love; to speak with all softness and tenderness; with the most endearing expression which is consistent with truth and sincerity. Let us, thirdly, resolve to harbor no unkind thought, no unfriendly temper toward each other. [35]

"You have heard ten thousand stories of us who are commonly called Protestants, of which, if you believe only one in a thousand, you must think very hardly of us. But this is quite contrary to our Lord's rule, 'Judge not, that ye shall not be judged,' and has many ill consequences, particularly this—in inclines us to think hardly of you. Hence, we are on both sides less willing to help one another and more ready to hurt one another. Hence brotherly love is utterly destroyed, and each side looking on the other as monsters, gives way to anger, hatred, revenge, bitterness, whether in us or in you, in our hearts or yours, are in abomination to the Lord? Be our opinions right or be they wrong, these tempers are undeniably wrong."[36]

Such insight was unique in the eighteenth century. The clarity it implies is not common today. Wesley wanted Catholics and Protestants to learn from one another and to work together for Christ whenever possible. He encouraged common events which did not compromise matters of faith, often joining in prayer requests and contributing to the physical well-being of Roman Catholics. It was Wesley's prayer that Christ Himself would heal the divisions within Christiandom. [37]

SECTION II
DISCIPLINES OF LAY MINISTRY

Until 1840 Methodism was essentialy a lay movement. The greatest of all John Wesley's contributions was his unique ability to involve a majority of those who joined his societies in the mission and ministry of Jesus Christ. His methods of recruitment, assimilation, and common discipleship were modeled after the Biblical witness and the experience of the primitive church. When Christianity was new there no divisions between laypersons and clergypersons. Every person was involved in a common mission with Christ. All were held accountable just as all shared equally in the abundance of God's grace.

In the last one hundred and fifty years, Methodism, in concert with all other Christian Churches, has quietly and gradually lost Wesley's genius of lay involvement in a complete ministry of mission and discipleship. In every Christian communion the process of decision-making has been substantially retained by the clergy and other full time professionals. National church policy and administration has been directed in a primary way by boards, agencies,and conferences, staffed and administered substantially by clergy. Lay persons in thousands of local churches of all denominations have felt more and more uninvolved with the decisions and proclamations of their national church. Most grant that the statements of the national churches are made by able and dedicated people and, very often, clearly reflect the teachings of scripture. Yet these statements are often ineffective because lay people, especially at the local level, have not been sufficiently involved in either the decision-making process or in the ministries themselves.

It was Wesley's genius to set no artificial limits on God's use of all the people within the covenant community. Early in his ministry, when he was bothered by lay preaching, his mother asked, "Johnny, who are you to limit the spirit of God?" He found the task of ministry too large and the challenge of mission too great to be undertaken by ordained clergy alone. The study of scripture and the experience of the primitive church, coupled with the urgencies of practical need, led him to break barriers and enter into creative new disciplines of lay ministry.

He found in scripture a clear call to discipleship, mission and ministry issued to every person. Neither Christ nor the prophets made any distinctions between people. From the time when Moses complained to God that the burden of leading the people of Israel through the desert into the promised land was too much for him, the image of ministry has been progressively opened to a wider and wider circle of people. In retrospect the original limits have always appeared to be provincial and self-serving. There is nothing in the New Testament that divides those that follow Christ. The fourth chapter of Ephesians and the twelfth chapter of First Corinthians know nothing of laypersons. When Jesus chose those closest to him—those who were to become disciples and apostles according to His grace—He chose ordinary people from the secular society of his time. They were judged by their faithfulness and by their fruits. When any sought special status in the kingdom they were gently corrected. None were called because they were Priests or Pharisees. Encouraged by his study of scripture and the practice of the early church, Wesley sought helpers who had the gifts of grace. In practice he ignored both formal academic and ecclesiastical standards. For him authority was granted to any person who followed Christ, with faith and functional gifts of leadership being the only requirement for receiving apostolic authority. With the great reformers he believed that every person received a spiritual calling which could be fulfilled in almost any vocation. Agreeing with Luther, he believed that a shoemaker can serve God as fully as the priest at the high altar. Calvin had taught that instead of retreating into a monastary to serve God, the Christian should see the world as God's monastary, and serve Christ in the midst of life. In its doctrine of the priesthood of all believers, reformation theology reaffirmed the sacredness of the secular. All work was invested with meaning and all life was invested with purpose. Wesley was one of the first to see the implications of the priesthood of all believers for lay ministry.

Wesley's disciplines of spiritual formation FULLY REQUIRED every member to be involved in ministry, for Wesley believed every person is called to minister by God's own plan of redemption and sanctification. He recognized the normative validity of ecclesiastical orders but as he witnessed frequently in his JOURNAL, the Holy Spirit breaks through this model again and again to lift up new forms of ministry, both charismatic and pastoral.[1]

Wesley's disciplines of lay ministry have ironic implications for today's church which has allowed lay persons a much smaller share of ministry, church government and spiritual vocation:

(1) Wesley dealt primarily with uneducated, uncultured, and provincial laity and yet he found great work for them to do in ministry. Today's churches deal with a highly literate, articulate, and very well-educated laity which has broad cultural and travel experience

and yet most of them are relegated to support roles at the edge of ordained ministry.

(2) Wesley's theology was grounded in life and in experience. It was not just the work of theologians but the work of every society, cell, band, class, and conference. He taught that theology was the task of the whole body of Christ and believed that it must grow out of the community life of Christ's disciples. Today, theology is primarily an academic discipline, undertaken by professors, directly involving only a very few clergy and laypersons.

(3) Wesley refused to quench the Spirit with rigid forms. He went into the fields and to the mines. He allowed Biblical words to be set to tavern songs. He allowed laywomen and laymen to preach and teach. He encouraged a remarkable variety of social and evangelical ministries, initiated and carried out by lay persons. And, he aimed at the heart as well as the head in his own preaching. Today, many ministries that have been traditionally carried out by volunteers in all churches are now carried out by paid workers (youth and teaching ministries, evangelism, visitation, various forms of mission, stewardship, finance, etc.). One must look to the secular culture (Vista, the Peace Corps, hospitals, rest homes, colleges and universities, Chambers of Commerce, service clubs, the Shrine, etc.) to find examples of volunteers taking on major levels of responsibility and decision-making. Often they involve laypeople in more significant forms of ministry than do our churches.

(4) Wesley was unable to do his work with the help of the clergy and ecclesiastical leadership of the institutional church of his time, so he organized a parallel ministry, almost exclusively made up of lay persons. He was perfectly free to go around and beyond the clergy because they had limited their own ideas of ministry. Today, some of the most creative ideas and a great deal of faithful witness come from the clergy and ecclesiastical leadership. But, often they seem unwilling to trust the laity with ownership of these ideas and seem even less open to directions which come from laity. (One of those who helped edit this book, a laywoman who is very active in her church, commented, "The greatest irony is that laity has been excluded for so long that it has lost interest! They really believe they are not needed and that mainline Christianity does not care for their ideas.")

In my own ministry, the Spirit came alive and the ministry became effective in the churches exactly at the time that I realized that I did not need to be part of everything that was going on in the church. Not only did I *not* have to lead in everything, I didn't have to initiate everything either! If I was open and encouraging, I could trust the laity to be active members of the body of Christ. Even the high-churchman, Charles Wesley, could quote the following in his JOURNAL with approval: "The calling of God never leaves a man un-changed; neither did God ever employ any one in His service whom He did not enable to the work He set him; especially those whom He raises up to supply of His place, and the representation of Himself."[2]

CHAPTER 4
THE METHODIST TRADITION
OF LAY MINISTRY

From the beginning, Methodist lay persons were the foundation for the church's ministry. They were given many places of significant authority. Rarely before in church history, since the apostolic period, had such a variety of ministerial functions been performed by lay persons. I do not believe it is coincidental that no church in the history of Christianity ever grew so rapidly. In the hundred years following 1750 the church grew substantially more than two thousand fold. Even more remarkable were the variety of ministries performed by lay persons. No ministry provided in any church by an ordained minister was not accomplished by a lay person in ministry during those years. Before the end of the nineteenth century, in the United States alone, Methodism established more than a thousand schools, colleges and universities, including more educational centers for Black Americans than organized by all other churches put together.

The church of the laity, which had not stressed an educated ministry, established some of the best schools and seminaries in the country. Alaska, American, Auburn, Baker, Boston, Denver, Dakota, De Pauw, Drew, Duke, Emory, Illinois Wesleyan, Iowa Wesleyan, Kansas State, Kansas Wesleyan, Maryland, Nebraska Wesleyan, Northwestern, Ohio Wesleyan, Southern California, Southern Methodist, Syracuse, Texas, Valpariso, Vanderbilt, and Wesleyan universities all have United Methodist origins. Albion, Albright, Allegheny, Baldwin Wallace, Bethune-Cookman, Birmingham-Southern, Centenary, Claflin, Emory & Henry, Florida Southern, Lycoming, Otterbein, Randoph Macon are some of the colleges. Seventy percent of these schools were started before 1870, and most of the rest were in the western part of the country which had not been settled. In addition the church started colleges for Indians, Spanish-speaking, and other minority groups. Hundreds of hospitals and other health care facilities were also established. Whenever you see the name "Deaconess" on a health institution you can be reasonably sure that it was started by United Methodism. No church was more active in caring for ethnic minorities, the poor, the oppressed, and the handicapped. No church was more active in world-wide missions.

This long line of achievement was possible only because all the members of the church were involved in all aspects of ministry. Wesley established a pattern of a wide variety of lay ministries. At the very beginning one of his companions as a missionary to Georgia was a lay person, Charles Delamotte, who was "American Methodism's first church school teacher and lay leader"—possibly her first lay preacher. "On February 16, 1737, John Wesley wrote to a friend in Oxford: 'I have now no fellow labourer but Mr. Delamotte, who has taken charge of between thirty and forty children.' These he not only taught to read, write, and cast accounts, but also instructed them in the Christian faith. After the three ordained ministers, one by one, left Georgia it was Delamotte who kept the spiritual work going, and who welcomed George Whitefield as their successor."[1]

Nor did he seek any payment for his services. So dependable was Charles Delamotte that on one occasion Wesley left the complete care of the parish in his hands for nearly three weeks. And, on his return noted, "I found my little flock in a better state than I could have expected. God having been pleased greatly to bless the endeavors of my fellow labourer while I was absent from them."[2] Delamotte played the part of a trusted friend in urging caution on Wesley in his infatuation with a young woman who did not appreciate his affections.

During his first five years of Wesley's itinerant ministry, from 1739 to 1744, of the forty-five preachers who gathered in his service only "three or four were clergymen." All the rest were lay pastors. Without exception they maintained themselves by working at their secular callings. They would itinerate as long as they were able, as often as not paying their own expenses, and then attempt to earn needed funds in "the intervals between their journeys." At the end of just five years these volunteers had led in building a society of several thousand members (more than two thousand in London alone), the class meeting style had been fully developed, the rules for the United Societies had been printed, the quarterly visitations already a regular practice, places of worship secured, and in some cases the "sacraments administered." In almost every case it was lay persons, both male and female, who did the preaching, taught the Bible classes, supervised the society in the time between Wesley's visits, and did the evangelizing that built the movement.[3]

In the United States the story was the same. At the Christmas Conference of 1784 not one member of the conference except Thomas Coke had a formal college education.[4] Methodism in America was begun as a lay movement. Historians disagree as to the exact beginning, but there is no disagreement to the fact that Methodism in America was begun by a lay person. It might have been in 1766 when Barbara Heck demanded that Philip Embury, a local preacher who was a carpenter by trade, begin preaching and start a Methodist class in New York. Or, it might have been earlier in the 1760's in Maryland where an Irish immigrant farmer, Robert Strawbridge, began his lay ministry. Before he was through he had begun Methodist ministries throughout Maryland, Delaware, Pennsylvania, and Virginia and helped with other Methodist beginnings throughout the South. During his ministry he preached and served communion to thousands of new Methodists. (Asbury disapproved of his serving the sacrament, but he continued to do so.)[5]

The early leaders all had to be lay persons because the ministers Wesley sent, with the exception of Asbury, returned to England before the start of the Revolution. Robert Williams sold his horse to pay his debts and his passage "embarking for the New World with the magnificent capital of a loaf of bread and a bottle of milk—and his trust in God."[6] This Irish layman not only converted many to Wesleyan beliefs but can be called the founder of the United Methodist Publishing House for he printed and sold the first Wesley Books and tracts in America.

The first native preachers were recruited by Strawbridge whose spiritual sons included Freeborn Garrettson, Philip Gatch and William Watters. Garrettson, like many lay preachers before him, paid an awesome price for his ministry. He was beaten by mobs. He saw one of his friends shot for giving him lodging. And he was driven from state to state by those hostile to enthusiasm, lay preaching, and a religion which changed the way people thought and behaved.[7] These early lay ministers were usually spent before they were thirty-five years of age, worn out by their sacrificial struggles. The first Methodist martyr was Willian Seward a lay minister who accompanied Whitefield as he evangelized.[8]

The most colorful lay preacher of all was perhaps Captain Thomas Webb who preached with a patch covering an eye which had been torn out by a musketball at the Siege of Louisburg. It was his habit to preach in full uniform, often taking off his sword, laying it on the pulpit as he preached. He had a hand in stabilizing the New York society and was the founder of societies in New Jersey, Pennsylvania, Delaware, and on Long Island.[9]

Initially almost everyone in the established churches looked down on these lay Methodists, believing that their efforts would amount to nothing because they did not have either proper orders or proper training. The remark made when Barrett's Chapel, a very small building in Delaware, was completed accurately summarized the common sentiment: "It's no use putting up so large a dwelling for Methodists, for after the war a corncrib will hold them all."[10]

Francis Asbury spent his life proving how wrong that estimate was. Utterly dedicated to sacrificial service, amazing self-discipline, and the teachings of Wesley, he taught himself the essentials of ministry. Although ordained by Wesley, in the eyes of every institutional church in the world of that time, Asbury was never anything else but a lay person. He had neither education nor recognized credentials for ministry. By the fruits of his ministerial labor he authenticated his Wesleyan ordination and his call to the ordained ministry.

By diligent study over many years he trained himself to be a minister. He had a reading knowledge of Latin and mastered Hebrew and Greek to read the scriptures in the original tongues. It was Asbury's fixed purpose, as recorded in his JOURNAL, to read no less than one hundred pages a day. Many other lay ministers were no less diligent, as they prepared for ministry. Captain Webb read the Greek New Testament daily; Jesse Lee kept a daily record of the titles of books and pamphlets he studied. From May, 1791, to August 1792, he read "in addition to the Bible, more than five thousand pages." Joseph Pilmoor recorded that he "studied Hebrew because of a desire to be more extensively useful . . . and more effectively promote the glory of God." William Winans record was even more impressive: "I have account of having read, since I began to travel, in 1808 up to this date (January 24, 1825), 318,095 pages of various sizes, from royal quarto to small 24mo besides occasional reading and many books of which I dare not set down the number of pages. This, of the books of which I have account, was an average of 50 pages per day; and yet, alas, how little do I know. Of the above number of pages, 30,000 have been in the Bible and commentaries on the Book." He stated that he had read the Bible through nearly one hundred times.[11]

Few lay ministers had such a substantial record of scholarship. "According to Peter Cartwright, who entered the Methodist ministry in 1804, there were at the time of the General Conference of 1844 fewer than fifty preachers who had more than a common English education, and scores of them not that; and not one of them was ever trained in a theological or Biblical institute."[12] It is interesting that it was about this time, 1844, that Methodism began to turn to ordained ministers, trained in theological schools, for their pastors. Soon the circuit system of itinerancy began a long process of disintegration and Methodism stopped growing as fast as the general population until 1950. Since that time it has been losing membership. Lay ministers gradually lost their places of authority. Throughout the early days of Methodism the preachers, lay and clergy, learned by the apprentice system. The senior ministers would act as instructors and tutors for the young preachers on probation. A minister's effectiveness on the circuit counted for more than any scholarly attainments. For the first time, the General Conference of 1816 prescribed a specific course of study on certain "practical subjects."[13]

Even in those days scholarship had little to do with ordination. Many lay persons were as well educated and as apt to be Bible scholars as clergy. Among the most influential United Methodist scholars of the nineteenth century was James Strong, a lay person. Famous for his CONCORDANCE which still sells thousands of copies each year, Strong had an expert's knowledge of Greek, Hebrew, and several other Semitic languages. He published several grammars, many scholarly books, and several Biblical commentaries.[14]

The dramatic story of lay ministry in United Methodism has yet to be recorded in a comprehensive way. It would surely be a storehouse of evidence of spiritual formation, effective evangelism, pastoral care, and social action that shaped generations. From Frances Willard to John R. Mott lay ministers have brought dynamics to United Methodism found in few other churches. Baron von Hugel felt that every true saint must have four traits: "He must have been loyal to the faith; he must have been heroic in times of testing; he must have shown the power to do what ordinarily would be impossible; and, he must have been radiant in the midst of the strain and stress of life."[15] The lay ministers of United Methodism were, by this definition, saints. They were full of a love that "beareth all things, believeth all things, hopeth all things, and endureth all things." (I Corinthians 13:7)

CHAPTER 5
A PRACTICAL PROGRAM OF
LAY MINISTRY TODAY

How can we build upon the inspiration of John Wesley and the example of two centuries of lay ministry today? In this section a few suggestions will be offered followed by an investigation of what lay ministers can do in the church at large and in local churches, with special reference to pastoral care, evangelism, lay preaching, social action, missions, and the fine arts.

One hundred years ago, the ordained minister was the best educated, the most influential, and the most articulate person in most local congregations. That would rarely be the case today. In every local church there are likely to be one or many members who know as much or more than the ordained minister on a given subject. If an ordained minister has neglected the academic foundations of ministry (the Biblical languages, theology, church history, Christian ethics, the sociology of religion, the psychology of pastoral care, and the philosophical and moral implications of major social issues), it is probable that some lay persons will be better informed in these areas as well.

In addition, there are now special areas of knowledge, deeply relevant to the mission and ministry of Christ, about which most ordained ministers will have little knowledge or sophistication. In areas of communication, when the ordained minister has little knowledge of radio, television, cable, computers, and motion pictures, the church is deeply dependent upon the laity for technical knowledge, production, and ideas for ministry. The future of effective evangelism, Christian education, and mission in society is at stake. In areas of social concern many lay persons have expert knowledge and experience without which the ordained ministry could, and often does, make either an ineffective or an erroneous witness. In areas of worship and evangelism, ignorance concerning the various arts and the contributions of national and ethnic cultures could be fatal to effective ministry. Since most ordained ministers are white and male, they must turn to laity for forms of authentic witness that should be absent from no local church. Many ordained ministers may be so out of touch with the forms of contemporary logic, scientific and technological training and thinking, and modern management methods that they cannot begin to communicate with those who have power in our society, or with other lay ministers.

The point is clear. Lay ministers are vital to the church at every level just as they were for Wesley. They have, collectively, experience, wisdom, ability, and a potential for effective ministry far beyond that of the ordained ministry alone.

Ordained ministers need to accept a new and radically Biblical image of ministry—one based on servanthood instead of intellectual or academic competence, upon a willingness to orient ministry according to function and task instead of authority and perogative. In the twenty-first century lay ministers are more likely to be those in the forefront of ministry ("the stars") because they are better tuned to the thought patterns (the rock music, the nature of the universe, and the dimensions of human need) that become new in every generation. Ordained ministers will more likely be the enablers (the coaches) supplying the service and disciplines of spiritual formation which will never be out of date. All effective ministries will be based on the common vulnerability of people who admit their own weaknesses, wounds, hurts, sins, and insecurities as they attempt to minister to others. Christ has been ill-served by an image of ministry which is "holier than thou." Some ordained ministers have cultivated a judgmental attitude in the pulpit which makes them unapproachable amid the pressures of life. The values expressed in the lifestyles of both ordained and lay ministries will become more important than performance skills or an ability to have *all* the answers.

I believe that no ordained minister should do anything at any level of the church that a layperson can do as well or better. There was a consistent rhythm in Wesley's own ministry. He attempted a ministerial task and found a layperson who could do that task well. Then, Wesley was concerned about the innovation. Finally, seeing the fruits, he gave his blessing and another area of lay ministry was born. The church needs to rediscover *that* method if it is to find renewal in this generation. Wesley did not do most of the regular preaching or lead any of the classes, cells, bands, and society groups. He rarely taught Bible study groups or directed prayer meetings, nor did he start the first church school. He did not organize the first prison ministry, the first orphanage, the mission to America or foreign missions to other countries, nor did he start the Holy Club at Oxford from which Methodism grew. He did not write much of the hymnal or initially approve of lay preachers, women in ministry, or lay preachers serving communion—but all these things were accomplished by dedicated lay persons!!

Perhaps it is time to reclaim the circuit model, with ordained pastors really being itinerants again, with lay ministers in complete charge of local ministries, of the building and forming of new churches, and of a great variety of specialized and new ministries. It may be that there should be an order of lay ministers similar to the orders of preaching friars or knights templar of the Middle Ages. In the spirit of St. Francis, laypersons might become, as many have always been, disciples, serving those in need with love as they work for justice. The class meeting in each local church could produce a great variety of new ministries, meeting freshly discovered needs in each community. There could be specialist, lay ministries in every discipline: preaching, visitation, pastoral care, social action, mission, communication, evangelism, chaplaincy, etc. Perhaps we could send out the sacrament of Holy Communion to every home, hospital, nursing home, and shut-in on a daily or weekly basis.

Wesley's standards for lay ministers were rigorous and practical: "1. Do they know God as a pardoning God? Have they the love of God abiding in them? Do they desire and seek nothing but God? And are they holy in all manner of conversation? 2. Have they gifts (as well as grace) for the work? Have they (in some tolerable degree) a clear, sound understanding? Have they a right judgment in the things of God? Have they a just conception of salvation by faith? And has God given them any degree of utterance? Do they speak justly, readily, clearly? 3. Have they fruit? Are any truly convinced of sin and converted to God by their preaching? As long as these three marks concur in anyone we believe he is called of God to preach. These we receive as sufficient proof that he is 'moved thereto by the Holy Ghost.' "[1]

The standards for ordained ministry today have become almost exclusively academic. In the long history of Christianity spiritual gifts have been considered more crucial. The Desert Fathers taught that prayer must be seen as "involving the laying aside of thought." They "made a distinction between the outward work, which they compared to the leaves of a tree, and the inward work, which they compared to the fruit. The outward work included study, spiritual reading and the celebration of the liturgy. The inward work is that which should occur throughout . . . prayer is the rejection and transcendence of thought."[2] Ministry must have an inward and an outward dimension. Both are equally important. In many church communities certain lay persons have wonderful gifts and graces to do all the outward work of ministry. They can preach, teach, serve prophetically, and as priests they have the wisdom and the maturity that knowledge and experience can give. Some also have the gifts of faith, purification, and love which support the inward work of ministry. They illuminate the gospel by their disciplines of the

Spirit. The church needs both kinds of ministry for spiritual renewal. In the liturgy of the Roman Catholic Church lay people "lay on" their hands as participants in baptism and confirmation. Many lay ministers participate in healing by the laying on of hands. Others use their skills to serve the weak and needy of society through ministries of love. They share with Christ service ministries in the world. Ministers are the hands and arms of Christ in the world. As servants of grace they offer the love of Christ to the wounded and suffering people who have no other friends. As St. Augustine wrote, "The laying on of hands is not something that can be performed only once like baptism. For what else is it but prayer over a man?"[3]

Perhaps more important than anything else is the gift some lay-persons have to teach, or enable, others to live as Christian ministers each day in the contacts of their regular, secular life. The laity realizes that it is not enough to "be saved" or to "witness" or to set aside "special times" for "being Christians." The important mission is to minister to the subway conductor who swears at you for being slow with the change. First, it takes discipline not to bite back. Then, it takes wisdom to form a caring response. Then, it takes courage to deliver it. It takes even more courage to minister to friends who put down those on welfare or display prejudice toward an ethnic group. The crucial ministry is *in the world* not at the church building. Only lay ministry can get it done!

How can the church spiritually form such a lay ministry?

I believe that every church body at every level must be made up exclusively of ministers. **If we believe in the priesthood of all believers, there is no Christian of any age or station who is not called to ministry.** Every church needs to train its lay ministers intentionally and trust the work of ministry to them. There could be a great variety of missional, evangelical, and social action ministries for volunteers of any age who would commit from two months (a trial period) to five years in lay ministry. Hundreds of new congregations in the United States and around the world, serving in love and working for justice, could be formed.

A local church model of lay ministry . . .

Every denomination should develop a formal program of lay ministry, involving special training and educational programs to equip the laity to carry out various functions of ministry at every level. The Wesleyan model would include the forming of lay ministers into teams with program and functional emphases. These teams could then serve local churches, enabling them to reach out in mission and ministry where the needs are. They would be made up of ten to twelve people who have the ability to complete whatever training is deemed necessary for each particular function and who have a "call" to that form of ministry. These lay ministers would, in the Wesleyan tradition, be volunteers who would be willing to commit from six to forty hours a week in ministry. They would work in their own local churches with the ordained ministry or they could commit themselves to ministries building new churches. They could serve in the secular world sharing the caring love of Christ and the Christian witness of social concern. As members of ministerial teams, they could bring renewal to other local churches through the sharing of specialized talent in ministry. The possibilities for ministry are as wide as the Gospel, our imagination, and inspiration.

I have had opportunity to be involved in an experiment in lay ministry in my own district. The seventy-two churches are recruiting and training two hundred and fifty lay ministers. It has been hard work, accomplished primarily by the lay ministers themselves. Every person who volunteered (we sent a lay recruiter to each of the seventy-two churches) agreed to give at least five hours each week to specific assignments of lay ministry in his or her own local church. Many committed to twenty, thirty, and forty hours of volunteer ministry. They plan to be on call for district and conference responsibilities in ministry four or five times a year. This call may involve sending a team of lay ministers specially trained in an area in which a local church needs help. For instance, we are training teams in the following areas to help local churches:

Worship and Celebration
Spiritual Formation
Christian Education for Children
Christian Education for Adults
Youth Work, Junior High Years
Youth Work, Senior High Years
Youth Work, College, Business, Service Years
Sharing the Gifts of the Heritage of Ethnic Minority Peoples and
    Churches
Improving the Image and Reality of Our Local Church (Visibility,
    Beautification, Publicity, Media, Advertising, Signs)
Stewardship and Mission
Evangelism and Mission
Preaching
Pastoral Care

Outreach Ministries of Mission and Social Action
Developing Support Groups for Singles and Parents
   Without Partners
Developing Programs to Combat Drug Abuse and Alcoholism
Developing Bible Study and Other Class Groups
Developing Programs of Social Concerns
Building Lay Ministry Teams for Ecumenical Cooperation
Building Lay Witness Missions

In addition, these teams of lay ministers hope to help other local churches in special projects or by a general call to bring two hundred or more lay ministers into one local church to accomplish special ministries. Our District Council chooses three or four churches in the district each year for intensive renewal upon application of the local churches. We attempt to do for local churches only that which they cannot do for themselves:

(1) Develop programs of social action or service ministries in the secular community.

(2) Conduct a massive religious survey of an entire area. On two successive Sunday afternoons all the district lay ministers will join with the laity of a particular local church and make some five or six thousand survey calls.

(3) Train local lay persons for responsibility as lay ministers in any one of the above mentioned program areas.

(4) Conduct team missions for spritual formation, worship or evangelism.

(5) Offer help in any area of weakness and need.

Strong lay ministry teams in each of these areas will inevitably renew the church. In the Wesleyan model, lay ministry involves every area of ministry.

For over ten years I experimented with lay ministry in a large local church. Since it was on Main Street in the center of the city, a team of experts made a study predicting that the church would die in fifteen years. That was over twenty years ago, and the church is much larger and more effective in ministry today than it was then. I am convinced that the program of lay ministry was what made the difference. We were able to be far more active in service and community ministry because we had many people in ministry.

The decision was made to invite carefully selected lay persons who would make a specific commitment of time (in this case from ten to twenty hours a week) to become members of the church staff. Those who made such a commitment as volunteers became regular members of the ministerial staff. The lay ministerial volunteers were treated in every way like the paid staff with the single exception of financial compensation. They came to all staff meetings, shared confidential discussions, carried out regular ministerial assignments, voted as equals concerning all decisions, and planned and shaped our mutual ministry. During most of the time the regular staff included six paid members and seven to nine volunteers. In addition some forty to fifty people at any one time gave at least ten hours a week as "part-time" extended staff members. Their responsibilities were project-oriented and sometimes were not ministerial in nature. But, their work was no less important.

Without question our church was able to survive and grow and be far more vital in mission primarily because of the lay ministry program. A majority of the lay ministers were technically "retired." Nevertheless, all had skills, energy, and ability equal to paid staff members. All were under the same committee supervision as were paid ministerial staff members.

Those who worked more than twenty hours a week as volunteer ministers had specific areas of responsibility:

Preaching and worship leadership
Pastoral care (some had professional training as counselors)
Co-ordinator of social ministries
Co-ordinator of prison ministries
Administrator and business manager
Building superintendent
Supervisor of ministerial visitation (including the visiting schedule of the ordained ministers to eliminate duplication and assure everyone's needs were met.
Supervisor of hospital visitation
Supervisor of home visitation

One lay minister proved so valuable that we persuaded him to leave secular employment and come to work full time for the church. He accepted one-third of his previous salary. He worked full time with me over sixteen years in two different churches. He was as valuable as any person I have ever worked with in ministry for he had a contagious faith and a self-giving love for all around him. Although I had much more education and training, I often watched people go past my door to seek counseling with him because he had so many interpersonal gifts. Our lay ministers did not do "busy-work" but the work of Christ's ministry at the highest levels. In my book, NO

GOLDEN AGERS HERE, I describe the local church lay ministry program in detail.[4]

Every person who entered the lay ministry program was chosen because he or she had already demonstrated gifts of ministry. They were people who displayed the fruits of the faith in their own lives and who demonstrated a spirit of loving care for other people. We defined a lay minister as a "lay person who feels a call to ministry and wishes to perform the functions of ministry (except the sacramental functions restricted by church law and those functions controlled by state law)." Every volunteer was asked to attend at least three two-hour general training sessions, and one three-hour session that would concentrate on the emphasis of the program team he or she had chosen. They also attended the regular lay speaking course offered by the denomination if they wished to share in public worship ministries.

Each was assigned to an ordained minister for an apprentice-type ministry of learning while in ministry. (Less than a quarter of our lay ministers wanted to be active lay speakers or preachers.) Some of them were better trained as pastoral counselors, as administrators, in areas of social concerns, in technological ability, and, in one case, in the Biblical disciplines than any ordained minister on the staff. The volunteers agreed to specific apprentice training in a specific ministerial assignment. They were challenged to be creative, not to be limited to what had been done, and to develop extensions of ministry in short and long-range projects.

I cannot remember any program that has generated so much excitement or which has produced so many positive results. The training, which concentrated on spiritual formation, assured a large number of committed lay ministers in each local church. The ordained ministers in the district co-operated enthusiastically for they realized how much practical help they might receive.

We shall briefly review some of the ministerial roles in which lay people have demonstrated great ability. I am drawing heavily on my own experiences in the local church described earlier.

Pastoral Care

Lay ministers, in common with most ordained ministers, are not usually psychoanalysts, psychiatrists, or psychologists. Thus, they were not encouraged to be involved in long term counseling sessions. Unless the minister was dealing with a clearly defined spiritual problem, the person needing help would be referred to a professional counselor after a maximum of three one-hour visits. Of course, if loneliness was involved or if the person was a shut-in, home visits would continue indefinitely. We had to extend beyond our rule because people could not afford professional help on their own and waiting lists for public help were too long.

Each person was assigned from four to fifteen people for pastoral care. The lay minister would establish at least one regular monthly visit in the home. The purpose of that visit was to monitor the person's feelings and physical, psychological, and spiritual needs. The person was contacted, at least weekly, by telephone. Many individuals became special friends. Often the lay ministers would take the person shopping, on errands, to the doctor, or to a movie. Many experienced new healing, joy, and spiritual renewal in their lives. Often the new relationship spanned generations. However, the lay ministers were more than friends. They were pastors sharing in their ministry the healing, loving care of Christ. They shared lives full of prayer and spiritual gifts. They saw members when they were at their weakest and most vulnerable, and often when they were not feeling friendly. They were good listeners. They were trained to be accepting and loving even when they were rejected themselves. They were patient when others were purposely trying to break their patience.

We tried to match people as closely as possible. Often a lay minister was much more successful than were members of the ordained staff in meeting the needs of our parishioners. They had time to listen and build bridges of common interest. They did not claim to have ready answers and they were accepting and affirming. Most of them knew what it was to suffer. They had faced death and had felt the emptiness of grief. Some had been abandoned and lonely. They had the common bonds of faith, similar experiences, and mutual love.

Evangelism

Relatively few lay ministers elected the ministry of evangelism or preaching, but those who did were as effective as any ordained minister could be. The lay minister who was with me full-time for sixteen years brought more than a thousand people into church membership. His methods were not fancy, but they were very Wesleyan as they were based on the power of the Holy Spirit combined with hard work. He never made less than two thousand in-the-home visitation calls a year. He would find the names of new people to visit in BANKER-TRADESMAN, a publication which lists weekly changes of property by geographical area. If there was an indication that a person or family would be responsive to the ministry of our church, this lay minister would call. He was a master at involving people in issues of social concern and in Bible study and prayer meetings. He offered his own life experience to those he met. He devised telephone methods to open the doors of those living in apartments and in the three-deckers.

Those involved in evangelism will soon come up against a contemporary phenomena not faced by Wesley—a greatly mobile population. It is the itinerant system in reverse—the pastor may stay longer but the congregation changes every three years! Mobile people especially need spiritual roots because they have little chance to develop geographic ones, and they are often far away from family and other moral support structures. We made clear that people did not need just another friend. They needed a pastor! Our lay ministers represented not only themselves, but came in the name of Jesus Christ. They came with the same humility and authority as an ordained pastor. They did not have spiritual power themselves, but they knew the source of spiritual power.

They tried to involve each person in the total program of the church. They were encouraged to respond to family needs and to offer prayer if that was appropriate. They were on the lookout for the special needs of single people and lonely people. Lay ministers were our most effective and energetic evangelists, radiating their faith and love until it was contagious.

Lay Preaching

More than seventy-five percent of our lay ministers did not have a call to preach. They had a call to serve Christ in other forms of ministry. Occasionally a lay minister developed a call to preach after service as a minister, but that usually came out of a corporate, spiritual experience.

I have a prejudice against a program of "Lay Speakers" which is not tied into a program of lay ministry. While it is authentic to minister without being a preacher, the reverse is not true. No person can be an effective preacher over an extended period of time without being committed to and deeply involved in, spiritual ministries of other kinds. This was confirmed by an experience I had in my assignment as District Superintendent. Since I am involved in helping churches when ordained ministers are appointed, I am often asked if I had heard a particular pastor preach. Consequently, I attend as many different churches as possible as a member of the worshiping congregation. Thus far, I have heard over sixty different ordained ministers in the district preach.

One Sunday morning I drove for an hour and a half to worship at a church served by a pastor with an especially strong reputation. I was very disappointed in the quality of the sermon he preached. I went back to worship in the same church two weeks later. The second sermon was only marginally better than the first. Six months later the pastor, feeling that he had completed a long and rewarding ministry at that church, wanted a new challenge. I went to visit with the Pastor-Parish Committee for the purpose of building a profile of the type of new pastor needed. The first item they listed was: "We have to have a pastor who can preach as well as Pastor _____; he is, by far, the best preacher we have ever had. His sermons are so inspiring and helpful to us." I wondered if I had gone to the right church! During the rest of the meeting they described many other accomplishments of his excellent ministry. He was extraordinary in pastoral care. His was a ministry of love. If you were in any kind of need he was there. If you went on vacation, he would pray for your safe return. If you were hurting, he would care enough to sit quietly holding your hand in love. One woman said, "He has three qualities: he knew and cared for us as people; he took time to show that he loved us; and, he brought us close to God every time he was with us."

I did not understand until I had driven almost home, and then the obvious hit me: They were listening to a preacher they loved and who loved them! That's why they so appreciated his preaching. He practiced daily what he preached. His *life* was his sermon.

Therefore, I do not believe that any person can be an effective preacher, at least in the same geographic location, unless he or she is also an effective minister in other ways as well. I believe that Wesley's language demanding a clear "call" and specific "fruits" of ministry before accepting a person as a preacher is still relevant. The person he considered an ideal preacher, John Fletcher, believed that Apostolic preaching "is urgent, simple and direct. It is a diagnosis of human misery, a warning of danger, and an application of the Christian remedy with gospel realism."[5]

The lay ministers in early Methodism were very "modern" in one sense. They were narrow specialists. Few had any broad liberal arts education or much experience with culture or any other intellectual discipline. Many learned both Greek and Hebrew, and all gave significant blocks of time each day to Bible study, meditation, and prayer. Wesley's system produced a remarkable self-reliance and encouraged innovation, which at times extended to eccentricity and rebellion. Lay preachers were apt to be interesting, full of surprises, and Biblically literate. For them the Bible was the preacher to the preacher and their messages grew from the Word itself. They had to preach ten or twelve times a week, having no alternative as they traveled their circuits. Methodist preachers were also famous for preaching without notes, a practice that was then fresh and new.[6]

In what was a major break with tradition, Wesley allowed lay women to preach. Mary Bosanquet presented him with such a strong role model, that he responded to her call. He wrote, "My dear sister: I think the strength of the cause rests there — on your having an extraordinary call. So I am persuaded as every one of our lay preachers; otherwise I could not countenance his preaching at all. It is plain to me that the whole work of God termed Methodism is an extraordinary dispensation of his providence. Therefore, I do not wonder if different things occur there which do not fall under ordinary rules of discipline. St. Paul's ordinary rule was, 'I permit not a woman to speak in the congregation.' Yet, in extraordinary cases he made a few exceptions; at Corinth, in particular."[7]

The stories of the early lay preachers show them to be involved in a constant dialogue between real life (praxis) and God's Biblical revelation. Contemporary theologian, James Cone, could have been writing of early Methodists when he wrote: "In the black tradition, preaching as prophecy essentially is telling God's story, and 'telling the story' is the essence of black preaching. It is proclaiming, with appropriate rhythm and passion the connection between the Bible and the history of black people. What have the Scriptures to do with our life in white society and the struggle to be 'somebody' in it? The answer to that question depends upon the preacher's capacity to tell God's story so that the people will experience its liberating presence in their midst."[8]

Their essential theological commitment to free will and free grace placed tremendous ethical and moral responsibilities on all Methodists. The militant Arminianism which marked the preaching of the laity with even greater emphasis than it did the preaching of Wesley, gave new Methodists the sense that God was in control of their lives, even in a rotten, unjust society. The preachers molded this theology into the hearts of the simple, trusting members of the society.

Extravaganzas in the pulpit were repressed. **Wesley sent many letters telling his preachers to stop shouting, start studying, or to demand that they get their own lives in tune with their words.** This was also a major theme for Francis Asbury whose attitude is recorded in his JOURNAL. One presiding elder who worked the frontier wrote, "He (Asbury) would not suffer anything which as manifestly enthusiastic or extravagant in religious assemblies to pass without rebuke." Peter Cartwright states, "The Methodist preachers generally preached against this extravagant wildness . . . I did uniformly in my ministrations, and sometimes gave great offense."[9]

Almost all the early lay preachers of United Methodism presented a New Testament message, strengthened by Old Testament law and prophecy. They made their claims directly and strongly without apology and with deep conviction. It is no surprise that people responded violently for and against. But, almost none remained indifferent. It is difficult to think of a better recommendation for them. They gave a great deal of attention to ethical and moral standards. Lay ministry today can carry on this powerful tradition.

The Lay Ministry of Social Action

The single key to effective social action is lay leadership and lay ministry. Everything John Wesley accomplished in this area was done primarily by his lay preachers and societies. Methodist lay ministers had a remarkable number of "firsts" in social action during his lifetime: the first hospital for the poor, the first public school for poor boys, the first orphanages, the first foundling home, the first Bible society, the first church school, the first organized society for prison reform, the first call for foreign missionaries (Webb's "spirited appeal"), the first home for unwed mothers, the first sailors' relief society, and the first public health clinics. In addition, each society, band, cell, and class was the center of moral and ethical teaching and outreach. There was not a single injustice or social concern of the eighteenth century that was not addressed at some Methodist meeting. The context of the society structure enabled effective social action because it revealed human needs. The hurts and pains of society in general were in the midst of Wesley's society as well. They could not be avoided because Wesley's society was heterogeneous and members' lives were a regular topic of spiritual discussion.

Dr. Stephen Mott's extraordinarily helpful book BIBLICAL ETHICS AND SOCIAL CHANGE, which outlines many Wesleyan principles for the twentieth century, discusses the problem when this involvement in society is lacking: Often we think, "I am too busy with the more important affairs of my 'calling' in life. But the call for help of course does not come because the extent of my love is not seen; it remains within me, unexpressed. The following illustration wryly expresses the point. A cartoon once showed a picture of a woman lying in her sick bed, obviously in misery. In the sink were stacked piles of dirty dishes. A huge basket of clothes to be ironed sat nearby. Two dirty children were fighting in one corner, and in the other sat a cat which was licking milk from a bottle that had been broken. A smiling woman stood in the doorway, and the caption under the cartoon pictured her as saying: 'Well, Florence, if there is anything I can do, don't hesitate to let me know.' Jesus's account of the active love which breaks out of in-group limits is the story of the Good Samaritan (Luke 10:29-37)."[10]

The Lay Minister in Mission

Involvement in mission results, of course, in an extension of social concern around the world. Few people recognize how innovative Wesley was in the field of missions. The Anglican church shared the view of most of the great state churches of Europe (Lutheran, Calvinist, and even Roman Catholic). In each case these churches reserved by legislation the work of evangelism and missionary witness to those who had been given the authority to preach by the civil authorities. They taught that although the Apostles had preached the gospel to the whole world in the first century, that commission had been exhausted. They believed that "the heathen outside Christendom are under the judgment of God because their fathers rejected the faith when it was offered to them." The missionary role was strictly limited and controlled by the church order and civil appointment. The great missionary commission (Matthew 28:15-16) was considered completed because the heathen had showed themselves not to be among the elect. Thus, it was the duty of the ministry to share the faith with church members at home rather than to seek converts.

Wesley, who saw the world as his parish, felt the call of the great commission again. Influenced by his Arminian theology, he wished to give every person the opportunity of grace and the chance to hear the call to sanctification. The lay ministers who followed him shared his zeal.

Thomas Taylor who left Plymouth in September, 1767, for America wrote while in passage, "I made a new covenant with the Lord that I would go to the utmost parts of the earth, provided he would raise up a people with whom I might join in his praises. On the great deep I found a more earnest desire to be united with the people of God than ever before."[11] Later is was his famous letter to John Wesley which painted the possibilities for growth in the New World, and asked for financial aid, legal advice, and leadership.

Lay ministers shaped the work on the mission field often adding a ministry of social concern to that of evangelism. Joseph Pilmore, within a month of his arrival in America, began a ministry among "the poor prisoners in the gaol in Philadelphia." His JOURNALS are filled with numerous other accounts of extensive prison ministries.[12] Because of the class system all lay ministries became "centers of philanthropy" because Wesley was constantly "organizing schemes of social improvement which are characteristic of modern city missions and institutional churches."[13] Every class, at home or on the mission field, collected food and clothes for the poor and entered into active social work. Wesley devised many of the schemes. But, he expected the lay ministers to carry them out. In London, for instance, "the society room was actually turned into a workshop for four months where the poorest members were employed in carding and spinning cotton. Soon after, all the women who were out of work were employed in knitting, for which they were paid the ordinary price. A gratuity was added to the earnings in cases where the family need was great. Twelve persons were appointed to inspect the work and to visit the sick." In 1743 Wesley appointed forty-six visitors whom he judged to be sympathetic, and capable for this delicate work. They were selected from a company of volunteers. Dividing the metropolis into twenty-three districts, they went two by two into the homes of the sick three times a week, relieving their wants and inquiring concerning their souls. Their accounts were presented weekly to the stewards. Four rules were laid down: (1) Be plain and open in dealing with souls; (2) Be mild, tender, and patient; (3) Be clean in all you do for the sick; and, (4) The golden law: "If you cannot relieve do not grieve the poor; give them soft words, if nothing else; abstain from either sour looks or harsh words. Let them be glad to come, even though they should go empty away. **Put yourself in the place of every poor man, and deal with him as you would feel God should deal.**"[16]

Lay ministers often discovered new areas of individual and social need in the general community and reported them with suggested plans for action. This challenge for mission and social responsibility on the part of lay ministers has continued. In the twentieth century the leading voice for missionary and ecumenical involvement in the world was the lay minister, John R. Mott. One of the most effective lay ministers in mission during the second half of this century was Dr. Harry Denman. Like the earliest lay ministers he did not water down his message. Addressing a large United Methodist gathering in 1971 he "assailed American churches as social clubs and American society as flaccid: In the thirties, individuals went on welfare. Today, corporations are going on welfare. . . . I may be too pessimistic, but I don't think the United States can evangelize the world. We are imperialist, we are militant, and we are still dropping bombs."[15]

Women have often been the most able and effective lay ministers. One of the most effective church organizations in the world today in both the areas of social concern and missions is, and has been for more than half a century, the United Methodist Women. Their programs of social outreach and Christian responsibility have transformed many lives and attitudes, including many ordained ministers. The publications of the United Methodist Women have consistently been sensitive to issues of peace, world hunger, economic injustice, and the oppression of ethnic peoples, women, and the aged. They have been informed by Biblical scholarship and Christian commitment. The program, policies and missionary outreach of the United Methodist Woman are perfect examples of creative lay ministry.

To Celebrate The Arts

The arts are a form of revelation, a medium of worship, and the best means of communication available to human beings. Because the arts communicate through indirection and inspiration they may offer the most effective vehicle of evangelism, education, and prophesy in the twenty-first century. The arts represent an area in most churches in which lay persons have far greater skill and more experience than most ordained ministers. If the church is to become active in the arts again, it will need the initiative and the creativity of lay ministers.

Theologians in the Arminian-Wesleyan tradition of free will and free grace have historically been open to the arts as a source of inspiration for implementing social change. Lambertus Jacobus van Holk, an Arminian scholar writes: "This openness to culture did not degenerate into mere identification with the world even during the nineteenth century, which was an almost complete disappearance of the prophetic spirit . . . The Arminian interest in secular culture . . . has been a grateful adaptation of cultural treasures to the religious life. Novels, poetry, and drama have had a great place in sermons, lectures, and religious instruction among the followers of Arminius."[16]

Wesley treated the scriptures as the unique record of God's revelation. But, he did not imprison God within it. Frequently, Wesley found himself in interaction with God in his daily life in both his spiritual experience and in his relationships with other people. His God addresses and makes claims upon individuals often through the love and witness of other people. He translated this openness to God in the world into an openness to all forms of artistic creation. Thus, early Methodism, when considered in the context of its birth during the most severe Puritanical period in history, was remarkably influenced by and interested in the arts. Wesley sought a wide intellectual inheritance for himself, including the world of philosophy, history, the theater, literature, music, the Reformation, the Renaissance, and scientific thought. He published works and commentaries of his own and reprints of the classics in all fields. He read Shakespeare and the Greek classics as well as the most popular literature of his time. By bringing in tunes and songs that had previously been barred at the church door, he and his brother, Charles, gained their initial fame as they reshaped worship through music and hymns. Warned by his mother, he resolved not to limit God in any of his thinking.

Christianity had been the patron of the arts for more than a thousand years until the Reformation and the Renaissance. Before that time almost every artist worked exclusively "for the glory of God." In reaction to humanism and in response to the enormous excesses of the institutional church, Reformed theology, particularly in its Calvinistic and Puritan forms, decried and neglected the arts. Not everyone smashed the artistic inheritance as Oliver Cromwell did, but all the arts eventually had to seek other sources for support. This removed art from the censorship of ecclesiastical control. As they stripped off layer after layer of external control, they revealed new truths about life. Both the revelation of a harmonious, integrated world symbolized by Mozart's music and the broken, shattered demonic nature of sinful human beings revealed on a Picasso canvass, present images of truth with a clarity possible in no other medium.

Tragically, many Christians have self-righteously celebrated their aesthetic starvation. Not realizing that fine art recreates the human soul, bringing visions of God which can make the spirit clean and unify the most pluralistic congregation in the love of Christ, many churches act as if they are locked into artistic expressions in worship and in life that were ordained to serve a preliterate world which accepted on authority all that was proclaimed. That world grew out of the plague, the Inquisition, the Black Death, and constant civil war. It was a world full of fear, responsive to threats of damnation. Art was considered irrelevant because church leaders thought all truth had been clearly revealed.

This self-satisfied, dogmatic, and judmental world view held complete power only as long as the Bible was secluded in mystery as the exclusive province of high priests and ordained ministers. Although few could realize it at the time, the invention of the printing press, enabling general circulation of the Bible in the vernacular, made it inevitable that the church would one day again become the patron of the arts. As soon as lay persons began to read scripture for themselves, they realized that it included within its narrative an entire world of possibility. God's word was one of faith and creation, of human understanding and literary beauty, of hope and reassurance meant to combat anguish and despair. It was a book of questions as well as answers. In it God is revealed "through a glass darkly."

In the twenty-first century God's revelation in Jesus Christ will be inadequately communicated without a revival of the arts in the church led by lay ministers. The word of preaching alone is not enough to effectively communicate either the necessity for salvation or a call to obedience. Only the corporate disciplines of the arts can effectively issue God's clear word of peace, justice, and joy. The sacramental ministry has to highlight its symbols in a world of economic injustice, starvation, and oppressed peoples. The liturgy and responsive readings alone may not be the answer for a skeptical world unaware of ethical questions or corporate responsibility. The committee meeting and the conference may not be the only way to get business done or to communicate in a pluralistic, ethnically informed church.

The fine arts offer alternative ways of expression. In a world moving away from highly directive communication, perhaps art with its essential method of indirection is the only way to convert a society from spiritual, intellectual, and emotional prejudices. (The preacher can tell us the story of passive resistance, but a motion picture like GANDHI brings a different level of communication.) Art is simply a means of expression. It can carry the good or the bad. Many have been fully aware of how powerful its pornographic and demonic messages can be without recognizing the "call" to present the Gospel fresh to every new generation with greater power. When we decry rock music and the power its beat and lyrics have over young people, we might remember again that the Wesley brothers took their music from the beer halls and used it to help bring the church alive for Christ.

Is it possible that the Gospel can be preached in forms other than in a sermon? A brief walk through a museum or a thumbing through an art book reveals ways in which God communicates with people. Kathe Kollwitz, an artist who has helped a great many people in this century to see the truth about themselves and others wrote, "I agree that my art has purpose. I want to be effective in this time when people are so helpless and in need of aid."[17]

The suggestion that art is a vital field for lay ministry is as old as Christendom. The early church changed the way people thought about God. The Jewish world thought of God as being free of all bodily form. The priests of the temple legislated that all representation of God was forbidden. In contrast, the Greeks thought of God in anthropomorphic form as the perfect man or woman endowed with superhuman powers.[18]

Early church artists, during the period when Christianity was forced underground by persecution, represented Christ in the flesh, attempting to show his suffering, compassion, sacrifice, and shepherding care. Since none of the evangelists gave any description of the appearance of Jesus, and no reliable tradition about his physical presence has survived, there was a freedom to present his teaching rather than his form in art.

Throughout the patristic period, until the year 1000, God was presented as King, Judge, and Creator. There was no effort to portray beauty, just power. Christ was never beautiful. St. Augustine would have thought a beautiful Christ absurd and sacrilegious. From the year one thousand through the fourteenth century, art became primarily the province of lay persons. Its highest flowering took place just before the institutional church reinstated its control. For almost three centuries the creations of artists, far more than, the efforts of theologians or preachers, shaped the form of revelation:

(1) The great Romanesque and Gothic cathedrals presented the awesome majesty of God. Early in the period, before inside walls were open to light and to the majesty of stained glass, little artistic interpretation occurred. Then, the arches came and the walls of the cathedrals were opened to light. At Chartres, from the workshops of Saint Denis, came the stained glass windows that Violet le Duc and Paul Durand consider the greatest in the world. The windows have the vivid color and joyful brightness that distinctively belong to the stained glass of the twelfth and early thirteenth centuries. Almost without warning most people changed their thinking about God. The brilliance of medieval illuminations in rare nobility, suddenly blazed in stained glass for all to see. The windows were the comic strips of the Middle Ages, revealing the content of scripture which laity had not been allowed to see and could not read. They began to know and understand the Bible. As they discovered the Bible, laity were able to reclaim the seasons of the church year (Advent, Christmas, Epiphany, Lent, Easter, and Pentecost). And, they began to celebrate a relationship to God, which for the first time since the apostolic church, was personal and saving.[19]

(2) The very image of God changed. The sculptors made their statues come alive. Christ was presented as risen and alive, expressing love and emotion. Eyes of figures were now open as art expressed not only the subject matter, but also interpreted emotions and spiritual depth. The fine philosopher of art, E. H. Gombrich, writes: "The work of the drapery and of the background looks as if it had been done in a mood of intense excitement . . . the emergence of a new medieval style which made it possible for art to do something that neither ancient Oriental nor Classical art had done: the Egyptians had largely drawn what they knew to exist, the Greeks what they saw; in the Middle Ages, the artist also learned to express in his picture what he felt. One cannot do justice to any medieval work of art without keeping this purpose in mind."[20] In response the mystics spoke of love, and the people dedicated their lives to the service of Christ in amazing numbers. God was now seen, for the first time in a thousand years, as a *loving, caring* father.

(3) Suddenly the austere, elevated Christ who for so many centuries had been viewed as ruler and Lord became a human, divine subject of personal devotion. God was presented in a way that common people could relate to a deity for whom they shared a personal love. For centuries no image of Christ had appeared on the cross. The early Christians dared not have a corpus for they were under persecution. The Bishops and priests who were in control from 313 to almost 1000 A.D. acted as if they were a bit ashamed of so weak and human a Christ. They allowed a fish, or a Greek word, or an abstract symbol, but no human presentation. Perhaps the fact that crucifixion remained a dreaded punishment for crime until the fourth century made its terror too real. Perhaps the pictoral representation of the Redeemer was forbidden because of doctrinal differences. But, the fact remains that no crucifix of devotion was used until lay artists turned a terrifying image of God into a loving, personal Savior and the crucifix symbolized the extent of the sacrifice and the depths of the love.[21] For the first time in Christian history, through the mother love of Mary, the feminine aspect of God was portrayed in art.

(4) Lay artists changed how people thought of themselves. As long as the artist was in control there were "four centuries of superlative beauty" and great growth in faith and in the strength of the Christian church. The art of the early church and of the years following 1000 A.D. had a vitality that was totally absent from 300 to 1000 when art was under the dominance of the state and the church. During these years artists spoke God's word in their work. The church was filled by people excited about spiritual formation and ready to sacrifice themselves for the loving Christ. To be sure, the institutional church sent them on crusades, and segregated them in monastaries and took total power over their lives. Nevertheless, these were years of positive outreach. A small group of Knights Templar established the first hospitals, and a very few monasteries present ed the heritage of civilization by establishing the first libraries, universities, and art galleries. Romantic love was born. Family life as we know it began to evolve. There came a new conception of the worth of human beings and of the value of life and a new appreciation of the majesty of God's creation.

As the medieval period came to a close, a figure of Christ at Amiens, was called "Le Beau Dieu." Everyone noticed the difference between the sculpture and the fully human, Christ at Chartres. The way people thought about Christ was affected by the way He was presented in art. "Three things," wrote Thomas Aquinas, "are required for beauty: first, integrity or perfection, because what is incomplete is ugly on that account; next, true proportion or consonance; lastly, brightness because we call beautiful whatever has a brilliant colour."[22]

The great freedom that artists had enjoyed for almost four hundred years was now restructured:

(1) All art was now commissioned and clergy prescribed its subject matter, its iconography, and its symbols.

(2) Because the content was predetermined, the artist was able to concentrate exclusively on the medium in which the work was created. As a result, craftsmanship rose to heights never before, or since, equaled.

(3) The artist had little opportunity to be either original or creative. In less than a century art took on the same repetitive and exact commonality it had known before (at the same time practices in worship and liturgy were shaped into the forms generally used today).

(4) Art was taken over from the lay person by the monks and brothers; those with "spiritual vocations," who did the illuminated manuscripts, the stained glass, and all the crafts.[23]

From then until the twentieth century much church art was decorative rather than illuminating or inspiring. During the Renaissance the church began to lose control. Yet, the lay ministry of the Van Eycks, Durer, Rembrandt, Grunewald, Botticelli, Da Vinci, El Grego, Goya, Blake, Gauguin, Rouault, Chagall, Picasso, Munch, and other artists is an eloquent and effective expression of spiritual power.

To individuals living in the twentieth-century, with shadows of the Holocaust, Viet-Nam, and the mushroom cloud, fine art is not just a medium which helps us to comprehend agony and terror. It can be the vehicle of proclamation which helps people to relate to the atoning love of "the lamb of God who taketh away the sins of the world." In a pluralistic world we find fresh images of Christ and salvation within every ethnic culture. African sculpture presents Christ as a powerful black man who has the strength to control the fury of the world. In Japan an artist has presented God as a loving mother, protecting her children from the hurts of society.

In every generation, fine art can take formless, spiritual essences and give them shape from which new life can spring. In the deepest poetry, in the communication of ideas, in the wisdom of literature, and in the majesty of musical harmony, God is revealed and Christ's word communicated. The supreme question about any Christian worship, preaching, sacrament, or act, is not whether that act is presented by clergy or lay ministers, or even how well it corresponds with church dogma, but from how deep a spiritual experience does it spring. The church must allow artists freedom to reach for the best that is within them. George Maritan, writing from a Roman Catholic point of view, understood "that the first duty of the artist . . . is to be unshakably faithful to his own truth, to the individual and incommunicable truth about himself, and about things which are obscurely revealed to him and which must take shape in his work."[24]

The artist's gift is always that which is most similar to God's—that of a new creation. Thus, the artist's calling is to give life itself in the service of the truth found within. Every creative person is in ministry.

Paul Klee wrote in his CREATIVE CREDO, "Art does not reproduce what we see. It makes us see."[25] That is why good art is always a revelation of that which hasn't been seen or heard before in the same way.

What is true in architecture, painting, and sculpture is true in all the arts. They all can help individuals to worship God, celebrate life, and sensitize each other. How many times have music and dance brought individuals close to God in worship? The world of the theater has opened new horizons of life, made people ashamed of their insensitivity, and helped them in spiritual growth.

Wesley showed appreciation of several of the arts. But, it was to literature that he made his personal commitment. In his Christian library he published thirty literary volumes, including such classics as Milton's PARADISE LOST, Young's NIGHT THOUGHTS, and PILGRIM'S PROGRESS. A list of his own works from the first one in 1733 to the revision of his NOTES ON THE NEW TESTAMENT in 1789 would fill a large volume.

It would be hard to think of a preacher in the nineteenth century who means as much to spiritual life as Melville, Hawthorne, Dostoevsky, Tolstoy, or Thoreau. It would be hard to find a pastoral counselor who could teach us as much about ourselves as can Jane Austen, Lewis Carroll, or Mark Twain. Few ministries of social action had the impact of Charles Dickens, Harriet Beecher Stowe, or Hendrik Ibsen. The lay ministers in literature in the twentieth century would make a long list, including Albert Camus, Franz Kafka, Graham Greene, John Steinbeck, Marcel Proust, William Faulkner, John Updike, Willa Cather, Emily Dickenson, T. S. Eliot, and many others. James Joyce portrayed modern culture accurately a half century in advance as he mirrored the visual closeups of television, the "camera" angles of movies, the intensity of pop art, the power and repetition of advertising, the humor of futility, the emptiness of sex without love, the triviality of possessions which turn to rubbish, and the horror of violent death.

Culture and art have penetrated people's lives. Yet, those in ministry often seem less and less aware of the serious questions and shared purposes of secular life. The Christian faith speaks to the meanings of life, the limits of human existence, and the formation of the human spirit. All these concerns are themes of twentieth century art. Many lay persons, individually and collectively, know more about the culture and the potential of artistic ministries than do most ordained ministers. That dimension of ministry is crucial as we enter a new century. The creative use of modern, artistic media for all the spiritual disciplines may be more important for the church than the use of the traditional arts. Twentieth century means of artistic expression totally dominates the lives of most people in the United States—the younger the person, the greater the domination. Motion pictures, television (including the abundant variety of cable stations, videodiscs, and tapes), rock music, audio records and tapes, the computer, and the paperback revolution put the input of a great variety of art into every home, every automobile, every geographic area, and every economic class. Those with skills and creativity in modern media must be won to the ministry of the church just as those with great speaking ability were recruited as preachers in past generations.

SECTION III
THE DISCIPLINES OF ORDAINED MINISTRY

CHAPTER 6
THE RENEWAL OF THE CLERGY

Wherever possible Wesley preferred to work through the ordained clergy, believing in a called ministry, by divine appointment. God's call was not only absolute and unconditional, but to "some particular work in the world." All ministry is directed and empowered by the Holy Spirit. For Wesley, any plan for revival would include a renewed, ordained clergy.[1]

Each year at the installation of the President of the British Methodist Conference the outgoing President hands to his successor John Wesley's "Field Bible."[2] The Bible was the dictionary, encyclopedia, and guidebook of renewal for Wesley. It was the standard for the spiritual community and the "road map" for fledgling ministers. Every aspiring preacher was first examined according to theological knowledge and purity of faith. A public exhibition of preaching before Mr. Wesley was followed by a written or an oral examination, also by Wesley, concerning "his reason for thinking that he was called of God to the ministry." The best proof, according to the founder "was that some persons should have been convinced of sin, and corrected by the preaching." Only the three marks of right belief, ready utterance, and demonstrated fruits were deemed sufficient evidence of a divine call. Then, the candidate was "admitted on probation, with a caution that he was not 'to ramble up and down, but to go where the assistant should direct, and there only; and, at the ensuing Conference, he might be received into full connection.' After a while the time of probation was found too short, and was extended to four years."[3]

No means of renewal is more important than the reinstatement of a method of rigorous selection of ordained ministers. Every Christian church should have spiritual standards which honestly represent it to the world. Only when individuals are in substantial and fundamental agreement with these standards can they be welcomed into ministry. Many denominations are now admitting individuals to the ordained ministry with the single prerequisite of academic qualifications.

This generation has been trained by all major denominations to see theological standards as somewhat irrelevant. Such lack of principle has reduced the witness of many churches to a general edification of "the American Way of Life." In the name of politeness, all rough edges are worn away. The Gospel has turned into a self-service, intellectual option. Church membership has become an alternative to a service club. In a renewed church, the ministry will be loyal to a Christological, New Testament standard:

(1) Everyone called to minister must make a confession of faith consistent with the standards of the church that issues the call. He or she must be willing to hold to that standard for as long as orders are retained.

(2) Everyone should undergo a definite period of probation in which his or her ministry should produce fruit in the Wesleyan sense of the term.

(3) Lay persons should be involved in all aspects of call, admission, and evaluation of ordained ministers.

(4) The ordained minister must have the spiritual disciplines of discipleship and a readiness to follow the direction of the corporate community. No person can effectively work in ministry without supervision. The same corporately defined objectives that one takes for granted in business and industry should be part of the program of the church. Accountability for ordained as well as lay ministers, which Wesley insisted upon, is basic for any renewal. As long as the standards remained based on Christology and the Biblical word, there would be no limits on prophetic ministry.

Empathy and tolerance on matters not essential (for Wesley this meant not in the twenty-five articles of religion) was essential. He tried to avoid theological controversy. No one was ever excluded from the loving care of the Christian community.

Wesley warned against dissension and division: "Let us not then trouble and embroil ourselves and our neighbors with unprofitable disputations, but all agree to spread, to the uttermost of our power, the quiet and peaceable gospel of Christ."[4]

Co-operation and conciliation were seen by Wesley as a form of holiness.[5] In this chapter we shall briefly review his thought on ministerial orders, the spiritual disciplines of the ordained ministry, and his principle of ministerial accountability.

Ministerial Orders

Although a high churchman, wedded to Anglican tradition and Episcopal forms, Wesley was spiritually open. He accepted the three-fold system of orders as an historical, but not an exclusive, arrangement. Patristic studies convinced him that the orders for Priest and Bishop were originally the same and that it was the practice of the Alexandrian Church for presbyters to elevate one of their members to the episcopacy. Nevertheless, he ordained Coke, "thereby showing that a third order was involved. On the basis of the Alexandrian precedent this third order had no exclusive rights to ordain, and there could be no thought of succession through the episcopacy."[6]

On some issues he did not bend. Throughout his life he insisted that only an ordained priest could administer the Lord's Supper.[7] Places of importance in the English structure of Methodism were always reserved for ordained clergymen, despite many learned and gifted lay preachers.[8]

In the beginning of the movement, the majority of his preachers had to support themselves and their families through some secular occupation. By 1768 this option was forbidden to full-time traveling ministers, a hard action (for many never had enough to live on) deemed necessary to allow itineracy, an undivided purpose, and complete independence of spirit.

These early preachers, lay and ordained, led lives of self-sacrifice and discipleship. Rule nine in the TWELVE RULES OF A HELPER was: "Take no money of any one. If they give you food when you are hungry, or clothes when you need them, it is good. But not silver or gold. Let there be no pretense to say we grow rich by the Gospel."[9]

The annual wage for their work was at poverty level. "Sixty-four dollars, and the same amount for his wife, with sixteen dollars for each child under six years, and twenty-two for each child above six and under eleven." Each minister, regardless of age, experience of ability, received the same compensation.[10] Wesley limited himself to the same recompence and then gave it away. How did Wesley convince himself of a candidate's suitability? In his STANDARD SERMONS the process is outlined: "By settling them to construe a sentence of Greek, and asking them a few commonplace questions. O amazing proof of a minister of Christ. Nay; but by making clear, open trial (as is still done by most of the Protestant churches of Europe), not only whether their lives be holy and unblameable, but whether they have such gifts as are absolutely and indispensably necessary in order to edify the Church of Christ."[11]

In 1777, he wrote to Alexander Matgher: "Give me one hundred preachers who fear nothing but sin and desire nothing but God, and I care not a straw whether they be clergymen or laymen, such a one will shake the gates of hell and set up the Kingdom of God upon earth."[12]

When an ordained minister failed to arrive for a preaching assignment in Kingswood on April 6, 1739, John Cennick stepped in to become the first Methodist lay preacher. In 1745 he published his reasons to all the world in his FURTHER APPEAL TO MEN OF REASON AND RELIGION, arguing that " 'the Scribes who preached among the Jews were not priests, that neither our Lord nor His apostles were priests, and yet were freely allowed to preach in the synagogues.' (Acts 8) Those that were scattered abroad went everywhere preaching the Word, and there is no suggestion that they were ordained; that in all the Protestant churches in Germany, Sweden and Holland, candidates for the ministry have to preach for a year before they are ordained, even as deacons, that laymen in the Church of England read the lessons, and even the whole service in many cases."[13]

Wesley extended the privilege to many women, at least as early as 1787 when he wrote on October 27th: "We give the right hand of fellowship to Sally Mallett, and shall have no objection to her being a preacher in our connection so long as she continues to preach the Methodist Doctrine and attends to our Discipline."[14]

Neither was he afraid of the preaching of youth, finding his justification in I Corinthians 16:10: "Without fear—of any one's despising him for his youth. For he worketh the work of the Lord ... Those who do so, none ought to despise."[15] Once he accepted his lay helpers, Wesley did not underrate them. At the first Conference "assistants were recommended to read the Greek New Testament, and more than a dozen books of Latin and Greek authors."[16]

In the address, ADDRESS TO THE CLERGY, Wesley proclaimed: "There is yet another branch of knowledge highly necessary for a clergyman, and that is, knowledge of the world; a knowledge of man, of their maxims, tempers, and manners, such as they occur in real life. Without this he will be liable to receive much hurt, capable of doing little good; as he will not know, either how to deal with men according to the vast variety of their characters, or to preserve himself from those who almost in every place lie in wait to deceive."[17]

The system of itineracy was instituted so that preachers would always have fresh challenges and new beginnings, and laity able to concentrate on mission rather than personality. The rule was that no preacher would stay in a circuit for more than one year. Most moved every year. Such practice was possible because the preachers upheld a strong, common standard, preventing great differences in pastoral quality and each received equal compensation.[18]

After a period of trial, Wesley insisted that his preachers give up any secular employment to spend full-time in the ministry. They depended on the societies for their food and shelter and had permission "to depart from the work whenever they wished," while Wesley retained "the right to dismiss" them. Many, even in the early days, criticized Wesley's autocratic nature. But, remarkably few left, and free criticism was allowed as long as "the work was done."[19]

Wesley's simple rules concerning their conduct toward one another were strictly enforced and proved remarkably effective:

(1) Let them beware how they despise each other's gifts; and much more how they speak anything bordering thereon.

(2) Let them never speak slightly of each other in any kind.

(3) Let them defend one another's character in every point to the utmost of their power.

(4) Let them labor, in honor, each to prefer the other to himself.[20]

Remembered as a harsh taskmaster, Wesley directed as much by example and love as by command. He wrote in A PLAIN ACCOUNT OF CHRISTIAN PERFECTION: "There is no love of God without patience, and no patience without lowliness and sweetness of spirit. Humility and patience are the surest proofs of increase of love."[21]

The Hard Work of Discipleship

More than any other principle, the human factor which brought success to the evangelical revival was the dedication and amazing grace possessed by Wesley's ministers both lay and ordained. For Wesley, to be a Christian was to be a servant of Christ, and to be a minister was to be the servant of servants. As Dr. David Steinmetz has reminded us, the most highly prized virtue of a servant is not originality, but fidelity! In both A CAUTION AGAINST BIGOTRY and in LETTERS TO A CLERGYMAN, Wesley makes clear that his ministers are to be judged by the extent and quality of their service. "Leisure and I", said Wesley, "have taken leave of one another. I propose to be busy as long as I live, if my health is so long indulged to me." His teachings on self-denial indicate that he expected the same for all members of his societies.[22]

He required hard work and continuing dedication: **"Eight hours for sleep and meals, eight for study and retirement, and eight for reading, catechizing and visiting the people."** This seemingly rigid pattern gave the preacher time and spiritual energy, providing intellectual stimulus, social opportunities, and the courage to tackle all areas of English life. Wesley claimed his to be "a more excellent way," which "promotes health of body and mind."

Wesley developed study habits as complete as they were systematic. On a regular timetable he studied the Bible, the church fathers, the classics of world literature, the textbooks of contemporary science, history, poetry, drama, logic, ethics, Hebrew, Greek, Arabic, metaphysics, natural philosophy, etc. One of the very few men of his time to study all major intellectual disciplines, he read Sir Isaac Newton's PRINCIPIA in the original Latin, Dranke and Le Clerc's PHYSICS, Dr. Halley on magnetism and gravity, and Bartholins' PHYSICS, as eagerly as Cave's HISTORY OF THE CHRISTIAN CHURCH or Shakespeare.[23]

He required of all his leadership, lay and clergy, a most serious and continuing study of scripture. Everyone who taught God's word was required to make it a lifetime study. All had to answer the same difficult questions: "Am I acquainted with the several parts of scripture, with all parts of the Old Testament and the New? Upon the mention of any text, do I know the context, and the parallel places? . . .

"Do I understand Greek and Hebrew? Otherwise, how can I undertake, (as every minister does) not only to explain books which are written therein, but to defend them against all opponents? Am I not at the mercy of everyone who does understand, or even pretends to understand, the original? For which way can I confute his pretence? Do I understand the language of the Old Testament? critically? at all? Can I read into English one of David's Psalms; or even the first chapter of Genesis? Do I understand the language of the New Testament? Am I a critical master of it?"[24]

While today's clergy consider themselves better trained and more scholarly than their eighteenth century counterparts, the fact is that most have not studied either Greek or Hebrew. In addition, they have not maintained a lifetime commitment to serious Biblical or theological scholarship.

No calling has more built-in opportunities for either unlimited sacrificial service or laziness than the ordained ministry. No one systematically evaluates or sets goals for most ordained ministers. Professional priorities usually have little to do with either performance or faithfulness. In many cases, the larger the responsibility, the less the accountability. Often professional advancement is a reward for skills and accomplishments which have little to do with ministerial service. The minister who is primarily a professional can become so skilled in interpersonal relations that parishioners celebrate his or her ability without getting involved in matters of faith, ethics, or moral responsibility. Those who treat ministry only as a profession usually neglect either the prophetic or the pastoral ministry.

One of the advantages of Wesley's authoritarian ways was that there was no room at the top. Wesley feared the effects of fond musings about success. He instructed his brother to inquire of each preacher, "How do you spend your time from morning to evening?" After hearing the answer, Charles offered this choice, "Either return to your trade, or resolve before God to spend the same hours reading, etc. which you used to spend in working." A little later he wrote, "If our preachers do not, nor will not, spend all their time in study and saving souls, they must be employed in other work, or perish."[25]

In the letters, whenever Wesley mentions a preacher he speaks of two basic requirements: zeal and activity. His discipline rooted out any who became too comfortable. More than any other particular, Wesley urged hard work in pastoral care. How can a pastor teach or help people he or she does not know? He wrote, "The sum is, go into every house in course, and teach every one therein, young and old, if they belong to us, to be a Christian inwardly and outwardly."[26]

Other churches employed an educated ministry, but in both England and America, Methodism, while sometimes falling behind in terms of a learned clergy, emphasized the education of the laity. Since every lay person was called to minister according to Scripture, Wesley felt that the first task of every ordained minister was to equip the laity. It is not surprising that Methodist ministers without formal education became so well educated because one learns much more as a teacher. Asbury was typical as he worked and studied in the Biblical languages in an effort to teach others.

The Methodist system was designed for an equipped laity: class and prayer meetings, institutions of primary, secondary, and higher education, the book concern and the traveling preacher, the lay leadership and the emphasis on mission. This crucial difference —the sharing of the intellectual as well as the spiritual heritage— made Methodism effective. Renewal in mission came as the Spirit blessed the hard work of discipleship.

Scriptural Foundations

A minister without spiritual resources is hopeless. Knowledge of Scripture has to be accompanied by both scriptural commitment and spiritual experience. Wesley persistently recommended fasting, prayer, intercession, meditation and Bible study.[27]

Wesley did not insist on theological trivia. He did insist upon a defined minimum content of faith for both ordained and lay ministers: "Who is a Gospel Minister, in the full, scriptural sense of the word? He alone, of whatever denomination, that does declare the whole counsel of God; that does preach the whole Gospel, even justification and sanctification, preparatory to glory. He that does not put asunder what God has joined, but publishes alike, 'Christ dying for us, and Christ living in us.' He that constantly applies all this to the hearts of the hearers, being willing to spend and be spent for them; having himself the mind which he, in Christ, and steadily walking as Christ also walked; he, and he alone, can with propriety be termed a Gospel minister."[28]

Accountability

Wesley believed that his ministers must be accountable for their work. No major Protestant denomination has a working system of accountability for either the professional or personal lives of its ordained ministry. Although some churches have some financial or numerical (membership) accountability, chances are that most ordained pastors are evaluated on social or professional graces instead of Biblical categories. Wesley described a situation which has not greatly changed: "But as these young preachers grew in years, they did not all grow in grace. Several of them indeed increased in other knowledge; but not proportionately in the knowledge of God, and less in devotion to Him. They were less zealous in his service. Some of them began to desire the praise of men, and not the praise of God only; some to be weary of a wandering life, and so seek ease and quietness. Some began again to fear the faces of men; to be ashamed of their calling; to be unwilling to deny themselves, to take up their cross daily, 'and endure hardship as good soldiers of Jesus Christ.' Wherever these Preachers laboured, there was not much fruit of their labours. Their word was not, as formerly, clothed with power: It carried with it no demonstration of the Spirit. The same faintness of spirit was in their private conversation. They were no longer 'instant in season, out of season.' Warning every man, and exhorting every man if by any means they might save some."[29]

Worried about the pressure of success, Wesley insisted that there could be only one test—that of discipleship. He specifically condemned any system of "honour, money or preferment."[30]

For the renewal of the church, the ordained ministry must reclaim both the breadth and the full dimensions of its apostolic power. It is no easy responsibility because the ordained ministry must espouse causes which are in direct conflict with some dominant interests, success images, and prejudices of contemporary society. John Wesley held a high standard for ordained clergy because he knew how crucial they were for reformation. It was their job to see to it that the mission of the church was carried on. They had no monopoly on ministry, but they were responsible for spiritual faithfulness and for the definition of discipleship.

On September 15, 1771, the young Francis Asbury was asked, "Are you worried about the difficulties a preacher faces?" He answered, "I look at it this way, when others suffer so much for their temporal interests surely I may suffer a little for the glory of God, and the good of souls. . . . The more troubles I meet with, the more convinced I am that I am doing the will of God."[31]

CHAPTER 7
THE PREACHING OFFICE

Few contemporary observers would argue that preaching is as important today or as influential as it once was. A great deal of twentieth century Biblical illiteracy can be directly traced to the loss of authority and the shifting away from the Biblical word in the Christian pulpit.

In Wesley's England preaching was also in decline and most clergymen were without significant influence. The rhetoric of dry rationalism had taken over the leading pulpits. Even the greatest preachers read their sermons as Deists or philosophers interested in their intellectual and social reputation. Early in the reign of George III, the famous jurist William Blackstone conducted a personal survey of "every clergyman of note in London." In every sermon he listened to, he found "not a single discourse which had more Christianity in it than the writings of Cicero," and that "it would have been impossible for him to discover from what he heard whether the preacher was a follower of Confucius, of Mohammed, or of Christ."[1]

All historical evidence points to a lack of conviction and effectiveness in the Christian pulpit when Wesley came on the scene. At the end of his ministry there had been a transformation in the public attitude toward preaching all over England. A revival had taken place and a golden age of preaching was the result.

Wesley constantly re-evaluated his own preaching:

(1) "From the year 1725 to 1729 I preached much, but saw no fruit of my labor. Indeed, it could not be that I should: for I neither laid the foundation of repentance nor of believing the gospel; taking it for granted that all to whom I preached were believers and that many of them 'needed no repentance.' "

(2) "From the year 1719 to 1734, laying a deeper foundation of repentance, I saw a little fruit. But it was only a little; and no wonder; for I did not 'preach faith in the blood of the covenant.' "

(3) "From 1734 to 1738, speaking more of faith and Christ, I saw more fruit of my preaching and visiting from house to house more than ever I had done before; though I know not if any of those who were outwardly reformed were inwardly and thoroughly converted to God."

(4) "From 1738 to this time—speaking continually of Jesus Christ; laying Him only for the foundation of the whole building, making

Him all in all, the first and the last; preaching only of this plan, 'The Kingdom of God is at hand; repent ye, and believe the Gospel.' "[2]

The text for Wesley's first sermon was "Seek ye first the Kingdom of God and His righteousness." Nearly seventy years later, he turned to a companion text for his last sermon, "Seek ye the Lord while He may be found: call ye upon Him while he is near."[3]

In these texts he exposed his method of preaching. **He brought people into God's presence by exploring their needs and giving answers for them.** He was not always successful, but he was constantly evaluating his efforts and reaching for an effective witness. Richard Watson, the most able Methodist theologian of that time, described the process: "His (Wesley's) attitude in the pulpit was graceful and easy; his action calm and natural, yet pleasing and expressive; his voice not loud, but clear and manly; his style neat, simple, and perspicuous; and admirably adapted to the capacity of his hearers. His discourses in point of composition, were extremely different on different occasions. When he gave himself sufficient time for preparation he succeeded; but when he did not, he frequently failed. It was indeed manifest to his friends, for many years before he died, that his employments were too many, and that he preached too often, to appear with the same advantage at all times in the pulpit. His sermons were always short; he was seldom more than half an hour in delivering a discourse, sometimes not so long. His subjects were judiciously chosen; instructive and interesting to the audience, and well adapted to gain attention and warm the heart."[4]

Although form was important, content was crucial for Wesley. Interestingly enough the standards found in Wesley's own SERMONS and in his NOTES were established for the public's protection and not to limit study or to control personal belief. So far as he was concerned, the preacher was free to believe what he or she liked, provided he or she did not preach anything contrary to the standards. A preacher was at perfect liberty to preach new doctrines, provided they followed the standards.[5]

Wesley's honesty about his own situation allows all of us, who have theological doubts or weaknesses in ability, to hope for a new spirit. He faced constant challenges of doubt and self-confidence, writing in his JOURNAL on October 14, 1738: "I cannot find in myself the love of God, or of Christ . . . I have not that joy in the Holy Ghost; no settled, lasting joy. Nor have I such a peace as excludes the possibility either of fear or doubt. When holy men have told me I had no faith . . . I have often doubted whether . . . I had or no. . . ."

Almost a year after Aldersgate, on January 4, 1739, he recorded: "My friends affirm I am mad, because I said I was not a Christian a year ago. I affirm I am not a Christian now. Indeed, what I might have been I know not, had I been faithful to the grace then given, when, expecting nothing less, I received such a sense of forgiveness of my sins as till then I never knew. But that I am not a Christian at this day, . . . For a Christian is one who has the fruits of the Spirit of Christ, which . . . are love, peace, joy. But these I have not."[6]

The doubts that Wesley expressed have been known by all honest preachers. The journals of his followers, as traced in the LIVES OF EARLY METHODIST PREACHERS, include many accounts of doubt, discouragement, and despair. The early Methodist preacher was given unheard of (in those times) personal freedom in faith as long as he or she maintained restraint in the exercise of the office.

Denominations have lost their identity over the last one hundred years because common standards are no longer found in either the Roman Catholic or the main line Protestant churches. Few parishioners know the denomination's theology and ethical standards. Even fewer understand the denomination's unique offerings in terms of the practical implications for their lives. Particularly in Protestant America there has been a common theology more reflective of the "American way of life" than of either the denominational dogma or scripture preached from most pulpits. People choose churches by "shopping" interdenominationally. They look at the personality and the charisma of the preacher, the social graces of the congregation, the age and economic mix, the size of the parking lot, the dominant political stance, and the type of facilities among other sociological factors.

One of the reasons that sect churches are growing is that people know what to expect. They come to hear the preacher because he or she will be faithful to conservative or fundamentalist Bible preaching.

Although Wesley would have severely criticized the narrow concept of mission and ministry and the overt judgmentalism of many sect churches, he did insist that his preachers were not to proclaim themselves in any form. Their task was, in Wesley's word, "to offer Christ" or in Luther's "to portray Christ." Effective preaching is sacramental, offering the word of God in the same manner and under the same grace as the sacraments are offered, with authority, proclaiming the great saving acts of Jesus Christ.

He counseled study to an extent matched by no other church father. Wesley found that ineffective preaching could be directly traced to insufficient study of scripture. To one man he wrote: "What has exceedingly hurt you in time past, nay, and I fear to this day, is want of reading. I scarce ever knew a preacher read so little.

And perhaps by neglecting it you have lost your taste for it. Hence your talent in preaching does not increase . . . It is lively, but not deep; there is little variety; there is no compass of thought. Reading only can supply this, with meditation and daily prayer. You wrong yourself greatly by omitting this. You can never be a deep preacher without it any more than a thorough Christian. O begin. Fix somepart of every day for private exercises. You may acquire the taste which you have not; what is tedious at first will afterwards be pleasant. Whether you like it or no, read and pray daily. It is for your life; there is no other way; else you will be a trifler all your days, and a pretty, superficial preacher. Do justice to your own soul; give it time and means to grow. Do not starve yourself any longer."[7]

Reading Wesley's sermons makes one wonder why they were so popular. Dr. Dinsdale T. Young explained that "the printed sermons were specially prepared as doctrinal standards for his preachers and people. Face to face with the multitudes John Wesley preached in a very different style."[8] John Lawson believes that this explanation, while plausible, does not take into account the spiritual force and authority in Wesley's personality, and the power of his theology. Wesley spoke frankly of his intention: "I design plain truth for plain people: therefore, of set purpose. I abstain from all nice and philosophical speculation; from all perplexed and intricate reasonings; and, as far as possible, from even the show of learning, unless in sometimes citing the original scripture. I labor to avoid all words which are not easy to be understood, all which are not used in common life; and, in particular, these kinds of technical terms that so frequently occur in Bodies of Divinity; those modes of speaking which men of reading are intimately acquainted with, but which to common people are an unknown tongue. Yet, I am not assured, that I do not sometimes slide into them unawares; it is so extremely natural to imagine that a word which is familiar to ourselves is to to all the world."[9]

This principle cannot be overemphasized. Even in a society of universal education and a great deal of cultural sophistication, the fact is that most people are intellectual specialists. Their special fields rarely are in Biblical theology, religion, or Biblical studies. Therefore, any base of communication must depend upon a common vocabulary and contemporary illustrations. Wesley asked, "What is the best general method of preaching? To invite; to convince; to offer Christ; to build up; and to do this in some measure in every sermon."[10]

As one who preached sermons of much shorter duration than common in his time, he frequently gave advice concerning brevity of sermons and prayers. He recommended that no prayer take more than four or five minutes.[11]

In his LIFE OF WESLEY, Robert Southey highlights a major factor in Wesley's preaching style: "In pointing his exhortations and driving them home, he spoke as if he were addressing himself as to an individual, so that every one to whom the condition which he described was applicable felt as if he were singled out; and the preacher's words were then like the eyes of a portrait which seems to look at every beholder."[12] Preaching was, for Wesley, "the supreme instrument", a sacramental act in which God's grace works forgiveness and conversion. Just as in the Lord's Supper, the preached word was a converting ordinance.[13]

Although he preached the full range of evangelical truth, Wesley did not take a written sermon into the pulpit during the last fifty years of his ministry. He wrote his sermons, but he preached them in an extemporaneous manner.[14] This combination of personal ability coupled with supreme confidence in God's grace and power was a key to the evangelical revival. Wesley's practice was revealed in his commentary on I Corinthians 3:2: "I fed you, as babes, with mild food—the first and plainest truths of the gospel." So should every preacher "suit his doctrine to his hearers."[15]

What is exegetical preaching in the twentieth century? Wesley's printed sermons employ few illustrations, concentrating on interpretation and exegesis. Often he gives a new translation of the Biblical words and presents his ideas of textual exegesis. Yet his sermons are topical in style rather than strictly textual. Today, exegesis means "critical" studies, based upon historical, archeological, and contextual backgrounds. Often it does not refer to textual studies. In fact, some Biblical theologians see little possibility of a direct translation of Biblical thought to the present situation (Bultmann suggests the Bible can only be applied by demythologizing its contents.) Nevertheless, contemporary preachers must struggle to bring God's word to bear on everyday life and to bring people into a sustaining relationship with Jesus Christ. Exegetical preaching in the Wesleyan tradition:

(1) May be topical—responding to pressures, concerns, and responsibilities of the contemporary world.

(2) Is rooted in the Biblical word, dealing with whole sections, not proof-texting to substantiate a preconceived point of view.

(3) Is theologically, not sociologically defined. The great themes of revelation (salvation, redemption, reconciliation, righteous-

ness, justice, the Kingdom of God, atonement, sanctification, forgiveness, etc.) are proclaimed as the way of shaping the church and the world.

(4) Looks for decision and commitment (the vehicle through which the Spirit can convert, direct, and form lives and communities.)

Wesley credited the Methodist teaching of perfection with bringing prosperity to his societies. But, it was the preaching of judgment and repentance which is credited with winning converts. Especially when preaching, he did not worry himself or his people about God's business: that great mass of revelation, doctrine, and dogma that people can do nothing about. Instead he concentrated on the divine rhythm as it affected people: judgment, justification by faith, ethics, morals, regeneration, conversion, and sanctification. These were the great themes of his preaching.

As he believed in grace, he saw the first task of preaching as that of convincing the listener of the reality of sin and each person's dependence upon grace. Leslie Church records an anecdote about Wesley's mastery of adapting his message so that the congregation was forced to apply it to themselves: "Wesley had preached to an eminently respectable congregation on the text: 'Ye serpents, ye generation of vipers, how can ye escape the damnation of hell?' A friend protested. 'Sir, such a sermon would have been suitable in Billingsgate; but it was highly improper here.' Wesley's answer: 'If I had been in Billingsgate my text would have been: Behold the lamb of God which taketh away the sin of the world.' "[16]

In contrast to the preaching of modern sectarian evangelists, he knew little of personal "testimony," nor was he concerned with "visions and personal revelations." (II Corinthians 12:1) Instead, Wesley preached holiness of heart as well as holiness of life. His sermons ON JUSTIFICATION and ON THE NEW BIRTH show both sides of his emphasis. If one was convinced of the love and forgiveness of Christ, that love would be returned in gratitude and faith. By glorifying the Christ crucified and risen (c.f. II Corinthians 4:5 and the sermons in Acts), he limited himself to preaching the Kerygma, personalizing it according to the needs of his hearers. Franz Hildebrandt indicated that the Wesleyan hymns are our best clue to Wesleyan preaching:

> My heart is full of Christ, and longs
> Its glorious matter to declare.
> Of Him I make my loftier songs,
> I cannot from His praise forbear:

My ready tongue makes haste to sing
The glories of my heavenly king.

Methodist Hymn Book, 270

Wesley looked for preachers in whom the Holy Spirit lived: "Scripture is the letter that kills to men who are carnal, who have not been justified by the grace of God. The same Scripture is 'the spirit that makes alive' to those who come alive in the spirit . . . the real hermeneutical problem is man himself."[17]

When asked what should be done to keep Methodism alive after his death, Wesley wisely gave balanced preaching as his prescription for renewal: "Preach our doctrine, inculcate experience, urge practice, enforce discipline. If you preach doctrine only, the people will be antinomians; if you preach experience only, they will become pharisees; and if you preach all these and do not enforce discipline, Methodism will be like a highly cultivated garden without a fence, exposed to the ravages of the wild boar of the forest."[18]

We live in a world which looks at Christ indifferently, for we have made Him commonplace and predictable. "Incarnational" preaching is needed to enable the experience of grace. **In a time when most people are unwilling to take responsibility for anything, a call to sanctification and perfection could be a redeeming word. We live bombarded by media which glorifies trivia. Every preacher has a charge to keep and a cause to glorify.**

CHAPTER 8
THE SACRAMENTAL OFFICE

For the mature Wesley the sacraments, Baptism and the Lord's Supper, were converting ordinances through which God dispenses salvation by means of prevenient, convincing, justifying, and sanctifying grace. Christ's atonement is presented as a continuing event: "A continuous fountain from which all grace and blessings flow." In the same way as the preached word, the sacraments are the means of grace Christ has chosen to form his people into a saved community in the present moment. Because of God's love, Christ intercedes for each person bringing forgiveness, reconciliation, and a new birth. Grace is ordered in the sacraments as the power which can form a dynamic relationship between the believer and Christ, who has carried out the atoning act. In response, believers are challenged to offer themselves and everything they have to God. In the tradition of the church, the sacraments have been under the care of the ordained ministry.

God shares the power of atonement with each new generation through the grace (free gift) of a converting ordinance such as a sacrament or the preached word. Ole Borgen's JOHN WESLEY ON THE SACRAMENTS: A THEOLOGICAL STUDY is an excellent overview. He systematically presents a unified doctrine of the sacraments, demonstrating that Wesley integrated both Baptism and the Lord's Supper into his theology. The importance of the sacraments for Wesley lies in their function as: (1) effective signs; (2) effective means of grace; and (3) effective pledge of glory to come.

This interpretation is important for church renewal because it presents a vehicle of grace which can be fully effective in a contemporary world that responds to signs and symbols more positively than to objective proclamations. The world of the twenty-first century is as open to real spiritual power as at any time in the past.

The spiritual barrenness that Bishop Borgen describes can be addressed by a theology which, like Wesley's, concentrates on what God has done and is doing through Christ. Borgen finds a sacrament to have a threefold power:

(1) A confirming sign of God's faithfulness which points to the continuing act of atonement through Christ

(2) A confirming seal that the offer of salvation is continually offered through the word and confirmed in the sacraments which offer all necessary graces to qualify us for salvation

(3) A confirming pledge that the glory of eternal happiness and a part in God's work is possible for all who will accept gracefully the sanctified life.[1]

This theological structure can give us a unified framework by which we can look at the sacraments as Wesley understood them.

Baptism

Christian thought, before Wesley, saw Baptism from two radically different, but not mutually exclusive, perspectives. Those of Roman Catholic perspective looked upon Baptism from the point of view of the Creator, relying heavily upon New Testament revelation. This view sees Baptism as exclusively the work of God. It symbolizes what God has done and is continually doing in salvation history. The baptized share in Christ's death and resurrection, the reality of God's forgiveness, and the ability to make clean, by the outpouring of the Holy Spirit, and through the Spirit the incorporation of the individual into the Body of Christ, which is the Church. The entire process presents the regeneration of the individual. Baptism is then seen as a vehicle of grace.

Much of the Protestant tradition has taken a view from a different perspective, observing the fact that fruits are not visible in most cases and that people live in a state of sin, not purity. This viewpoint lays great emphasis on the faith of the recipient as being the crucial factor in making the sacrament effective. While not denying the reality of the power of the grace conferred by Baptism, many Protestants concentrate on a personal regeneration which must be freely and individually embraced. The Protestant understanding sees any other view of Baptism as too mechanical.

Wesley tried to combine the two views, just as he built his theology, checking his results by scripture and the experience of the early church. In the early years of his ministry Wesley simply inherited his sacramental theology. He did not question either the effects or the practice of infant Baptism or the meaning of Baptism itself. The anglo-Catholic tradition was his and he accepted it. The pressures of events forced him to evaluate his practice. He found: questions of order (who was qualified to baptize); questions of availability (large areas under his guidance were denied coverage by Anglican clergymen); and, questions of spirit (many of the baptized bore no fruits and showed no signs of renewal).

He wrote in his TREATISE ON BAPTISM: "If infants are guilty of original sin, then they are proper subjects of Baptism; seeing, in the ordinary way, they cannot be saved, unless this be washed away by

Baptism."[2] His father, Samuel Wesley, wrote a learned defense of orthodoxy which John edited and republished. It heavily influenced his own thinking for it presented Baptism as an extension of Puritan "covenant theology," in which children of Christians fully inherit the new covenant in the same way as the children of the Old Testament. Baptism becomes, with circumcision, a sign and a seal of inclusion. In his own treatise, John repeated his father's belief that Baptism is "washing away the guilt of original sin." Thus, "Infants are the proper subjects for Baptism." In his CATECHISM, Wesley claimed that Baptism was "a death unto sin, and a new birth unto righteousness."

He came to believe that the purifying acts of repentance and Baptism were but the inner and outer aspects of a single religious change, the only appropriate response to the Gospel. When asked, "What is the spiritual significance of Baptism?" He answered, "A death unto sin and a new birth unto righteousness."[3]

The baptized become "sons (and daughters) of God" who have, indeed, "put on Christ" and been made "alive to His resurrection." Baptism is a sign and a symbol of having been brought from death to life; not merely "justified" but also "glorified."

Because his major emphasis was on conversion, as an experience of a believer making a decision for himself, Wesley did not emphasize the sacrament of Baptism. When he wrote the ARTICLES OF RELIGION, he expunged any reference to the imputation of grace in favor of an understanding of Baptism which saw it as "a sign of regeneration and the new birth." Ernst Troeltsch, in describing Methodist practice, wrote: "At first, during the original period, the society consisted of adult members who came in from the outside; the question of infant Baptism did not need to be raised, since all the members belonged to the established Church which dispensed the Sacrament of Infant Baptism throughout the land. A probation period of six months preceded their final reception into the society. The members received their society ticket, which had to be renewed every quarter, and within the society they were divided up into classes of about ten persons, who gathered themselves together weekly under a lay leader, for mutual fellowship, guidance, and Bible study; the renewed grant of the Society ticket, and the final reception of candidates, were dependent upon the leader's report."[4]

It must be the divine word and not faith, as important as faith is, which is the basis for Baptism. Wesley shows "how one who regards faith, on the part of the candidate for Baptism, essential to its validity, can never, if consistent, administer Baptism; since there is no case in which he can have absolute certainty that faith is present. Or if one should have doubts as to the validity of his Baptism in infancy, because he has no evidence that he then believed, and, for this reason, should ask to be baptized in adult years, then if Satan should again trouble him as to whether, even when baptized the second time, he really had faith, he would have to be baptized a third, and a fourth time, and so on ad infinitum, as long as such doubts recurred. For it often happens that one who thinks that he has faith, has not whatever, and that one who thinks that he has no faith, but only doubts, actually believes. We are not told: 'He who knows that he believes,' or 'If you know what you believe,' but 'He that believeth shall be saved.' "[5]

The Sacramental Office—The Lord's Supper

In contrast to his ambiguous teaching concerning Baptism, Wesley looked at the Lord's Supper as the means of grace by which renewal might come to the Church and into individual lives. For him, Communion was "the grand channel whereby the grace of His Spirit was conveyed to the souls of all the children of God."[6] For him the Lord's Supper, a converting ordinance, was not a sacrifice, something which the church or the individual offers to God, but instead, it is a gift God offers which graciously nourishes and brings salvation to human beings. Wesley taught that any persons who failed to avail themselves of "constant" communion with God lost the primary agency of spiritual power, regeneration, and renewal. The original holy club from which the entire movement grew called itself, at Merton College, not "Methodists" but "Sacramentarians."[7]

Wesley believed that the central act of worship was the Lord's Supper. For him the eucharist "was not only a duty, but a joy" which should be "celebrated daily, if possible." In many Anglican churches of his day, the Lord's Supper was offered once every three years, and in most no more than twice a year, to the general congregation. Wesley demanded the privilege more frequently, for he felt the need of daily communion. He was personally expelled from the sacrament at Epworth church by the rector, who was drunk at the time, and the members of his society often found that the Lord's "table was fenced against them." Only under such provocation did Wesley decide to take the step toward a full ministry in order to provide the faithful with a service which they desperately needed.

In a sermon preached at Oxford as early as 1732 he insisted that Communion should be constantly taken by Christians. He entitled his message CONSTANT COMMUNION and felt so certain of its importance that when he repeated it in 1788 he gave it a preface, asserting that "he had no reason to change his views on any of the statements therein." He and Charles wrote at least 169 hymns on the Lord's Supper.[8]

In his ARTICLE OF RELIGION #16, he spoke of God using the sacrament to "strengthen and confirm." This article of faith is unquestioned in the long heritage of the Roman Catholic Church, the 13th article of the AUGSBURG CONFESSION of 1530, and the ninth of the THIRTEEN ARTICLES of 1538, the joint product of English and German divines, and confirmed by most of the patristic fathers. St. Augustine wrote: "Our Lord Jesus Christ has knit together a company of new people with sacraments."[9]

Many have stayed away from the table because they thought the Lord's Supper an ordinance for holy people, morally privileged to commune with God in a unique way. In his exegesis of Luke 22:19: "Do This in remembrance of Me," Wesley writes: "It is no wonder that men who have no fear of God should never think of doing this. But it is strange that it should be neglected by any that do fear God, and desire to save their souls; and yet nothing is more common. One reason why many neglect it is, they are so much afraid of "eating and drinking unworthily," that they never think how much greater the danger is when they do not eat or drink it at all. That I may do what I can to bring these well-meaning men to a more just way of thinking, I shall show that it is the duty of every Christian to receive the Lord's Supper as often as he can."[10]

In his effort to strike a balance between the Roman emphasis on the great gift and the Reformation insistence upon a person's free choice to accept or reject that gift, Wesley was not a pure "receptionist" for he saw the Supper as a converting sacrament. He did not insist that Communion be limited only to those with a "full assurance of faith."[11] Rather it was sufficient for them to be "sincere seekers," and willing to accept what God would give:

> "We only can accept the grace
> and humbly our Redeemer praise."[12]

As a child of his time Wesley fought the battles of sacramental form—the theological side streets which so delight those with literary power. He once denied Communion to one who had not been baptized by a minister with episcopal orders. Later, he publicly confessed this "fault" and reproved himself in his JOURNAL. He accepted the twenty-eighth Article of the Church of England which states that the unworthiness of the ministry does not hinder the validity of the sacraments.

Wesley initiated the practice of approaching the Lord's Table in groups to emphasize the communal nature of the supper. This allows an "open invitation" wherein believers decide for themselves the extent of their participation. Wesley provided that "all who will, may come, provided they love the Lord Jesus Christ." Methodist theologian Adam Clarke solidified this attitude into doctrine when he wrote, "Every minister of Christ is bound to administer to every man who is seeking the salvation of his soul, as well as to believers." Although the table was open, in theological theory, its openness in fact came much later. In the early days of Methodism, each communicant had to possess a "Communion note" which was dated and renewed only when satisfactory seriousness in life was in evidence.[13]

Wesley also reinstituted the Love Feast to symbolize "Christian unity, both vertically with our Lord and His apostles, and horizontally with each other."[14] Wesley reconnected the Agape Feast and the eucharist. Dr. Church summarizes the uniting of individuals spiritually with each other and with the risen Christ through the experience of Agape: "During the first fifty years, since the sacrament of the Lord's Supper was not celebrated in Methodist chapels, and many hesitated, for various reasons, to make their Communion at the parish church, the love-feast grew in importance . . . There was in the love-feast no question of consecrated elements, of any priestly act of sacrificial offering, but, in so far as it was a common meal whose participants gave thanks to God and to his son Jesus Christ through whom they knew their present salvation, it was probably some satisfaction to many who felt themselves debarred by circumstances from Holy Communion. Nevertheless, where attendance at Holy Communion celebrated by a clergyman could be secured without conscientious scruples, the love feast was regarded as a supplement rather than as a substitute."[15]

Without complete success, Wesley attempted to combine the richness of the Patristic period and Roman Catholic practice with the theology of the Reformation. He did, however, succeed in forcing his contemporaries to reconsider the meaning of the sacrament, to serve it much more frequently, and to open themselves to its spiritual power. His teaching is vital in ecumenical discussion because it offers a bridge across the major traditions.

With Roman Catholics Wesley found Christ really present, conveying grace to the recipient through divine activity, without implying spiritual worthiness on the part of the communicant. With the Reformation he claimed, true to his evangelical spirit, that full efficacy depends on the free choice of the recipient and results in a fruitful response: "I found much of the power of God in preaching, but far more at the Lord's Table."[16]

To what extent can Wesley's view of the sacraments help in the renewal of the Church today? Is such a compromise of Catholic and Reformed positions possible? The basic questions are: Is the concept of "sacrament," which Wesley inherited and which is so central for him, truly a New Testament concept?

Theoretical talk about the "real presence" is only relevant as a faithful community is in constant contact with Christ. It is the reality of a living relationship with the saving Christ, no theological construction, that brings renewal. Let us read the Word, witness to it, interpret it, and try to faithfully live it. Only then can we share the table, along with prayers, testimonies, and celebrations, and find there a converting ordinance instead of a theoretically defined "sacrament."

> Come, to the supper come,
> Sinners, there still is room;
> Every soul may be His guest.
> Jesus gives the general word;
> Share the monumental feast,
> Eat the supper of your Lord.
>
> In this authentic sign
> Behold the stamp Divine:
> Christ revives His sufferings here,
> Still exposes them to view;
> See the Crucified appear,
> Now believe He died for you.[17]

CHAPTER 9
A CONTEMPORARY VIEW OF
ORDAINED MINISTRY

When the disciplines of John Wesley are considered in the light of contemporary ambivalence about the ordained ministry and the pressures of the modern world, his views at first glance seem out-of-date. Yet, they seem to be crucial to the renewal of the contemporary church. He believed that:

---

(1) The ordained ministry should be a calling, not a profession.

(2) The ordained ministry should concentrate on servanthood.

(3) The ordained ministry derives its authority exclusively from God's grace working through personal and professional skills.

(4) The ordained ministry is a corporate, not an individualistic calling.

(5) The ordained ministry is a quest for spiritual perfection through a never ending spiritual formation and a disciplined lifestyle.

The Ordained Ministry Is a Calling, Not A Profession

Originally, in the early medieval period, the concept of a "profession" involved a commitment of one's life to a religious order. There were no "professionals" in the secular society and would not be any for over five hundred years. At the dawn of the Renaissance, medieval universities began to develop professional disciplines for the secular world in divinity, law, and medicine. "In this classical conception of a profession much emphasis was placed on the service rendered by the practitioner. The important thing about a profession was that expertise was placed at the service of individuals or communities who needed it. This is what distinguished the professional from the artist, scholar, banker, or businessman. The artist or scholar attended to a discipline for its own sake. The question of applicability or practicality was not primary. If others enjoyed or learned from the results of their work, that was fine. The work was not however, fundamentally shaped by the needs or concerns of persons."[1]

Dennis Campbell continues his very clear and persuasive analysis of a "professional" ordained ministry: "Today the idea of what it is to be a professional bears little resemblance to its medieval heritage. The idea has been secularized. The medieval cultural synthesis, in which all of society was understood in relation to Christian theological categories, broke down. Along with it went the idea of profession as Christian service. Profession gradually came to be associated with occupation. A profession is something one does to make a living. This secularization of the meaning of profession is one aspect of the general secularization which defines contemporary Western culture."[1]

Of course many fine pastors use the word "professional" in reference to the faith they "profess," proclaim, and vow to uphold. For such an interpretation, many of the following comments are unfair. Nevertheless, secular society does not see a "profession" in such a light. There it is defined in terms of rights, benefits, and peer control. Campbell analyzes a view of ministry which is common in many denominations. Few views of ordained ministry could be so opposite to that of John Wesley. His concept will gradually slip away if such a position becomes normative. The itinerant system, a spiritually centered lifestyle, and a noncommercial system of evaluation and accountability, all become impossible if ministry is seen as a profession in the modern sense of the word. There are images of professional success deep within our culture which are sure to subtly corrupt any professionally styled, ordained ministry. Attention inevitably slips toward matters of personal skill and accomplishments, compensation and work conditions, privileges and prerogatives, status and success.

The Wesleyan position for the called ministry was expressed in the Episcopal address at the General Conference of 1912: "For such heroic consecration it is profane to quote money values. The eloquence that may be hired, the learning that may be subsidized, the pulpit style that may be paid for in coin, cannot be of this type, and is spiritually impotent. The Christian ministry is not a profession. Nothing can be more inimical to the spirit of a God called ministry, nothing more utterly subversive of the sacredness of the pastoral office, than to place soul-winning and soul-shepherding on the secular basis of compensation. No prophet of God ever prophesied for wages. No apostle ever sold his inspiration to the highest bidder."[2]

The 1980 Book of Discipline makes clear that the "called" ministry is still that sanctioned formally by the United Methodist Church: "The ordained ministers are called to specialized ministries of Word, Sacrament, and Order. Through these distinctive functions ordained ministers devote themselves wholly to the work of the church and to the upbuilding of the general ministry. They do this through careful study of the Scripture and its faithful interpretation through effective proclamation of the gospel and responsible administration of the Sacraments, through diligent pastoral leadership of their congregations for fruitful discipleship and by following the guidance of the Holy Spirit in witnessing beyond the congregation in the local community and to the ends of the earth. The ordained ministry is defined by its intentionally representative character, by its passion for the hallowing of life, and by its concern to link all local ministries with the widest boundaries of the Christian community."[3]

The call is given by God but authenticated through the covenent community which is the church. If a person believes that he or she has received a call to be an ordained minister, that claim must be accepted by a spiritual community if ordination is to take place. Wesley believed that there was an "inner" call which is incomplete without the confirmation of an "outer" call. He tested the authenticity of a call by means of "graces, gifts, and fruit." The professional view of ministry may overemphasize intellectual gifts and academic training. Although we would not want to depreciate the importance of such factors, other elements are just as essential for ordained ministry.[4]

Since the call is from a community of believers and implies a lifetime commitment of service within that community and as a representative of that community in the wider world, significant attention must be given to spiritual graces and the individual's personal commitment of faith. Does the candidate for ordained ministry uphold and live according to the content of faith of the spiritual community in which ordained ministry is sought? The answer to that question always involves at least three areas of concern. Stated in a personal way they are:

(1) Am I committed to the spiritual teachings and values of this covenant community? (This does not imply conformity with an extensive list of theological trivia, but it does suggest that there are theological essentials that any member of a church might expect from an ordained minister of that church.)

(2) Are my ethical standards, personal habits, family life, and moral behavior consistent with the beliefs of the church in which I wish to become an ordained minister? This implies that there is a connection between one's faith and one's life that cannot be avoided. Ordained ministers, in common with all other Christians, will fall short of their ideals and stand in need of forgiveness, reconciliation, and new beginnings, but at least they must have those moral and ethical ideals and be willing to struggle to uphold them. Any thought that the private life of an ordained minister is not the business of his or her spiritual community cheapens both the minister and the community. Unless the Christian faith effects every aspect of one's life, it is not the faith of the Gospel. Those who are ordained must regularly urge members of their congregations to put every segment of their lives under the control of Christ. They must be willing to live by the same standard themselves. Anyone who has had experience with many churches knows how devastating immorality can be to witness and ministry.

(3) **Has my life and previous attempts at ministry convinced me that I have the spiritual strength and personal discipline for ministry?** (This implies that there have been fruits of faith in the lives of others as a direct result of discipleship. Wesley insisted that a record be established in lay ministry before one could begin training for ordained ministry.)

Among the earliest Wesleyan preachers the one mark which was commonly expected was that of utter dedication and commitment to the cause. Francis Asbury wrote early in his ministry: "The Lord has graciously assisted me in preaching every day; and my desires to be entirely devoted to do so still increase. But alas, what cause have I to mourn the want of life and zeal, both in public and private duties. Nevertheless, it is my determination to offer all I have to God. May he give me more to offer, and graciously accept the offering made."[5] During the next year he was again testing the call, as every minister constantly does: Saturday, May 7, 1774, "My soul longeth for God, my heart and my flesh cry out for him. O that I were wholly devoted to my God." July 11, 1774, "My soul is not so intensely devoted to God as I would have it; though my desires for more spirituality are very strong, Lord, when shall my poor heart be as a rising, active, holy flame?" September 18, 1774, "Losing some of my ideas in preaching, I was ashamed of myself, and pained to see the people waiting to hear what the blunderer had to say. May these things humble me, and show me where my great strengths lieth."[6] Every minister, lay and ordained, can expect to blunder, fail, and be subject to folly. Nevertheless, every church has the responsibility to expect that its ministers will continue to strive to be faithful to their "call." Several of the earliest Circuit Riders carried in their saddle bags a paper on which they considered was divine direction. It read: "Nec propter vitam, vivendi perdere causas." Wesley found the phrase in Richard Baxter's THE REFORMED PASTOR and recom-

98

mended it to his preachers. It is translated, **"Let us not, for the sake of life, sacrifice the only things worth living for."**[7]

The Ordained Ministry Should Concentrate On Servanthood

The ordained ministry is one of the few responsibilities where, because of confidentiality, the greatest accomplishments and the most obvious failures are never disclosed. (There are few ways to effectively evaluate all types of counseling, intercessary prayer, personal spiritual formation, or many social or prophetic ministries.) The ordained minister shares with all members of the church the task of ministry. If there is to be any difference at all in "calling," it must revolve around ministerial service that no one else is willing or able to attempt and in the ability to teach, enable, and equip others for ministry. John Fletcher, who taught Wesley so much about the disciplines of ministry, suggested that there was no stronger vow than that already given to every priest in the charge of ordination: "See that you never cease your labour, care and diligence until you have done all that lieth in you, to bring all such as shall be committed to your charge into that agreement of faith and that ripeness and perfectness of age in Christ, that there be no place left among you for error in religion, or viciousness in life."[8]

The Wesleyan tradition makes clear that there is no higher status than one's Baptism and that all Christians share the functions of ministry. In common with most other ecumenical communions, the Wesleyan tradition lifts up an ordained ministry to see that God's word is truly preached, that God's sacraments of Baptism and the Lord's Supper are duly administered, and that the saving grace of Jesus Christ is made available to every person. The first requirement of an ordained minister is not the ability to perform such functions well, although that is of crucial importance; but, in the example of Jesus Christ, it is a commitment to a ministry of servanthood by means of sacrificial love.

In such a common ministry, the ordained minister is the enabler, the helper, the coach, but not the star player. Every ministry of servanthood shares two qualities:

(1) It seeks out those in need to share the grace and the love of Jesus Christ.

(2) It is secure enough in grace to live sacrificially, helping the weak to be strong and the strong to be less satisfied.

Visitation

Perhaps the single greatest danger to an effective ordained ministry has been a general neglect of regular, systematic parish visitation and regular systematic involvement with the poor and the oppressed in the local community. John Wesley took both of these concerns with utter seriousness. Early in his ministry he wrote, "Through a man preach like an angel, he will neither collect, nor preserve a society which is collected, without visiting them from house to house." At seventy-one years of age he recorded in the JOURNAL, "I began at the east end of the town, to visit the society from house to house. . . . This (visiting) is so grievous to flesh and blood, that I can prevail on few, even of our preachers to undertake it."[9]

Visitation is a primary spiritual discipline just because it makes us unsure and uncomfortable. We are often too polite with the powerful and too proud with the weak. Sometimes we patronize when we should squirm and squirm when we should be prophetic. Visitation is that experience that makes preaching come alive and helps the preacher get in touch with his or her own vulnerability. John Fletcher wrote concerning visitation, "The most powerful nerve of the sacred ministry is ecclesiastical discipline." He was known in every house, and so was his "Helvetic bluntness." Each visit was a challenge to the lapsed, an instruction to the children and a prayerful encouragement to the faithful to press on to perfection. Wherever the pastor was he bore his parishioners—all of them—before God in prayer. His greatest energies were for the least deserving. "The more sterile the soil appears which he is called to cultivate," he wrote, "the more he waters it both with his tears and with the sweat of his brow; the more he implores for it the dew of heaven and the influences of that divine Sun which spreads light and life through every part of the Church."[10]

There are many examples of Wesley's sacrifice for his people. When the deadly "spotted fever" had swept over Bristol, Wesley spent days going from house to house, ministering to both body and soul when everyone who could had fled the city. When a protracted frost resulted in hundreds of people in London being thrown out of work, he fed a hundred and fifty people each day at his own expense. He cared for the poorest people. He knew them by name. Often they were living in his home. He started at least thirty businesses to employ them, began schools to educate their children, designated hospitals and homes to care for their bodies, and built religious societies to give them mutual spiritual strength for body, mind, and soul.[11]

Although education and a polite lifestyle have produced many material advantages for ordained ministers and their families, most of us would confess that we have been quietly conditioned not to embrace daily contact with the poor we talk so much about. We spend even less time listening to those we call oppressed. In honesty, many of us get the bulk of our information second hand. We read about the hungry, the oppressed, the unemployed, the exploited, the drug culture, and the world of the criminal. We are intellectually fascinated, but often not enough to get personally involved over a long period of time, except as advice givers.

There is no substitute for face to face contacts. We are often "brave" in our sermons but it is a cheap bravery. Individuals in a congregation often become anonymous and many preachers tend to preach past them to the world. Unless we are *active visitors* we must rate our sermons by artificial standards for we will never know for certain how they are being received by other worshippers.

In contrast, a witness made in visitation is likely to be far more effective, and a more courageous way to involve others in social responsibility than the preached word. A one-to-one recruitment approach will get both the minister and the church involved in doing the work of righteousness.

Visitation for the purpose of *listening* is of equal importance. As the preacher listens, the spiritual, psychological, and physical needs of the congregation, are uncovered. The spiritual concerns that need to be addressed in sermons can best be discovered through visitation. When crisis comes, pastoral care is often effective in direct proportion to the relationship that has been built through caring visitation.

The Ordained Ministry Derives Its Authority
Exclusively From God's Grace Working Through
Personal and Professional Skills

Christian ministry of all types, according to scripture, is to be judged exclusively by its fruits. Wesley rated authenticity of call, complete personal commitment to service, and the willingness to submit to rigorous personal disciplines above everything else. His work was phenomenally successful in both England and in the United States because Wesley's preachers shared spiritual experiences and preached to those who could easily identify with them. As they gave themselves to their tasks, their weaknesses and vulnerabilities often turned into strengths. It was obvious that they could not accomplish their ministries alone. They needed the help, prayers, and compassion of lay persons. Because there were many people in the societies as able as the circuit riders, the sharing of responsibilities came naturally. Everyone realized that the preacher, who had to immediately ride on to another responsibility, would have to share the tasks of ministry. The contemporary church needs to learn the value of a pluralistic ministry and to recapture the priesthood of all believers as a pragmatic doctrine. The great variety of talents within the church can be better harnessed by ministers who admit their needs for help and who do not hide their vulnerabilities.

What type of ministry will be best equipped to recruit such help? Wesley often admitted his weaknesses and his dependence on others. His JOURNAL has many references to his own doubts, weaknesses, mistakes, and inconsistencies. The "fair summer religion . . . (effective) while no danger is near" haunted him all of his life. Yet, he also records many incidents where ministerial and pastoral success rose out of adversity. The entire mission to America is a marvelous example. Wesley failed in his own attempt; he doubted the wisdom of an organized attempt by his followers; and he chose the losing side in the Revolutionary War. In addition, he disapproved of the experiment in episcopal government, of making the American mission a church, and of the extensive use of "uncontrolled" lay preachers. Despite an almost perfect record of poor decisions and poor judgments, he parented the most numerically successful mission in the history of the Christian church.

A "workaholic" who could not stand leisure, Wesley accomplished many of his most important ministries because of enforced illness. Many think his NOTES ON THE NEW TESTAMENT his finest work. He chose it himself to be one of the standards of doctrine, and referred to it as something "which I could scarce ever have attempted, had I not been so ill as not to be able to travel or preach, and yet so well as to be able to read or write." Luke Tyerman describes his persistence "in the face of his bleak environment and his debilitating illness" at Hot Well: "With the exception of the time prescribed for his taking exercise on horseback, two hours for meals, and one for private prayer, he spent sixteen hours a day on this—the greatest work which he had yet attempted." In ten weeks he completed a rough draft of the translation as well as notes for the four Gospels.[12] One wonders what he might have accomplished if he had been well.

People are best ministered to by a person who is intent on imitating the one who was willing to "make his own wounds available as a source of healing." Paradoxically, such vulnerability makes a ministry more faithful. Those who serve without illusions do not have to pretend in their own lives. Only those who humbly give the service of pastoral care can afford to be bold in the pulpit for they will be believed.

Philip Otterbein's favorite preaching theme, "God's Grace," gave him the opportunity to restore the confidence of those needing more vital inner assurance by sharing what God can do with weakness and vulnerability. This Wesleyan image of ministry is particularly important as we approach the twenty-first century. The spiritual quest of prayer, devotional meditation, and the study of scripture that all of us follow in spiritual formation implies, of course, that there are no clear cut, easy to discover religious answers. Ministers who pretend to have all the answers to the meaning of life as well as to the pains and problems of existence, have a most difficult task indeed, for they claim to know more than the scriptures reveal. How many times did Abraham, Moses, David, the prophets, and the disciples stumble in confusion? For an agonizing moment, even Christ felt forsaken.

Local churches have come alive in response to the suffering and the needs of their pastors. For example, two pastors in Massachusetts had strokes. Both were lovingly cared for, supported for eighteen and twenty months at full compensation, and came back to their respective congregations much stronger in spirit and mission. Since the need for the members to share ministry was conspicuous, they began to effectively minister.

Humor is that vital quality that allows a person to move through periods of weakness. Most of us take ourselves too seriously and life itself too seriously. It is our relationship with God that we don't take seriously enough. If we can laugh at ourselves and share the joy around us, that attitude will open us to the power of God's grace. Is it possible to receive the good news and not be full of joy? No task of ministry is completely on the shoulders of those "called" to be ordained ministers. They are never alone in their work.

The Ordained Ministry Is a Corporate, Not an Individualistic Calling

Wesley found, as has every church administrator before or since, that some ordained ministers want the advantages of a connectional ministry without the responsibilities. In the United Methodist system, for instance, the professional advantages of a connectional church are easy to list:

A lifetime guarantee of employment at minimum salary, plus parsonage, all utilities, health insurance, modest pension, telephone, some transportation expense, and other advantages

A common support base of peers in emergencies

Significant power, in a representative form of church government, in setting policy for the church and the rules and benefits for clergy

A support system for the loneliness and isolation which is increasingly the lot of an ordained minister in a society which no longer honors or depends upon ordained clergy as much as it did in the past

An educational support system which provides initial training and opportunities for continuing education, travel for enrichment, and conferences for learning and sharing

Significant help in local church programing (Church school and youth materials, national and international organizations for women, men and youth. Financial and advisory resources for specific needs, music for choirs and organists, Bible study aids)

Nothing in the above list is unique to the United Methodist Church. Many of the advantages are available at any church or synagogue. Nothing in the above list generated directly from John Wesley. His unique contributions to the disciplines of ordained ministry are now not commonly assumed. In terms of *renewal* these contributions may be the most valuable of all:

(1) The idea which evolved into a connectional church was based on democratic principles. Many local churches are pushed to be more active in mission around the world and in social concerns than they would themselves choose to be because their representatives establish a corporate vision, enabling local churches to be involved in world-wide programs of caring service. Such connectional cooperation is the only way a local church can be involved in effective discipleship in such a complex and secular socity. It may be the only system which enables local churches to escape the dangers of provincialism and parochialism.

(2) The idea of an itinerant ministry which moves frequently from place to place, preaching the word and administering the sacraments while involving congregations in Christian mission was born. Many historians would claim that this mode of organization of the

ordained ministry, more than any other single factor, was responsible for the growth of the United Methodist Church.

The itinerant system, as developed by Wesley, had several advantages for ordained ministry and mission not found today in any mainline Protestant church:

(1) Ordained ministers were frequently sent to new assignments, causing the development of new ideas, fresh leadership, different perspectives, less artificial dependence on the ordained ministry, the stimulus of new situations for the minister and congregation, and a regularity of preaching, teaching, and devotional leadership for the local church

(2) Since the ordained pastors were on circuits, the congregations learned to be in ministry by themselves. They grew in size and in mission because they were dependent on the ministry of the laity. The growth pattern of the United Methodist Church shows an inverse curve in response to the advent of a "settled ministry." As a percentage of the population in the United States the United Methodist Church showed phenomenal growth as long as it kept a system of circuits dependent on lay ministries. As soon as that system was dropped, the church began its long period of membership decline.

(3) The emphasis was naturally centered on Christ and the call to discipleship rather than upon the personality and abilities of a particular ordained minister.

(4) The major expenses in stewardship were not spent for the custodial care of ordained ministers. Today, many churches spend more than eighty percent of their entire budgets to pay salaries, to take care of parsonages and manses, and to maintain their local church buildings. A very large percentage of money collected in all Wesley's societies, bands and classes went directly into mission—at home and around the world. Bishop Asbury made the point with remarkable clarity. He believed that the itineracy constituted "a sheriff's sale" of all earthly things that pertained to him in this world. It shattered "into fragments everything out of which an idol could be made." It cut him wholly "loose from the world." It prepared him to live a heavenly life, "without even a shred of the earthly, the sensual, or the devilish." Asbury's JOURNAL makes it clear that he expected his preachers literally to despise the riches of this world and it was doubtless considerations such as these that influenced him not to be deeply concerned over the lack of stable

financial support of the ministry. He had many opportunities to observe the moral havoc wrought by state support of the ministry of the Established Churches and he was determined to avoid anything even remotely resembling a similar evil.[13] Obviously early Methodism had expectations that are totally irrelevant today in our society where most ordained ministers are married and have financial responsibilities for a family. It may be, however, that the recent trend toward second incomes for some ministers will become more general, releasing smaller churches from the burden of full support.

(5) The program of the local church had an element of vitality and constant innovation. The preacher and the leadership were constantly renewed. This model of the early church built up the same relationships described in the Acts of the Apostles, the Letters of Paul, and in the works of the Patristic fathers.

(6) There were opportunities for effective challenge to ministry and for the freedom to preach the Word as it is (without the conforming influence of financial pressure by a congregation).

The person called the most effective practical theologian in history showed that practical theology did not primarily involve the building of an institutional structure, but the ORGANIZATION OF PEOPLE IN MINISTRY. His genius was pointed toward meeting the spiritual needs of individuals, toward meeting the missional needs of the community, and the social and ethical needs of the world. **HIS ENTIRE EMPHASIS WAS PUTTING THE GOSPEL TO WORK IN THE LIVES OF PEOPLE, CALLING THEM TO MINISTRY AND TO SERVICE IN THE WORLD. HE ORGANIZED SOCIETIES TO MEET THE NEEDS OF PEOPLE. HE NEVER ORGANIZED PEOPLE TO MEET THE NEEDS OF HIS SOCIETIES.** This fact, more than any other, is Wesley's contribution to the renewal of today's church. Is it possible that institutional churches are losing their effectiveness because people think that they exist to serve themselves (perhaps as benevolent clubs) and not primarily to serve the needs of people? Do churches exist primarily to support their own institutional programs rather than to support the people in their communities or beyond?

Where Are We Now?

Is it possible to reclaim these essentials of a connectional church in today's society which is based on democratic principles? Practical steps are available for any church to move in the directions Wesley indicated if they are so motivated:

(1) A willingness to cut down on the overhead of the institutional church must exist. When we need so much money to support ourselves there is little hope of substantial service to others. The Wesleyan model would have lay ministers in charge of each local parish (perhaps twelve, with each person responsible for a different program area or ministerial service). These would be grouped in a circuit (co-operative parish) of from twelve to fifteen local churches, depending on membership. They would be served by a staff of three or four ordained ministers with complimentary skills. This would dramatically reduce overhead expenses (three of four parsonages and three or four salaries shared by twleve to fifteen local churches; shared secretarial, staff and office expense, etc.).

(2) A willingness to reclaim St. Paul's model of a tentmaking ministry is necessary. The fact that a person is paid to minister and works "full-time" in a narrowly defined institutional model is certainly not the only Biblical model of ministry. It may be that many forms of secular employment and involvement are equally valid extensions of ordianed ministry. Gustavo Gutierrez suggests that "new ways must be found to support the clergy. Those who do not wish to live on stipends or from teaching religions should be allowed to experiment . . . A secular job could be very healthy: they would find themselves in the real world of men; it would lessen the temptation to servility on the part of those who depend totally on the clerical institution: It would likewise diminsh the financial problems of the institutional church."[14]

Wesley himself was the great example. From the beginning it was his financial independence that gave him freedom to witness and work in the way he did. "The foundation stone of his first preaching room was laid on May 12, 1739, with 'the voice of praise and thanksgiving.' The eleven trustees whom Wesley appointed did very little to raise the necessary funds, and Wesley took on himself the payment of the builder. Whitefield urged Wesley to get rid of the trustees, on the ground that they would have power under the deed to turn him out if he displeased them by his preaching. Wesley took this advice, canceled the deed, and became the sole proprietor. This, though insignificant at the time, was a matter of great importance, for in this manner nearly all the chapels built in the early years of his ministry were vested in himself."[15] Throughout his life he was a tent-maker—writing, publishing, and selling his books. He gave all of his earnings to mission and ministry. His freedom to innovate was earned by the removal of any possibility of selfish motivation.

(3) There must be a willingness on the part of the leadership of the church to set the example. Bishop Asbury had been in America a little over a week when he began "to implement Wesley's insistence upon an intinerant rather than a settled ministry—much to the dismay of Richard Boardman and Joseph Pilmore, who were inclined to develop pastorates in the cities." To his JOURNAL he confided: "I am fixed to the Methodist plan, and do what I do faithfully, as to God . . . My brethen seem unwilling to leave the cities, but I think I shall show them the way. I am in trouble, and more trouble is at hand, for I am determined to make a stand against all partiality. I have nothing to seek but the glory of God; nothing to fear but his displeasure . . . I am determined that no man shall bias me with soft words and fair speeches."[16] It was this kind of dedication and self-discipline that made a disciplined system work.

Tragically, Asbury sought to keep his preachers poor, and he was able to do so for he remained poor himself. Several United Methodist historians have rightly commented that the terrible suffering of the early itinerants and their premature location and death may be directly attributable to Asbury's policy of planned hardship. Stewardship is judged fairly not by the amount of money that is earned but by how it is used. The ordained minister deserves the support of the leadership of the church when he or she has financial needs. Lay persons have exactly the same responsibility for stewardship in their own ministries.

(4) A willingness must be developed to change one's attitude concerning ordained ministry. Ordained ministers have been judged according to secular standards by others for so long that many now judge themselves by those standards. If the world is to define what a good minister is, we are not likely to have many "good ministers." Some ordained ministers have begun to judge their "profession" in terms of the biggest salaries, churches, sanctuaries, memberships, parsonages, staffs, budgets, etc. Such a system eventually corrupts everyone.

When Bishop Asbury preached his first sermon in New York he intentionally chose the text form I Corinthians 2:2: "I am determined not to know anything among you, save Jesus Christ and him crucified." This was his lifetime practice in ministry, an attitude which earned him a great deal of freedom. Any minister who judges the work of ministry from secular perspectives takes on great additional burdens. The Biblical view of ministry brings with it awesome responsibilities. But it also brings great freedom because ulti-

108

mately it is God's grace that shapes, informs, and empowers. Once that fact is accepted, ordained ministers are free:

To witness without fear
To love those they don't like
To be full of doubt as well as full of faith
To be weak as they point to the strength of God
To be wrong as they point to the truth that is in Christ
To give up control as they share ministry with laity
To fail in the knowledge that the victory already has been won
To burn-out in the knowledge that nothing, ultimately, including salvation depends upon them.

The Ordained Ministry Is a Quest For Spiritual Perfection By Means Of Spiritual Formation And a Disciplined Lifestyle

When a person is ordained that act marks the end of a process of divine selection and the beginning of a lifetime of continuing and never-ending spiritual formation (or disintegration) and of spiritual disciplines (or license). It is possible to relax so much after completing a long and difficult path that one never gets going again. Henri Nouwen who has written many books of great spiritual power, helps us begin: "Ten years ago it was clear that the church called and that it was an honor, privilege and election to be ordained to the priesthood. The representatives of the church made it clear: 'If you can't live up to the expectations, we ask you to leave.' But now the student seems to say to the church: 'If you don't live up to my expectations I am leaving.' And in many subtle ways it is communicated to the student that nobody wants to lose him and that he can make more demands on the church than the church can make on him."[17]

A great part of Wesley's secret lies in the fact that he passed on a very demanding call to a lifelong quest for spiritual formation. He provided the context for spiritual formation for all his preachers. They were not left to struggle alone. His methods built on the experiences of the early church and the Eastern Fathers. They taught that to be spiritually formed implied that each person had a spiritual director. St. Basil (330-379) told of the necessity of finding a spiritual director "who may serve you as a very sure guide in the work of leading a holy life," one who knows "the straight road to God," and he warns that "to believe that one does not need counsel is great pride." St. Gregory Nazianzen (330-387) spoke of spiritual direction as "the greatest of all sciences." St. Jerome (340-420) told his disciple, Rusticus, that it was impossible to progress spiritually without a spiritual guide, and many of his epistles gave explicit direction for his followers. St. Augustine (354-430) insisted that "no one can walk without a guide."[18]

It was the Desert Fathers in Egypt, Syria, and Palestine who provided a model for spiritual formation that has been an inheritance for those in ministry. They were spiritual directors for disciples who sought them in the Desert. Those looking for "holiness and purity of heart" found in them necessary guides. Their method is seen most clearly in the APOPHTHEGMATA or SAYINGS OF THE DESERT FATHERS. In warning St. Anthony writes, "I know of monks who fell after much toil and lapsed into madness because they trusted in their own work." Another elder wrote, "Go attach yourself to a man who fears God, humble yourself before him, give up your will to him, and then you will receive consolation from God."[19]

Wesley wrote and preached on the necessity to constantly renew the "spirit of holiness." God's grace is that force that empowers the renewal of the spirit. That grace wounds us at points we consider ourselves the least vulnerable. As we are filled with pride in our accomplishments and our abilities, spiritual discipline reminds us of our utter dependence. As we moralize and judge others, spiritual discipline reminds us of our own guilt. As we are indulgent with ourselves, spiritual discipline records our need to confess. As we become confident in ministry, spiritual discipline reminds us that grace is that which can be given but never possessed. Grace remains a spiritual mystery. It can provide the spiritual strength for ministry and faith. Yet, if we become acquisitive and try to manipulate our new found spiritual strength, we lose it.

Every person does not need the same form of discipline. For the most part we are able to motivate ourselves concerning the things we enjoy doing. As a young minister I never had to discipline myself to allow sufficient time for study and meditation. That is what I most enjoyed. I needed discipline in pastoral services—in home visitation and in social events. I would much rather stay home and read than attend a meeting or make a visit. When I discovered that the Methodist discipline of 1784 advised preachers not to let their studies interfere with soul saving: "If you can do but one, let your studies alone!," I felt it was speaking to me.

For me a most important rule of spiritual discipline is the necessity of emphasizing the opposite of our desires and natural inclinations. If we are comfortable carrying out ministries of pastoral concern, we may need to apply the spiritual disciplines of study and turn to the Biblical languages, Bible study, and the devotional classics. If we love to preach, perhaps we should discipline more time for personal involvement in social action. If we find ourselves excited by the adventure and sense of personal accomplishment of being daily in mission and involved in social action, perhaps we need to apply as much discipline to our prayer lives, our stewardship, or our personal morality.

The need to use spiritual disciplines to counterpoint desires and natural inclinations is as important within functions as well. If we find ourselves using all our study time concentrating on the Bible, perhaps we need to open ourselves up to other cultural areas: fiction, the theater, the fine arts, psychology, history, and the various sciences. If we find ourselves on the liberal side of most social concerns, we need to be especially well-informed concerning conservative positions. Both lay and ordained ministers will be serving those who disagree with them. Ministry is more effective when an honest respect for differing points of view is possible. It is equally necessary to be well-informed concerning theological and ethical standards which differ from our personal inclinations.

John Wesley modeled this approach throughout his lifetime. Hebrew, Arabic, Greek, Latin, ethics, logic, metaphysics, oratory, natural philosophy, poetry, and divinity were carefully entered into his weekly plan of study.[20] He felt himself strongly opposed to many of the principles of Roman Catholicism on the one hand and Puritanism on the other. So, he made a disciplined study of both communions making him the most ecumenical of the major reformers. He initially disliked the idea of preaching without notes or in the out-of-doors but so disciplined himself that he became one of the most productive extemporaneous preachers in history. The Oxford Don with his elitist education so disciplined himself that he was the most effective ordained minister in history among uneducated working people. He who was primarily a scholar at the beginning of his ministry became more active in social and missionary ministries than any theologian before him. Wesley's long ministry was a model of the discipline of counterpoint—letting the grace of God shape those parts of life that are too much under the control of personal desire.

SECTION IV
DISCIPLINES OF THE CHRISTIAN CHURCH
CHAPTER 10
THE MISSION OF THE CHURCH

Although Wesley's thinking on the church is expressed in an unsystematic, nondogmatic way, he spoke in an age when a strong doctrine of the church was presupposed. Born into the national church, he took for granted that his activity would not be schismatic. In addition, he lived in the afternoon of the Reformation when the great questions of doctrine were live, public issues.

In his eyes the church had one mission—obedience to the Word of God. For him, the church, formed by the Holy Spirit, is both Catholic and Reformed, united in Christ, and judged by its fruits alone. As expressed in the New Testament, the Word calls the church to evangelize, to nurture, to heal, and to serve. Mission becomes the distinguishing mark of any church which reflects the will and way of God. Christ continually forms His people into a community, the church, which exists to carry out His purposes and is defined by His presence.

Wesley taught that the will of God is known only by "consulting the oracles of God." Only by studying scripture could one know what is "the holy and acceptable will of God."[1] While clearly a "man of one Book," he was not wedded to any one theory of revelation or inspiration. His emphasis was Christological.

His dual call to mission, back to the Bible and out into the world, was very unpopular with the leaders of the established church and with the vast majority of "religious" people. Richard Green in his BIBLIOGRAPHY OF ANTI-METHODIST LITERATURE OF THE EIGHTEENTH CENTURY (1902) lists 606 anti-Methodist items, written almost exclusively by clergy of established churches, an incredible number in a century when books were comparatively expensive and not popular and when the great majority of the people could not read. With the reformers, Wesley claimed that corruption had entered the church itself. His stress on the corporate community contrasted with the revolutionary spirit of his age—a spirit which stressed the importance of the individual and freedom from groups built on discipline.

For those who followed him, Wesley distinguished five areas of mission. The church is: (1) to spread scriptural holiness throughout the world by leading all who would follow to the experience of sanctification; (2) to proclaim God's Word in preaching and in witness until the Word of assurance is available to all; (3) to effect conversion by changing lives and reorienting them along the way to salvation; (4) to serve as God's agent in assuring justice in love for all; and, (5) to institute a world parish with no geographical, national, secular, racial or sociological boundaries.

To Spread Scriptural Holiness

"What may we reasonably believe to be God's design in raising up the preachers called Methodists?" Wesley did not stumble for an answer to his own question: "Not to form any new sect; but to reform the nation, particularly the church; and to spread scriptural holiness over the land."[2] In contrast to dead formality that was all about him, Wesley found that only scriptural holiness could reform the church and nation. He looked for an inward and outward holiness, in imitation of the perfection which was Christ, and found, instead, meaningless superstition, conspicuous immorality, and a studied ignorance of the Biblical Word.

When the Moravian Brethren objected that he did not speak often enough of Christ and of Faith, Wesley indignantly informed them that the Bible was his "standard of language as well as sentiment." As one who endeavoured "not only to think but to speak as the oracles of God," he challenged them to produce any inspired writer who spoke of either Christ or faith as "frequently or as fervently" as he did.[3] Wesley argued that "whatsoever is not read therein, nor may be proved thereby, is not to be required of any man that it should be believed as an article of faith, or be thought requisite or necessary to salvation."[4]

His class meetings were formed so that individual experience would not corrupt scriptural truth. God's Word was studied until collectively understood, as a check on individual experience and indulgence. No experience was left without the corrective of intensive examination according to Biblical principles. The classes and societies were his means for spreading scriptural holiness.

The Proclamation Of God's Word Of Assurance

In his societies, Wesley taught a communal discipline of devotion, dedication, and service. This discipline led to an assurance of salvation. Wesley often challenged individual experience as a criteria for truth. Those who were "fleeing from the wrath to come" and who wished to "be saved from their sins" (and these were the only preconditions required of those who would join Wesley's society), were offered not a doctrine of experience but a message of assurance.[5]

Since salvation is open to every person and assurance the condition of the saved, evangelism is a major mission of the church. One witnessed and evangelized not because experience led in that direction, (in fact experience was often forbidding), but because the Word of God clearly commands such activity.

The Conversion Of The World

Wesley's missionary goal was the conversion of all peoples. Those who were saved by the undeserved love of Christ could not afford to wait for individuals to come to Christ of their own accord. Faith was contagious. Each Christian had a share in the redemptive ministry of God. Wesley's view is remarkably consistent with that of many twentieth century theologians: salvation is complete health and wholeness. "What is salvation? The salvation which is here spoken of is not what is frequently understood by that word, the going to heaven, eternal happiness. It is not the soul's going to paradise . . . It is not a blessing which lies on the other side of death, . . . in the other world. The very words of the text itself put this beyond all question: 'Ye are saved.' It is not something at a distance: it is a present thing; a blessing which, through the free mercy of God, ye are now in possession of. Nay, the words may be rendered, and that with equal propriety. 'Ye have been saved,' so that the salvation which is here spoken of might be extended to the entire work of God, from the first dawning of grace in the soul, till it is consumated in glory."[6] Thus, for Wesley the real question became: WHAT ARE THE RESPONSIBILITIES OF SAVED PERSONS IN THE WORLD?

In his NOTE ON MATTHEW 3:2, Wesley saw the Kingdom of Heaven in a present/future context, making the common distinction between the Kingdom of Grace and the Kingdom of Glory. These taken together form one kingdom, but the Church here on earth can work only in the Kingdom of Grace. By proclaiming and living the law and the prophets, the Church makes a wider community aware of the need and necessity for redemption and reform. By initiating a sacramental life of service, discipline, worship, preaching, and prayer, the Church forms the context of the Christian life. By finding the cause and means for existence in God's revealed Word, the Church is able to find renewal through the forming work of Christ in each generation. Through its sacraments, preaching, teaching, publishing, missions, social action, and pastoral serving, the Chruch undertakes to share in the mission of the Holy Spirit.

114

The Service And Love Of All Peoples

Personal commitment to human beings in love is the hallmark of the church. In his conflict with the Moravians, Wesley thought them mystical and ineffective precisely because they were unwilling to perform the work of service and love which were marks of the primitive church. Wesley turned his back on them "because they not only do not practice but utterly despise and decry self-denial and the daily cross; because they, upon principle, conform to the world in wearing gold and gay or costly apparrel" and (fundamentally) "because they are by no means zealous of good works; or at least, only to their own people . . . because they make inward religion swallow up outward in general."[7] Nothing is more common in his JOURNALS than his call to the service and love of all peoples.

The World Parish

Wesley's claim that the world was his parish presented not only the extent of his missionary concern, but the fullness of his gospel. What Christ had done was good news for Wesley in great part because it offered salvation to all and gave every individual, without regard to circumstance, the hope of a meaningful and realized life. His mission was to proclaim this message, in word and deed, throughout the world. This remains the essential mission of any church today.

Wesley's experience in America not only led to his conversion, but it taught him how renewal begins. Dedicated to the conversion of Indians, Wesley found himself unconverted. How many have followed in his footsteps and found themselves "in a fair summer of religion"? He proclaimed: "I can talk well; nay, and believe myself, while no danger is near. But let death look me in the face, and my spirit is troubled." The first step toward spiritual renewal is to honestly face present conditions. In absolute need for a savior, with no resources of his own, Wesley found no magical or easy way. A wise man advised him to "be still, and go on." His mission answered his need. He wrote: "Perhaps this is best, to look upon it (his unconverted state) as my cross; when it comes, to let it humble me, and quicken all my good resolutions, especially that of praying without ceasing; and at other times, to take no thought about it, but quietly to go on 'in the work of the Lord.' "[8]

Wesley's conception of mission was world-wide, but the breadth of the responsibility he accepted is often overemphasized. Mission for him was not something out there—in another country—but a responsibility which surrounded him wherever he found himself. Significantly, he never went back to a foreign field, but mission followed him all his life. He never forgot world need, but that need did not place limits on his missionary concern as it so often does in the contemporary church. He would be horrified if he could see powerful church congregations give to spread the gospel in foreign lands while at the same time ignoring the responsibilities of mission in their own communities. For Wesley mission was total, involving a full commitment both to world needs and to immediate surroundings.

Wesley's experience in America not only led to his own conversion, but it also taught him how renewal begins. Dedicated to the conversion of Indians, Wesley found himself unconverted. How many have followed in his footsteps and found themselves "in a fair summer of religion"? He proclaimed: "I can talk well; nay, and believe myself, while no danger is near. But let death look me in the face, and my spirit is troubled." The first step toward spiritual renewal is to honestly face present conditions. In absolute need for a savior, with no resources of his own, Wesley found no magical or easy way. A wise man advised him to "be still, and go on." His mission answered his need. He wrote: "Perhaps this is best, to look upon it (his unconverted state) as my cross; when it comes, to let it humble me, and quicken all my good resolutions, especially that of praying without ceasing; and at other times, to take no thought about it, but quietly to go on 'in the work of the Lord.' "[8]

He saw the whole world as "only one great infirmary. All that are therein are sick of sin; and their one business is to be healed. And for this very end, the great Physician of souls is continually present with them."[9] Martin Schmidt concluded that Wesley "was possessed by the missionary idea in a manner rare in the whole history of the Church."

Wesley asked, "How could good news be proclaimed to all the world, if all the world were not concerned with the offer of salvation?"[10] Charles Wesley gave this summary of missionary theology:

Thy sovereign grace to all extends,
    Immense and unconfined:
From age to age it never ends;
    It reaches all mankind.

O let me commend my Saviour to you,
    I set to my seal that Jesus is true:
Ye all may find favour who come at His call,
    O come to my Saviour! His grace is for all.[11]

CHAPTER 11
MEMBERSHIP IN THE CHURCH

From the time of Constantine, membership in a Christian church was an assumed and rather unimportant fact in western civilization. Everyone in a given nation was a member of the national church according to the taste of the secular ruler. No one had to give much thought to membership. It was accepted and ignored as a matter of course. With the establishment of the Free churches and the advance of the doctrine of believer's Baptism, church membership became a matter for increasing debate. In a pluralistic society such as the United States, one's stand concerning church membership will go a long way toward determining participation in ecumenical affairs and the content of doctrinal thinking.

Surrounded by individuals who took pride in their agnosticism and reveled in living in a secular age, Wesley was one of the first major church leaders to give attention to the problem of church membership, a practical matter which lent itself to his particular genius. He alone set the standards of membership for Methodist societies and just as surely he defined the initial relationship of the society to the established church.

For Wesley, membership in a community of believers (a church) was "no optional luxury" in the Christian life. Rather, "every follower of Christ is obliged . . . to be a member of . . . some church."[1] Wesley was able to have a sole condition for membership in his societies ("to flee from the wrath to come, and to be saved from their sins") only because the full commitment of each member to an existing church was presupposed. In the formation of his society, however, Wesley took a giant step away from Dr. Horneck and others who had formed similar societies. In the case of all the others for which we have records, individuals could join only if they were already members of the Church of England. The bounds of the church established the bounds of the society. Although independents and dissenters occasionally attended the meetings, the conditions for attendance were strict, and membership was practically impossible. Wesley, who considered spiritual considerations alone crucial for membership in his society, declined to impose any ecclesiastical tests whatsoever on those who came to him seeking a path to salvation. He did, however, insist on ecclesiastical discipline after they joined. He believed that Infant Baptism by itself admitted a person into church membership. In his A TREATISE ON BAPTISM he wrote: "By Baptism we are admitted into the Church, and consequently made members of Christ, its Head. The Jews were admitted into the Church by circumcision, so are the Christians by Baptism. . . . It admits us into the Church here, so into glory hereafter. . . . In the ordinary way there is no other means of entering the Church or into heaven."[2]

For adults, an additional covenant-commitment confirmed by evidence of obedience to Christ was necessary for admission to the societies. No doctrinal test was ever required nor was any "confessional principal" allowed to define limits. As the 1980 UNITED METHODIST DISCIPLINE (page 41, paragraph 67) makes clear, this is still the standard for United Methodists.

Wesley criticized all churches of that day, including the Church of England, for neglecting the New Testament. The fact that the Anglican church was not as interested in the moral and spiritual qualifications of a member as in their social standing was anathema to Wesley. His guidelines for membership went far beyond the needs of a society and eventually forced the society to become a Church. These guidelines have relevance for us because Wesley was attempting to establish "a household of God, built upon the foundation of the apostles and prophets, Christ Jesus Himself being the chief cornerstone."[3]

Without embarrassment he established a dual standard for membership—one for the laity, one for the clergy. Believing in the possibility of universal salvation, he opened the doors of membership to all that would come. When one became a member he or she entered into a lifetime process of sanctification. Exceedingly liberal in his standards for lay membership, Wesley was doctrinally strict and theologically demanding of those who would preach and minister in his name. Believing in a called ministry, he reasoned that those called by God were thereafter bound by God's will, not their own. Anyone in the society should have the assurance that the message being proclaimed and taught them was that of Methodism, not of a particular preacher or teacher. Since no one was forced to be a Wesleyan minister, preachers were required to confess their faith and hold to it as long as they wished to retain the privilege of guiding and leading others.

Wesley summarized the basic requirements for lay members in 1742: "The distinguishing marks of a Methodist are not his opinions of any sort. His assenting to this or that scheme of religion, his embracing any particular set of notions, his espousing the judgment of one man or another, are all quite wide of the point. Whosoever, therefore, imagines that a Methodist is a man of such and such an opinion is grossly ignorant of the whole affair; he mistakes the truth totally." Forty-six years later, he said to a congregation in Glasgow:

"There is no other religious society under Heaven which requires nothing of men in order to gain their admission into it but a desire to save their souls. Look all around you; you cannot be admitted into the Church, or Society of the Presbyterians, Anabaptists, Quakers, or any other unless you hold the same opinion with them, and adhere to the same mode of worship. The Methodists alone do not insist on your holding this or that opinion; but you may continue to worship in your former manner, be it what it may. Now I do not know any other religious society, either ancient or modern, wherein such liberty of conscience is now allowed, or has been allowed, since the age of the Apostles. Here is our glory, and a glorying peculiar to us. What Society shares it with us?"[4]

Preachers had to meet much more rigorous tests. Wesley insisted upon a Biblically centered, Christocentric theology and that this be the foundation for all preaching and teaching. The Wesleyan balance of openness in the pew and orthodoxy in the pulpit, found in no other church, was Wesley's first contribution to the ecumenical movement. It presents a new nonjudgmental openness while assuring the source of truth in worship and pulpit. While no one has the whole truth, in the Scriptures Wesley thought he had found the "fountain of truth."

To have faith is much like being in love. No amount of intellectual concentration or rational dexterity can bring about either faith or love. Genuine love just isn't within conscious control. No rational gymnastics will lead to genuine faith. Therefore, one opens the self to the experience of faith as to the experience of love, by entering into relationships which bring opportunities for community and communion. For this reason joining a church in the Wesleyan tradition is similar to the act of getting married. At a marriage no one can pledge love in an absolute and continuing sense. One simply is not able to maintain the feeling of deep love at every moment of every day. One cannot rationally maintain that which is not intellectually controlled. However, a pledge of fidelity may be made, creating a climate of faithfulness in which love may grow and become mature. If the marriage is a holy one this commitment will lead to an experience of mature love which will grow with the years.

For Wesley membership was just as holy an obligation. When people came forward to join his society, they were not required to know all there was to know about faith, to certify that their beliefs were true and conformed to those of all others in the society, or pledge that they would never change. No such stamp-pad impression of faith was demanded. To join was to make a commitment of intention, of fidelity, not a declaration of arrival. Individuals are invited to build their theology corporately within a community of believers, not arrive with a theology fully formed. Infant Baptism may be sustained because the community, not the individual, holds the essentials of the faith. It is recognized that no person has a full and complete understanding of scripture. Yet, if the commitment of the new member is secure, and if the community performs its task as given by Christ; then, faith will ripen and mature over the years and in the grace of the Holy Spirit sanctification becomes possible.

This freedom of membership is possible only in the context of a clergy bound to the revealed Word. It is not the cheap freedom which comes in churches that count tolerance as the primary virtue. Wesley insisted that the community be ministered to by those called by and faithful to Christ.

Membership In The Context Of Wesley's Doctrine Of The Church

It is a denial of Wesleyan heritage to look upon the Church as an organization or a club rather than as a living household of God. Yet, it is easy to see how such a substitution could happen. Wesley taught much about both the church and his societies, and these teachings have been confused. Wesley read out of his societies numerous individuals for unChristian conduct, lack of obedience, faulty loyalty, or other reasons. But, he never read anyone out of the church. In exercising discipline "the question is not," wrote Wesley, "concerning the heart, but the life. And the general tenor of this . . . cannot be hidden without a miracle."[5] His standards were different for clergy because within any household, if it is to be strong, there must be a remnant, a core, which is completely loyal in love and service to the head of the house and in service to all the members of the household.

When Wesley formed his society he looked for "the inward witness." When he looked to the Church his criteria was outward need. Just as a person can be a member of a family and share in family love without returning that love, so a person can be a member of a church without being Christ-like.

We can see how easy it is to be confused, for by his own definition Wesley was not a Christian until he had been a member of the church for many years and an ordained clergyman as well. As an ordained minister however, he proclaimed his faith, not his doubts. When asked to define a Methodist, he pointed to those formed by Christ within his society; when asked about members of the church, he referred to all who belonged to the Church of England. Even within the society, full members did not always have an Aldersgate experience.

Why Should One Be a Member Of a Church?

Wesley was bothered by this question. The obvious answer is that everyone stands in need of salvation, of meaningful life, of sanctification, and of the love of the Christian community. When the church is the Church, when Jesus Christ is present existing as community and guiding and forming all activities and services, then, the Church becomes an agent of salvation. When challenged about the fruits of Christianity, he was quite frank to note that membership in the church was not one of them. **The goal of the Christian life was not to become a member of the church—that was only the beginning.** Wesley felt that the life of a church member should always be in forward movement toward sanctification—that it should never be productively static. Thus, members of the church were always either moving toward perfection or slipping backward toward indifference. This was particularly true with regard to Christian perfection. In 1789 Wesley wrote: "You do well strongly to insist that those who do already enjoy it (perfect love) cannot possibly stand still. Unless they continue to watch and pray and aspire after higher degrees of holiness, I cannot conceive not only how they can go forward, but how they can keep what they have already received."[6] His societies became communities of spiritual movement, places where sanctification was carried out.

The Standards Of Membership

While one could join easily, there was no cheap membership in a Wesleyan society. Love was expressed through discipline, not indulgence. When in 1948 the great Old Testament scholar Millar Burrows was translating from the Dead Sea Scrolls he gave the title "Manual of Discipline" to one of the major scrolls even though the words are not hinted in the text of the scroll. He wrote: "Noting the combination of liturgical directions with rules covering procedure in the meetings of the group and personal conduct of the members, I was reminded of the manual of discipline of the Methodist Church."[7] Burrows, although not a Methodist, identified discipline in spiritual affairs with Methodism. Such spiritual discipline has always been the mark of maturity within the membership of the church, just as discipline is the mark of maturity in the children of a family. In contemporary society, which has experienced the "shaking of the foundations," discipline should no longer be a threatening word. It is, in fact, the only key to renewal.

In his examination of the rules of Wesleyan societies, Dr. Ernest Rattenbury concludes: "There is nothing so amazing in this document as its omissions. Not one word is said about evangelical experience as a necessary qualification for membership in the society; it is assumed that it will be absent with some; the form of godliness was all that was essential, along with the resolution to seek the power. It was a society not for the converted only, but for the seeker. . . . But what is more amazing is that there was no intellectual or doctrinal test whatever. Anyone could belong to a Methodist society, whatever his theological convictions, so long as he proved himself a sincere seeker after God by doing good, abstaining from harm, and acknowledging the social character of religion by using the means of grace . . ."[8]

Wesley strongly defended those of weak faith. "By weak faith I understand: 1. That which is mixed with fear, particularly of not enduring to the end; 2. That which is mixed with doubt whether we have not deceived ourselves, and whether our sins be indeed forgiven; and, 3. That which has not yet purified the heart fully, not from all its idols. And thus weak I find the faith of almost all believers to be, within a short time after they have first peace with God. Yet that weak faith is faith appears: 1. From St. Paul, 'Him that is weak in faith, receive;' 2. From St. John, speaking of believers who were little children, as well as of young men and fathers; and, 3. From our Lord's own words."[9]

Wesley met the challenge of those within his societies who wanted to establish elaborate standards of ecclesiastical fitness and membership. Many wanted only those of a certain theological persuasion within the ranks. Persons joining the society had to be ethically pure, but the emphasis was on inner quality and not on moralism. Many a repentant sinner and notorious reprobate followed a path from the revival meeting into the inner sanctum of the society. It was Wesley's unvarying policy with respect to "the admission of members into the society, that no regard is had to any particular sect or party. Whoever is found upon inquiry, to be a good man is readily admitted."[10]

What About The Grouping Of Members?

Wesley's societies can be viewed in the context of the recent movement in church renewal which has turned to small groups as seeming panaceas for the ills of the church. Small groups have proven valuable for therapy, prayer, Bible study, service projects, intensive Christian experience, vocational guidance, and real conversion. However, rarely have such groups been organized along the Wesleyan model. As a theologian he used such groups only as tools to better express corporately what God had revealed. There was little stylization or formalization of them during his lifetime. He would be critical of the modern small group movement in at least three particulars:

(1) Many have not been structured within the framework (and under the guidance) of the church. This makes them much less effective in outreach, leavening, and durability.

(2) Few have shown sufficient concern for the wider community, within the arc but not the community of the Church. The groups have often been purely negative when dealing with the problems of the institutional church and have been very free to tear down the admittedly insufficient efforts of denominations. Often like spiritual gypsies they serve themselves while ignoring their obligations to others outside the immediate group.

(3) Many demonstrate what appears to be inflexibility and rigidity, allowing only one path to salvation, service, and truth. None have shown the methodological openness which was the mark of Wesley's success.

He demonstrated that intensity of personal experience does not demand withdrawal from the concerns and the working of the world. It was as he became vitally aware of the needs of the world that he became able to see the living word in his experience. Wesley gave the following advice to his leaders (of small groups and bands): "That it may be more easily discerned whether the members of our societies are working out their own salvation, they are divided into little companies, called classes. One person in each of these is styled the leader. It is his business: (1) To see each person in his class once a week; to inquire how their souls prosper; to give advice, reprove, comfort, or exhort them; (2) To receive what they are willing to give toward the expenses of the society; and (3) To meet the assistant and the stewards once a week."[11]

What would be the result if every church could be organized after this simple pattern? Its members could reclaim the inspiration of Bible study and the power of prayer. They could be helped into a new involvement with one another and a new honesty in all relationships. Most important, there could be a new spirit of appreciation for spiritual values and the richness of the experience of others.

Wesley's general rules remind us that there is little frankness in most church meetings today. It is no accomplishment to love and to be kindly toward those who always try to avoid anything controversial in discussion. Some churches have as members only those that share the same values and customs. It was the refreshing honesty of Wesley's meetings that made them so valuable. The first purpose of the group meetings was to "confess our faults, one to another, and to pray one for another that we may be healed." Wesley gave this guidance: "(1) To meet once a week at least; (2) To come punctually at the hour appointed; (3) To begin with singing or prayer; (4) To seek, each of us in order, freely and plainly, the true state of our soul, with the faults we have committed in thought, word and deed, and the temptations we have felt since our last meeting; and (5) To desire some person among us (thence called a leader) to speak his own state first, and then to ask the rest, in order, as many and as searching questions as may be concerning their state, sins and temptations."[12]

The Discipline Of Members

For many years it was the law of the Methodist Church that new members remain on probation for a period of six months. This rule allowed the church enough time to properly train and assimilate these members before making a judgment as to intention, performance and character and it gave the new member the opportunity to find whether or not he or she had found a spiritual home. Today, in some churches, membership is almost like membership in a "booster's club." While Wesley asked every person to participate in the life of the church, offered them its services, and asked each to make a commitment to Christ, he pressured none into society membership. He extended that privilege only to those willing to lead a new life in faith in accordance with the teachings of Christ.

The original Methodist discipline was modeled on the rules of the primitive church. Discipline was instituted, not for the benefit of the institution (society), but for the benefit of the individual Christian. Although Christians working together in discipline can accomplish much more for the Kingdom in this world, the primary blessings of discipline have always been to the disciplined person. Any church which fails to develop spiritual discipline doesn't care sufficiently for its people. If the love of Christ is shared, every member cares about the spiritual growth and moral strength of every other member. The Church has the same responsibility for its members as family members have for one another, and for the same reason, a community of love must be shared.

The Excluding Of Unworthy Members

For Wesley, forgiveness was always possible. Therefore, no person was ever excluded from the family of the church. The individual societies, groups, cells, and service groups within the church were another matter. No person had a right to leadership. Such an honor was earned, given in the grace of the spirit. Whenever necessary Wesley changed leadership, seeking new vitality in his societies. He wrote in his JOURNAL: "The next week we endeavored to purge the society of all that did not walk according to the gospel. By this means we reduced the number of members to less than nineteen hundred. But number is an inconsiderable circumstance. May God increase them in faith and love."[13]

Ultimately, Wesley expected the greater discipline of love: "I have a higher demand upon you who love as well as fear God. He whom you fear, whom you love, has qualified you for promoting His work in a more excellent way. Because you love God, you love your brother also; you love, not only your friends, but your enemies; not only the friends, but even the enemies of God. You have put on, as the elect of God, lowliness, gentleness, long suffering."[14]

CHAPTER 12
DISCIPLINES OF RENEWAL IN WORSHIP

In few places is today's Church more poverty stricken than in its worship. Too few congregations have developed creative ways of recognizing the worth of God. Some, often without realizing it, still fail to be inclusive before God. Their leaders are insensitive to women, older members, children, young people, and members of different ethnic groups and cultures. Experiments abound and readers should be encouraged to explore those that pertain to particular congregations or to groups within a congregation. Liturgical jazz, folk masses, rhythmic choirs, religious drama and dance, clown and mime ministries, and other creative forms have much to offer but often do not speak to the needs of the whole congregation.

As a priest, Wesley never questioned the shape of the liturgy nor the efficacy of the sacraments of the Church of England. He loved THE BOOK OF COMMON PRAYER and most of his own services of formal worship are taken from it. Frank Baker found that "for John Wesley THE BOOK OF COMMON PRAYER was only just less inspired than the Bible." His highest tribute to it was "I believe there is no liturgy in the world, either in ancient or modern language, which breathes more of solid, scriptural, rational piety, than the Common Prayer of the Church of England. And though the main of it was compiled considerably more than two hundred years ago, yet is the language of it not only pure, but strong and elegant in the highest degree."

Whenever Wesley changed from the regular practice of his church, he was careful to find sanctions for his action either in the Biblical Word or in the practice of the primitive church. When Wesleyans in America needed guidance, he furnished them with Articles of Religion and a liturgy taken from Anglican sources. Although deeply disappointed when the forms of ministry were broken by Asbury and others, Wesley was extraordinarily free in his attitude toward worship. He wrote in his STANDARD SERMONS: "I do not mean, 'embrace my modes of worship or I will embrace yours.' We must both act as each is fully persuaded in his own mind. Hold you fast that which you believe is most acceptable to God, and I will do the same."[1]

The basic form of worship familiar to Wesley was a corporate act which finds its source in New Testament times. In the Old Testament sacrifice was given special emphasis at times of great national and religious holidays. With the dispersion of the Jews, synagogues sprang up in local communities, and in each synagogue a pattern of worship developed. Since sacrifice was permissible only in the Temple, this crucial feature of previous worship patterns had to be abandoned. In its place came liturgical forms which are still in use. During the patristic period the pattern of synagogue worhip including a verse of praise, prayer, a reading of scripture, an exposition of scripture in the form of preaching, and a period of meditation. Through Roman Catholic influence, patterns of the Temple slowly reasserted themselves becoming dominant by the Middle Ages. The Mass reenacted the ritualistic sacrifice of Christ. The Reformation revived synagougue practice, while the Temple continues to provide the background of the Roman Catholic Mass.

The evangelical revival brought significant spiritual drama to worship. Wesley taught that the true end of public worship was celebration. Every service was an Easter event, lifting up love, both the love of God for individuals, and the love of individuals for God.

Scholars agree that there were three parts to the Wesley service: "The service of confession, the service of the Word, and the service of offering, rehearsing the three basic moods of Christian worship—repentance, proclamation and dedication. Confession comes first. This is broadly symbolic of the fact that all we bring to the service of Christian worship is our fragmented and broken attempts at goodness, and that the service is not for the purpose of self-congratulation, but for the purpose of rejoicing in the majesty and love of God who meets us with good news in the midst of our inadequacy."[2] In response to confession, the community of belivers share the forgiveness of Christ.

Through the converting ordinance of the preached word the community of believers gains access to the good news which enables life as God intended it to be, and as Christ lived it. Through the converting ordinance of the Lord's Supper, the community of believers share in the grace of Christ the gift of offering their souls and bodies to the service of God through participation in his work in the world.

The general pattern of worship in United Methodist Churches today is structured formally in a ritual which is approved by the General Conference at the beginning of each quadrennium. In recent years several creative options have been provided and experimentation encouraged. These patterns provided guides which can be locally adapted. Such is not always the case. Wesley felt himself bound by the canons and prayer book rubrics of the Church of England. The 1792 DISCIPLINE presented the first formal order of worship for use in Methodist churches. There it was "directed" that there should be "uniformity" in "Methodist public worship on the Lord's Day." The morning service was to consist of "singing, prayer, the reading of a chapter out of the Old Testament and another out of the New, and preaching." The afternoon service was similar except that one full chapter was to be read out of the Bible; and the evening service was to consist of singing, prayers and preaching without scripture reading. It was also provided that upon the days which the Lord's Supper was to be administered "the reading of the scripture lessons may be omitted."[3]

Wesley believed in both liturgical form and free expression. He also defended liturgy as giving the people more chances to participate and as giving the preacher good guidance. All sermons, Wesley mandated, were to be Biblical in both form and content. Richard Watson, the most esteemed Methodist theologian of the nineteenth century, devoted eight pages of his THEOLOGICAL INSTITUTES, published in 1826, in an attempt to prove that "those who object to the use of liturgy in public worship" are "illogical" and "contrary to scriptural teaching and Apostolic practice."[4]

The Church of England had no hymn book before the year 1736, relying mainly on the metrical versions of the Psalms by Sternhold and Hopkins or Tate and Brady. The English speaking world was introduced to hymns and to congregational singing by the Wesleys. Charles made use of both tavern tunes and the music of the great composers. "In the organization of the revival itself," wrote Dr. Diamond, "the hymns were of value in three directions. Their power of suggestion, their educational value, and the effect of the music with which there were associated contributed in a marked degree to the creation of the desired emotional experience, and to the permanent influence of the religious idea and impulses which were the psychological center and soul of the movement."[5]

The hymn, almost always representing a paraphrase of scripture, became a vehicle for God's Word in worship. Scripture was spoken through music so the worshipper would both understand and remember. Hymns have since become the liturgy of the free churches with the accumulated treasures of the hymnody their formal heritage. Bernard Manning wrote that "hymns are for the Dissenters what the liturgy is to the Anglican. They are the framework, the setting, the conventional, the traditional part of divine service as we use it."[6]

Charles Wesley and other hymn writers gave the unlearned person a theology which shaped both thought and action. Hymns became the best known writings of eighteenth century England, quoted and sung wherever Christians met; they possessed, for the most part, a musical quality now unlikely to be found in a popular hymnody, lifting the cultural as well as the spiritual standard of the people. A renewal of worship in contemporary America would have to involve a revival of our musical inheritance. Hymns no longer command the loyalty and the deep spiritual foundation that was once a dynamic factor of worship. With increasing frequency a majority of today's congregations do not participate in the "singing." The influence of the Wesleys on the hymnody has steadily declined for many of their hymns fell by the wayside when orthodox theological thinking went out of intellectual favor at the beginning of the twentieth century. The time for the renewal of the hymnody is at hand. Already there are signs of creativity. Composers have turned to substantial religious themes when writing anthems, oratorios, and instrumental music. There is a need for inclusive language, as well as the need of sharing the rich worship heritage of ethnic cultures. The church has to develop high standards of theological and musical integrity if the hymnody is to be revived and restored to its former importance in worship.

John and Charles Wesley would be excellent models for such an undertaking. The hymnody of early Methodism was notable as a storehouse of devotional aids, where prayer is suggested by a Biblical text, as an unmatched reservoir of Biblical instruction, and as the provider of astounding uplift in spiritual enthusiam, cultural taste, and personal spiritual formation. Worship without vital musical expression lacks its finest source of communication and communion.

When Wesley wrote the PREFACE TO THE SUNDAY SERVICE OF THE METHODISTS IN THE UNITED STATES OF AMERICA, he made four principle alterations from the practice of the English church: (1) The holy days were omitted for they took away from the importance of Jesus Christ and were misunderstood by the common people; (2) The Service of the Lord's Day was shortened to leave more time for the preached word and the expanding hymnody; (3) Sentences in Offices of Baptism, and for the Burial of the Dead, were omitted because they conflicted with Wesley's theological emphasis; and, (4) Many psalms were omitted as "being highly improper for the mouths of a Christian congregation."[7]

The most frequently heard criticism of the worship of the Wesleys was that it bred "enthusiasm," a euphemism for over-emotionalism and fanatical behavior. Something happened in worship in early Methodism (The people felt themselves to be fully in the presence of God), because something was expected to happen—faith was present. (Paradoxically, we exercise similar emotional reaction at football, basketball and hockey games, boxing matches, and other sporting events; a normal activity because the outcome of these games seem so important to us.) Charles Wesley writes of his experience in

Newcastle: "Many, no doubt, were at our first preaching, struck down, both soul and body, into the depth of distress. Their outward affections were easy to be imitated. Many counterfeits I have already detected. Today one who came from the ale house drunk, was pleased to fall into a fit for my entertainment, and beat himself heartily. I thought it a pity to hinder him; so instead of singing over him, as I had often done we left him to recover at his leisure."[8]

Falseness in any kind of religious expression must be avoided and exposed, yet no revival of worship will be possible until something happens to individuals during worship. We have the same experience with worship as John Wesley had with hymns; unless worship has a proper balance of the creative and the familiar, it looses its force: "I was reflecting on an odd circumstance, which I cannot account for. I never relish a tune at first hearing, not till I have almost learned to sing it; and, as I learn it more perfectly, I gradually lose my relish for it."[9]

Despite his efforts to champion forms and patterns of worship and his intention of maintaining the great liturgies of the early church and the influence of the **BOOKS OF COMMON PRAYER**, Wesley spent a lifetime fighting formalism and deadness in worship. He wanted worship to be both Catholic and Reformed, ordered and free. There is great difficulty in following his advice for the churches which give their ministers extensive freedom for liturgical and devotional improvisation are those which provide them with little or no training in worship practice or liturgical principle. There can be no realistic hope for renewal in worship until this paradox is corrected.

Wesley may have been able to maintain his loyalty to liturgical and formal order on Sunday morning because he expressed himself so freely in evangelical worship, private devotion, and prayer meetings through the week. He initiated the Watch Night Service and the Love Feast. Borrowed in part from the Moravians, these services became classic examples of Methodist practice. The former was a devotional expression of Wesley's theological emphasis upon salvation and the shortness of time. In a very special way it reminded men and women of their condition and lifted them beyond the limitations of the moment.

Building on that borrowed from others, Methodists made these two services uniquely their own. The first Watch Night was held in the United Societies in London. Wesley was fascinated by the practice of primitive Christianity of holding worship services "at the noon of the night." The service reflected his interest in eschatology and an expectation of an early return of Christ. He described a Watch Night Service on New Year's Eve: "We concluded the year at

West Street, with a solemn Watch Night. Most of the congregation stayed till the beginning of the year, and cheerfully sang together, 'Glory to God, and thanks and praise, Who kindly lengthens out our days.' "[10]

No worship pattern in Christian history has been more consistently misunderstood than the Love Feast. A Love Feast is a sacramental acting out of the horizontal relationship between Christians which God's love creates. A celebration of love which dramatizes acceptance of Christ's central teaching and act, the Love Feast in the twentieth century might represent for Protestants something similar to the Roman Catholic experience during the offering of the Mass. Something in addition to the subjective experience of worship is being done; an actual event is taking place. The event celebrated is the divine gift of salvation and love, not only the perpetual acting out of Christ's sacrifice on the cross. John Dungett describes such a Love Feast: "They commence with prayer and praise; in a few minutes a little bread and water is distributed, and a collection is made for the poor. The greater portion of the time allowed, which is generally about two hours, is occupied by such as feel disposed, in relating their own personal experience of the saving grace of God."[11]

As the father of the Evangelical Revival, Wesley will always be known first for his great evangelistic worship services. Their form was the same as the weekly service: hymns, scripture readings, prayers, meditation, preaching, call for dedication, and benediction. The spiritual response called forth from the worshipper was the same: repentance, receptivity, meditation, and commitment. At both types of services it was expected that conversion and new birth would occur. At both the same theological pattern was the rule. Differences were found in externals—in the evangelical services the congregation was always substantially larger; the setting was usually out of doors and the worshipers were a mixed company, with hecklers, atheists, and agnostics frequently present. In that day before electronic voice projection, the preaching and teaching was necessarily louder and at an intense pitch, the congregation was arranged at random, sitting, standing, and reclining while emotions were given much freer expression, and worship was not centered on an altar or a cross.

Every cell, band or society meeting was an experience in worship. Every marriage, every funeral, every pastoral call was a sharing of worship. Much of Wesley's writing was an effort to further private devotions, family prayer and meditation. No person was adequately prepared for corporate worship who was not privately committed to the discipline of regular and frequent daily devotions.

Wesley revived the prayer meeting and established the form which is still maintained wherever prayer meetings are a living force. Committed to the priesthood of all believers he encouraged lay persons to be worship leaders, preachers, and to be engaged in all forms of ministry. He taught them the value of fasting and appointed regular fast days for Methodists.[12]

Wesley's exciting witness leads to several conclusions for twenty-first century worship:

(1) Worship can be freed from narrow traditions. There is a danger that worship will become commonplace, and even manipulative if the same clergyperson chooses the theme, prayers, sermon topic, hymns, lessons, and liturgy for each service, week after week, year after year. The danger would be even greater if the ordained minister carried out all the forms chosen as celebrant. There must be positive models in leadership for every member of the congregation: children/adults, male/female, black/white, youth/senior citizen, healthy/ill, joyous/discouraged, poor/wealthy, etc. God can speak to many needs through many voices. Certainly representatives from all these groups should have a part in planning and leading in worship on a regular basis.

(2) Worship must be full of expectation and excitement. As did Wesley, we can learn from others. Ethnic churches and the traditions of other cultures have much to share. Most of us could learn more creative things about the possibilities of worship by worshiping occasionally with ethnic minority congregations than in any other way. There is power in what is fresh and new. Ethnic congregations teach us that worship can have different time frames, tones, participation levels, forms, etc. Worship in other countries is equally instructive. In Africa we would be reminded of the human heartbeat by hand-clapping and drums. In South America we would discover a new level of celebration and joy. Bishop James Armstrong describes worship in a large Pentecostal church in San Paulo, Brazil. Three thousand people were there. The congregation began with five minutes of thunderous applause welcoming the presence of Christ. The church had no paid clergypersons. Some were healed, others prayed in tongues, and elders of the congregation were led to preach. On the same day he visited another worship service where ten thousand were present.[13] Every nation in the world has something new to share, from the Pacific Islands to Orthodox Russia there are creative approaches to God.

(3) Worship must be free of the attitudes and language of sexism, agism and racism. Wesley opened the pulpit to women, gave positions of major leadership to those over sixty-five, and welcomed everyone of every race and station into his society and worship. As a person shaped by the eighteenth century, as the quotations in this book make clear, Wesley frequently used sexist language, and wrote sexist hymns and prayers. His spirit allows us to be certain that if he were alive today he would be sensitive to the damage that can be done in worship by insensitive people. I recommend highly the books of Sharon and Thomas Neufer Emswiler, especially WOMEN & WORSHIP A GUIDE TO NON-SEXIST HYMNS, PRAYERS AND LITURGIES, and WHOLENESS IN WORSHIP.

(4) All worship should share in the variety and the richness of the entire history of the Christian church. Wesley rediscovered the abundant grace in other worship traditions from the early church and the Eastern Fathers, and through different Catholic, Reformed, and Orthodox liturgies.

(5) Worship must make use of all the arts. Just as Wesley used new music, so the church should harness the great spiritual power of fine art, the theater, music (even with a beat that those under twenty will recognize occasionally), the motion picture, the dance, and multi-media presentations. Preaching is not the only valid mode of communicating the Word.

(6) Lay persons should have leadership roles in every part of worship. Some lay involvement in worship leadership and worship feedback should take place every week. Like everything else we do before God, worship should be evaluated regularly.

(7) Worship is first and last an act of service to God. The greatest act of worship is the expression of love carried out in meeting human need. The Gospel never tells of Christ leading a worship service, but it is full of his acts of love.

CHAPTER 13
THE DISCIPLINES OF STEWARDSHIP

Techniques for raising financial support have been refined to the point where the "fundraiser" can sometimes predict the amount actually raised in advance. Almost every church has an annual "every member canvass," pledge drive, Loyalty Sunday, countless "stewardship" meetings and mailings, and all the other "business-like" approaches which make for "successful stewardship." Many Roman Catholic parishes have embraced these "Protestant techniques."

Wesley's societies received financial support, in proportion with the ability of its members to give, unsurpassed in church history. Many principles of Christian stewardship, now taken for granted, were first developed during his ministry. Giving careful attention to the theological implications of stewardship, he established a discipline which did not depend upon techniques. Time was looked upon as "a small fragment of eternity" made important and meaningful as it was intentionally used in stewardship for God. As part of God's creation each individual is given life, a history, certain possessions, and a place in time. As steward and temporary custodian of these gifts, no one can claim anything exclusively for very long. **Every person owes God, not only a percentage of wealth and income, but all possessions including self. This is as true for the hours of life and for one's talents and abilities as it is for material possessions.**

Taking the reformers' emphasis on "redeeming the time" as his own, Wesley's personal goal was that of complete and unreserved stewardship. As Christ is the source of all that one has, so He is the redeemer who makes all things possible, all things valuable, and all things eternal. In such a perspective, stewardship, according to Wesley, is not a responsibility or a demand, but an overwhelming privilege: "God has entrusted us with our bodies, (those exquisitely wrought machines), so fearfully and wonderfully made, with all the powers and members thereof. He has entrusted us with the organs of sense; of sight, hearing, and the rest: But none of these are given us as our own, to be employed according to our own will. None of these are lent us in such sense as to leave us at liberty to use them as we please for a season."[1]

Although the rational of Wesley's thought is easily grasped, in practical terms it appears unrealistic. Who is going to take God seriously if everything is demanded? It is Wesley's contention that God will have it no other way—Nothing is accepted from anyone unwilling to give all. The rich young ruler had to go sorrowfully away.

"He that gives us all, must needs have a right to all; so that if we pay Him anything less than all, we cannot be faithful stewards . . . We cannot be wise stewards unless we labour to the uttermost of our power; not leaving anything undone which we possibly can do, but putting forth all our strength."[2]

Often success in "every member canvasses" produces stewardship difficulties. Although proportional giving has Biblical precedence, churches have presented it in a way which indicates to the giver that he or she has now fulfilled all obligations. The gift becomes God's portion and all the rest is used in any way desired. Stewardship in more personal areas of commitment—within the family circle, in building personal power, in living lives of morality and economic justice, in worship and devotion—is more important in the sight of God than material gifts. Wesley wrote: "We are now indebted to Him for all we have; but although a debtor is obliged to return what he has received, yet until the time of payment comes, he is at liberty to use it as he pleases. It is not so with a steward; he is not at liberty to use what is lodged in his hands as he pleases, but as his master pleases. He has no right to dispose of anything which is in his hands, but according to the will of his Lord. For he is not the proprietor of any of these things, but barely entrusted with them by another, and entrusted on this express condition—that he shall dispose of all as his master orders."[3]

The problem with such an approach is essentially one of attitude. A total partnership with God may be seen as a limiting, restricting, hopelessly binding covenant. For Wesley just the reverse was the case. Only in stewardship can life take on meaning and escape the hopeless bondage of selfishness, pride, and evil. The fact of stewardship was the other side of the greatest blessing, salvation. To be chosen as God's steward means that one has been invited into mission with Christ.

A person's stewardship defines both the extent and the depth of his or her relationship with God, replacing the sacrificial offerings of the Old Testament with the life of the believer. God claims living sacrifices, both souls and bodies, lifted up in love. We can actually share in the work of Christ, which makes us valuable and our lives meaningful.

Wesley seriously carried out his own teaching. Royalties from his books would have made him one of England's wealthiest persons, but such a fate was avoided by "squaring accounts at the end of every year." His only extravagance was books, and these were the tools of his trade and made available for general use. He believed that whenever one purchased something that was either unnecessary or extravagant, it was stolen from God: "When you are laying out that money in costly apparel which you could have otherwise spared for the poor, you thereby deprive them of what God, the proprietor of all, had lodged in your hands for their use. If so, what you put upon yourself, you are, in effect, tearing from the back of the naked; as the costly and delicate food which you eat, you are snatching from the mouth of the hungry. . . ."[4]

How relevant is such an argument for a society of relative affluence? It may, in fact, be a key to church renewal. As long as the church acts selfishly in the name of Christ, accumulating for itself and its leaders wealth, prestige and power, few will hear the worth in its preaching. Half of the world's people are still hungry, yet most ecclesiastical executives and many pastors exercise the expense account delights and the travel benefits of secular power. Few Christians seem ready to risk a substantial part of their capital in an effort to save or serve others.

Did his own practice square with his preaching? At the height of his temporal power, Wesley wrote a prophetic statement, "If I leave behind me 10 pounds; . . . you and all mankind bear witness against me that I lived and died a thief and a robber. . . . The income from the almost unprecedented sale of Wesley's tracts, pamphlets, and books was sufficient to make him a rich man; but never did he spend more than seventy-five dollars a year upon his personal needs. Always he wore cheap clothes; and . . . dined on the plainest fare. In a single year . . . he kept one forty-seventh of his earnings, and gave away nearly ninety-eight percent. Increased income, therefore, had no effect on his personal expenditure. He supplied his humble needs in the most modest manner, and gave away all the rest—or rather returned it to God, its owner."[5]

How can this teaching be applied in an affluent society, when wants become necessities in ten year cycles? May stewards allow for an increase in their standard of living? Certainly Wesley's thought is unsophisticated and uneffected by what has been learned in a capitalist economy which combines the elements of free enterprise with social welfare legislation and big government. Today's economic world is much more complex than his. Many would claim that Wesley should have invested his money and used only the proceeds or interest. In that manner many poor would still be receiving aid and the capital would be furnishing work for others. It may now be much more effective to provide employment than to give charity. To provide jobs, capital has to be accumulated and put to work. Yet every economic system, according to Biblical ethics and the prophetic word of righteousness, must be structured by both justice and compassion. Wesley was inventive and original in devising means of social action in his time. His followers should not be afraid of innovation today.

A Methodist barber, William Shent, was in financial straits after being publically expelled from Wesley's society for conspicuous sin. When he was down, the members of the society turned their backs on him. Wesley came to his defense: "And does nobody care . . . must he also be starved? Must he with his grey hairs and all his children be without a place to lay his head? Can you suffer this? . . . Where is gratitude? Where is compassion? Where is Christianity? Where is humanity?"[6] Wesley's humanity was the foundation for his mission. He worried about the effects of selfishness on spiritual life.

The primary motivation for stewardship, according to Wesley, was not institutional need but the condition of the soul and the personal happiness of the steward. He wrote, commenting on 1 Timothy 6:9, "They that will be rich fall into temptation and a snare, and into many foolish and hurtful desires, which drown men in destruction and perdition."[7] Concern for the welfare of the steward, instead of for the financial health of the institution or the cause benefited, is fundamental.

Wesley was careful to expand the discussion from finances alone to include all the habits, desires, wants and activities of life. To evaluate stewardship, all of life must undergo intentional investigation. Worried about the spiritual condition of the wealthy, Wesley formally proposed at annual conference, "Ought we not to have a longer time of probation for the rich before we admit them into our society?" After long and interesting debate the conference decided this would be unnecessary, but the discussion lead to passage of a resolution that "the time of probation for rich and poor should be three months."[8] Totally honest with the wealthy, Wesley never approached them under false pretenses. He could be completely frank with them because he thought of their spiritual well-being and not the extent of their financial support. Since he totally supported himself he had no vested interest in a compromised witness. This gave him independence of action while creating a genuine pastoral relationship. Stewardship was encouraged as a way of life, not induced by special recognition.

Bishop McConnell went to some lengths to track down a common misunderstanding of Wesley's most quoted piece of advice: "Gain all you can, save all you can, give all you can." This statement has been used to give license for the accumulation of wealth. Wesley recommended saving for the sole purpose of accumulating a reserve that could later be used for the larger demands of ethical responsibility. While his own giving seemingly had no limits, he found that his advice was misunderstood during his lifetime: "O that God would enable me once more . . . to lift up my voice like a trumpet to those who gain and save all they can, but do not give all they can! Ye are the men, some of the chief men, who continually grieve the Holy Spirit of God, and in a great measure stop his gracious influence from descending on our assemblies. Many of your brethern beloved of God, have not food to eat; they have not clothes to put on; they have not a place where to lay their head."[9]

This rigid doctrine of stewardship prevented Methodism from involving as many members of the upper classes as it might have done using a more conventional approach. Yet it enabled Methodism to establish the discipline, the accountability, and the spiritual drive which made it the most effective evangelical movement in the history of the church and a force in social welfare.

The Church of England in Wesley's time was state-supported through tax and land revenue. His adventure into voluntary giving was daring for it made its requirements of people who were already supporting the state church through taxation. Nevertheless, Methodists were determined that their financial needs would be supplied by the means of all the members rather than by the philanthrophy of the few. Monday, February 15, 1742, is an historic date in this connection. A conference at Bristol was called to discuss the proper method of discharging the public debt which burdened the society. Money which has been borrowed on demand notes might be called at any time, and several hints had been received that the creditors would soon foreclose. Facing the stewardship question, Captain Foy, whose ship sailed regularly from Bristol, suggested, "Let every one in the society give a penny a week, and it will easily be done." To the objection that some of the members . . . were too poor to give even a penny, the Captain replied, "True, then put ten or twelve of them together. Let each of these give what they can weekly, and I will supply what is wanting." The society was divided into groups, or "classes," with one person, the leader of the class, receiving the collection at each weekly meeting. Wesley appointed the "leaders" and assigned a "class" of twelve members to each of them. Wealthy members made up for the inability of the poor. Many poorer members of the society took over similar burdens for others as they prospered and took on leadership.

CHAPTER 14
THE DISCIPLINES OF CHRISTIAN MISSIONS

From both his parents Wesley learned Arminian doctrine and his missionary outlook. At that time, with the exception of the Order of Jesus in the Roman Catholic Church, only those influenced by Arminian theology had developed a doctrine of Christian missions. Among the state churches, interest was from the beginning centered on the local parish for most Calvinistic theologians emphasized predestination and election, providing little motivation to prioritize missions.

Tyerman, in his biography of Samuel Wesley, wrote, "The missionary spirit was a passion in the Wesley family when Christian missions to the heathen scarcely existed."[1] In 1705, before anyone else in England had even suggested a mission to any place except to English colonies and plantations, Samuel not only "suggested a scheme for the conversion of Jews, Mohammedans and heathens," but offered himself as a missionary to "Abyssinia, India, or China for the sake of the heathen whose language he expressed himself willing to learn as well as to any of the English colonies or to any existing native churches."[2] When Wesley himself wanted to go on a mission to the Indians in America, Susanna wrote to him, "Had I twenty sons, I should rejoice, were they all so employed though I should never see them more."[3]

Wesley looked upon America as a place where he could extend the ideals of the holy club and establish the practices of the primitive church (confession, frequent communion, fasting, etc.) Although his adventure in Georgia has been judged a failure by many, his experience there was influential on his thinking and spirit for the rest of his life. He never lost his apostolic and missionary obligation, and he stressed this same discipline in his society and in his preaching as an obligation of Christian obedience.

As John Vickers has described in his fine work, THOMAS COKE, APOSTLE OF METHODISM, Wesley's chosen American superintendent was Methodism's missionary ambassador. "Methodism was one of the first of the Protestant denominations to undertake overseas missions and one of the last to establish a missionary society. The interval was filled largely by the exertions of one man . . . spending his own fortune for expenses, Coke traveled over much of the world as a missionary. On May 3, 1814, at sixty-seven years of age, bound for missionary service in India, Coke died upon ship. On his lap was a Portugese grammar, for he was trying to learn a language then used in Ceylon. 'The body of the father of Methodist missions' was committed to its resting place in the Indian Ocean.''[4]

On January 7, 1814, Bishop Francis Asbury had written in his JOURNAL: "We learn that Bishop Coke, with seven young preachers, has sailed for the East Indies. The British society is poor as well as ourselves it would appear: This is a good sign. In less than one hundred years Methodism has spread over three quarters of the globe; and it is now about to carry the Gospel of salvation into Asia. Amen.''[5]

A commitment to world-wide missions came very rapidly. The 1820 General Conference officially recognized the Methodist Missionary Society and by 1832, historian Nathan Bangs had completed AN AUTHENTIC HISTORY OF THE MISSIONS, which was primarily an account of missionary work among the American Indians which by 1844 "expanded to include thirty-five indian tribes in sixteen states and territories, exclusive of Upper Canada.''[6]

In the same period worldwide missionary effort began. The first missionary to Africa, Melville Cox died soon after he arrived there in 1833. Work began in South America in 1835 and in China in 1848. The first United Methodist missionaries had assignments that required patient dedication and incredible personal sacrifice. The South American effort, which showed great promise and growth, was undercut by the financial crisis of 1837. By 1841 all missionaries had to be recalled and the work temporarily suspended.[7] In China dedicated missionaries waited nine years and two months before Ting Ang, their first convert, was baptized. A forty-seven year old craftsman with a wife and five children, he had attended preaching services for two years before he was baptized and admitted into membership.[8]

John Wesley understood the spiritual anguish involved for he wrote in his JOURNAL: "Oh let none think his labour of love is lost because the fruit does not immediately appear! Nearly forty years did my father labor here (Epworth), but he saw little fruit of all his labour. I took some pains among this people too, and my strength also seemed spent in vain; but now the fruit appeared.''[9]

It has been the women of the church who have taken the leadership and made the greater sacrifices in both missions and social concerns. In 1850 there were "not more than twenty Methodist foreign missionaries in the world." By 1920 there were over two thousand.[10]

The difference was a direct result of the involvement and dedication of women. The Woolston sisters were sent to Foochow in 1858 and when the Women's Foreign Missionary Society was organized in 1869 they were confirmed as its first representatives in China.

This was the story in every mission field. At great personal cost, women took the risks. From sixty to seventy percent of foreign missionary workers sent from the United States in the seventy-five years between 1850 and 1925 were women. Without question this was the period of the greatest growth of the church outside the United States and the period of greatest humanitarian service. Women went to serve abroad at a time when they were not welcome in the pulpit at home. Often they were not wanted and rudely treated. Mary Porter wrote in her Diary in Peking in 1871: "The presence of single women in China missions was an offence against all Chinese ideas of propriety . . . There were missionaries on the field . . . who believed that the introduction of women . . . was a mistake. In conference . . . Miss Brown and I agreed that we should be missunderstood no matter what course we might choose . . . We decided, therefore, that we should conduct ourselves in all our relationships according to the conventions of our own Christian land."[11]

These women, joined by thousands of others, by means of personal sacrifice, not only brought the good news of Christ but helped to bring the fruits of His love into the lives of people far beyond the modest limits of the missionary church. In China, as a direct result of Christian missions, the purposeful exposure and murder of infant baby girls and the practice of binding the feet of those that survived was abolished. Girls and young women were given the opportunity of education for the first time by these missionaries and given hope in society. Around the world the hungry were fed, the sick were healed, the outcasts were loved, and the poor sought out, all in the name of Christ.

The missionary enterprise was not entirely an endless line of splendor. Some were willing to compromise any Christian principle for institutional success. The finest China scholar of the twentieth century, John F. Fairbank, recorded that as it became successful the "missionary position became more ludicrous." Some missionary leaders even were willing to use the technique of war to win converts. Methodist Earl Cranston declared it "worth any cost in bloodshed if we can make millions of Chinese true and intelligent Christians."[12] This stance, to impose the gospel in association with armed force, was used all over the world. Eventually it proved to be futile and dangerous. Often institutional leadership made wrong choices, spoiling the heroic sacrifice of those serving in ministry in the field. Fairbank writes in his autobiography: "In the face of the anti-imperialist movement in April, 1922, alas, the Protestant missions in China set an all-time record for obtuse nonsalesmanship by publishing a book, entitled not CHRISTIAN HELP TO CHINA, but

THE CHRISTIAN OCCUPATION OF CHINA. It was full of militant maps and statistics and was so utterly foreign-minded it was a real giveaway. It must have made a lot of Chinese Christians feel they had been "had". From this time, T. F. Tsiang, like others, became less concerned about Christianity for China, and more concerned about national rights."[13]

Only gradually did the United Methodist Church rediscover an idea that John Wesley taught and preached more than a century before—that the goal of mission and ministry is not only individual salvation but also accepting the spiritual disciplines leading to sanctification. Wesley went so far as to preach that salvation without the fruits of righteousness, justice, and the loving, caring service of those in need was not salvation at all.

The United Methodist Church, and most other Christian churches, has come to understand that a missionary commitment involves:

• Respect for the people and the culture of the other country

• A commitment to service and the needs of people

• A commitment to national leadership in control of the work of the mission

• A commitment to the principles of righteousness and justice

---

Wesley's practice and his thought provides several suggestions for those in mission:

(1) Any program of Christian missions must be balanced between an equal emphasis on the Gospel revelation of individual salvation by grace through faith in Jesus Christ and the Gospel revelation that every saved person is called to the mission and ministry of discipleship and love wherever there is a human need.

(2) He had a passion to reach people who had not heard the Gospel of Jesus Christ and to meet the needs of people who faced any kind of personal or moral tragedy.

(3) He had a remarkable tolerance and willingness to enter into dialogue with other peoples. He was so secure in his faith in Christ that he felt no need to drag others down.

(4) Any program of Christian missions must be expansive enough to include within its scope:

(a) The involvement of many lay ministers, especially those with specialist skills not usually possessed by ordained ministers.

(b) The involvement of as many volunteers as possible. Massive efforts are needed to match the secular societies program of Peace Corps and Vista volunteers. Many, many people over sixty, or just out of high school or college, have the skills, energy, faith, and experience to be extraordinary missionaries and have the time and the spiritual commitment as well.

(c) The involvement of as many full-time volunteer lay or ordained ministers into the executive and policy-making positions of leadership. Because he earned his living independently Wesley was able to make his own decisions without financailly vested interest in mind. A balance between full-time volunteer and full-time paid staff executives would be healthy.

(d) The involvement of children and youth on a large scale. Many young people would learn more intellectually and spiritually through a year in mission away from home, in the United States or in any other country, than they could possibly learn at home.

(e) The involvement of trust at every level of mutual responsibility. Too often we have allowed our programs to be bogged down by mutual criticism and defensiveness. Just as an ordained minister should not be afraid to give up control of everything in a local church, so local churches and conferences do not have to "own" everything done by a national board or by missionaries in the areas of need. Nor does a national board have to control all involvement in mission and social concerns.

(f) The involvement of citizens of each country as leaders of missions in those countries, as those who define the need and who evaluate the results.

(5) Wesley heartily applauded risks taken to serve people in human need even when those risks resulted in serious mistakes. It is far better for national boards and executives to be under attack because they have attempted too much, or something controversial, than because they attempted too little, or only "safe" projects, in an effort to avoid criticism.

It is possible that Wesley, if he could have been present at the Assembly of the World Council of Churches in Vancouver in 1983, would have been among those giving a standing applause to Allan

Boesak, the minister from South Africa, during his speech responding to the theme of the assembly: "JESUS CHRIST—THE LIFE OF THE WORLD."

He said: "The realities of our world suggest the cold grip of death rather than the freedom of life . . . the Word is drowned by the ugly sound of gunfire, by the screams of our children and the endless cry of the powerless . . . Yet the Gospel affirms that Jesus Christ is the source of life. He is the giver of the sacred gift of life. He intends for us a life filled with abundance, joy and meaning. He is the Messiah in whose eyes our lives are precious . . .

"Is it really meant for the millions who lived without hope? Yes, because Jesus spoke to the despised and rejected: the Apocalypse of John was written to a weak, scattered, underground church, suffering under the persecution of a ruthless tyrant."[14]

Many express the fear today that the economy of the world may collapse. The third world countries, led by Brazil, Mexico and Polland, owe billions of dollars. If they default, the banking system of the western industrial countries may disintegrate. Then, there would be a world-wide depression. Most of us forget that the economy of at least sixty percent of the people of the world has been in a state of collapse throughout their lifetimes. They live each day in poverty with little hope of relief!

In his fine book, THE POWER OF THE POOR IN HISTORY, Gustovo Gutierrez writes theology "from the underside of history" in the Wesley tradition. Like Wesley, when discussing the mission of the church, he escapes from pastoral and institutional concerns by underlining the ethical, moral, and spiritual dimensions he learned from the working class people living in poverty in Lima, Peru. In the same way Wesley developed his conception of mission by contrasting the world he saw with the witness of the Gospel.

CHAPTER 15
THE DISCIPLINES OF EVANGELISM
AND WITNESS

An evangelist is one who brings the gospel to others. A witness is one who testifies by act or word to the truth of the good news of Jesus Christ. A renewed church finds its spirit in the contagious awakening of persons and not in a structured program meant to accomplish institutional tasks. A renewed person finds that Christ's claim is so transforming that it must be shared. The experience of faith is similar to that of love—when the condition is real, it cannot be kept to oneself.

There is no such thing as a "professional" evangelist in the Biblical record. Every person is called to be an evangelist and a witness.

Much contemporary theology is structured on sociological and philosophical foundations which assume that human beings are the objects to which all things in life, including the Word of God, must give account and that they are judge of all that comes before them. This combination of humanistic and rationalistic principles has resulted in a disintegration of the language of faith. If the Biblical "word" becomes an object for interpretation bent to suit convenience or completed action, then both evangelism and witness collapse, without power or conviction. Unfortunately, this is what has happened in contemporary theology, and, as a result, evangelism seems strangely irrelevant to the institutional church. Robert W. Funk describes this process with great clarity: "With man as the filter through which the Word must pass, or, if you like arbiter of the meaning, it is inevitable that he will censor out what he does not wish to hear and audit only what he is predisposed to hear. Yet the Word of God, like a great work of art, is not on trial . . . The text, too, although shaped by human hands, stands there to be read and pondered, but not manipulated. The view of hermeneutics which begins with the assumption that the text requires interpretation, that it is, so to speak, on trial, has the matter backwards. It is not the text that requires interpretation, but the interpreter!"[1]

This discovery is not particularly new. More than fifty years ago Karl Barth, in the Preface to the second edition of ROMANS, set the agenda for evangelism. Confronted by scholarship which proclaimed that the Biblical text is made up exclusively of human words, historically conditioned, and that the text itself is already an interpretation of the word of God. Barth, instead of denying the obvious, proclaimed that the process of interpretation must be reversed. Suggesting that we should read our daily newspaper with the Bible in mind, and the Bible with our daily newspaper in mind, Barth declared that Christians must live with the text until it disappears, leaving them in confrontation with the divine word itself, Jesus Christ. This is similar to the Christological approach to evangelism and witness that Wesley used to transform the religious life of a century.

Evangelism shares the converting word—the Gospel that converts a person from living apart from God to a life living in community with God. **Wesley believed in "prevenient grace," that love of God which acts before a person has any thought of salvation.** For him the purpose of evangelism was "to declare to all mankind what it is that God hath done, and is still doing, in our land. For it is not the work of man which hath lately appeared. All who calmly observe it must say, 'This is the Lord's doing, and it is marvelous in our eyes.' "[2]

If Wesley's contention that Christ died for all and not simply for the elect is true, then the call to evangelism is both broad and crucial. Complete trust in God did not prevent Wesley from carefully structuring his evangelistic commitment. Making no distinctions, he went primarily to the secular world with his message of salvation. Contemporary evangelism has increasingly limited its primary activity to the "churched." Without self-consciously abandoning the world, it has progressively developed a vocabulary and a technique which tends to prevent communication with those in the secular society. As society itself becomes more materialistic and sophisticated in attitude and lifestyle, traditional evangelistic appeals involve a smaller and smaller segment of the general community. The spectacular crusades of a Billy Graham are misleading for they seemingly include in their scope an ever-widening group of people. The fact is that the proportion of people involved each year is dropping even when statistics are limited to the "churched." This is partly true because the population has grown rapidly since Graham began his work. Although his crusades involve a great number of people, no scholar would question that a far smaller percentage of Americans are involved in such efforts than has been true at any time since the opening years of the nineteenth century.

It was Wesley's judgment that evangelism should try to reach the entire population since Christ cared for all the lost. Every person brought into membership in one of his classes became responsible for witness. When Methodism came to the United States it brought a zealous evangelism which set "the wilderness aflame," resulting in a forty year period of renewal. Wesley's methods are still viable for he concentrated on the idiom and the needs of those addressed. Such a wholistic emphasis is badly needed in a fragmented world. Open to the working of the Holy Spirit, Wesley knew no limits of socio-economic class.

Local Church Evangelism

Any local church may develop a plan for contacting every person in the community. Adapting Wesley's principles to today's world with all its complexities is not easy. In a mobile society, lay persons are as likely to itinerate as clergy once were. Under such conditions the newcomer to a geographic area must receive special attention. Often well-educated and quite sophisticated, new people are reached only by those who concentrate on the Gospel rather than upon the needs of the institutional church. The needs of the person, the family, and the society must be emphasized ahead of the needs of the church for growth.

It was Wesley's experience, consistent with the Biblical witness, that converted lay persons made the most powerful evangelists. They were communicators—those who could listen and speak in the action patterns of their day. They broke tradition, at a time when Church polity reserved both preaching and evangelism exclusively to clergymen. Wesley horrified the leadership by using laymen and laywomen for these tasks: "I allow that it is highly expedient (that) whoever preaches in His name should have an outward as well as an inward call, but that it is absolutely necessary, I deny." He lifted the practice of the apostolic age which was so important to him (Acts 8): "Therefore they that were scattered abroad went everywhere preaching the word." (Verse 4) "Now, were all these outwardly called to preach? No man in his senses can think so. Here, then, is an undeniable proof, what was the practice of the apostolic age. Here you see not one, but a multitude of lay preachers, men that were only sent by God."[3]

Wesley found that when God converts a person everything changes. A new life is born. The ego factor diminishes to the point where one needs not worry about competitive or individual conquests. For this reason, evangelical style, as it has been understood in the twentieth century, must undergo a radical transformation. Just as Wesley used books and pamphlets and the out-of-doors for the first time, effective evangelists today will use new methods. **Perhaps the computer will be seen in a hundred years as the greatest evangelistic tool in history! Cable television will soon be available,**

allowing two-way communication and a remarkable opportunity for witness. Indeed, social action (witness in the community) can be the most effective form of evangelism. Persons witness for God most completely in what they do than by what they say. Although this has always been true, the fact takes on special importance in a pluralistic society. Most people outside the institutional church, and many people inside, fail to understand what most evangelists are talking about. Indifferent to theological questions, secular individuals fail to identify with the institutional church and, most of all, have no felt need for salvation. Secular persons do, however, react to social action which meets their needs and to personal concern that brings them involvement in a caring, loving community. They notice acts of love and are able to understand both sacrificial service and hypocracy.

No ecclesiastic in the Church of England bothered Wesley in the days of the Oxford Club when conversion was being discussed. It was only when the consequences of conversion spread into the secular world with revolutionary effect, that anyone cared about Methodist evangelism. Wesley went among the mine workers not because he had read about their needs, but because God had called him to serve all people. He assumed that "if a man's soul was saved, fundamental social change would inevitably follow." Personally involved in every social revolution of his time, Wesley did not accept any pietistic division between spiritual and secular. Every meeting was an opportunity for reformation and change. "Those who have tasted of the goodness of God are frequently wanting in declaring it. They do not, as they ought stir up the gift of God which is in every believer by exciting one another to continual thankfulness and provoking each other to love and good works. We would never be content to make drawn battle, to part neither better nor worse than we met."[4]

This was exactly what witnesses were called upon to accomplish —to provoke each other to love and good works. So it was that reform in social life was the incidental, but inevitable, consequence of all Wesley's activity in prisons, among the poor, the slaves, the politically oppressed, the heathen, and the lower classes.

Evangelism brought an increase in membership and insured the assimilation or withdrawal of the new convert. Wesley gave an open invitation and then required a change in lifestyle. Too often we have reversed the process. We have given a narrow invitation to the secular society based on a presumptive moralism and then not required any change in lifestyle for those who politely respond.

In summary:

(1) Wesley was concerned with changing lives rather than with collecting impressive statistics. He organized the converted immediately into societies which made extensive demands of spiritual, intellectual, and moral discipline. This was the fruit of conversion which was seen as the beginning, not the ending of a process. It was follow through that counted most for him. He recorded the commitments kept, not the contacts made.

(2) Wesley gave real authority and responsibility to laity according to the witness of Scripture. Members of the society had the basic task of evangelism. Perhaps today's church should require that each member lead at least one other person into membership each year to maintain full connection in the community. Of course, exceptions would be made for those with special problems or other extraordinary difficulties. The church that took such a plan seriously might not grow in total membership, but the quality of its membership would be substantially improved.

(3) There was no secret to Wesley's great evangelistic success—he combined the puritan work-ethic and Christian witness. Each member was continuously and enthusiastically at work. Each made a witness before God. If people responded that was a bonus, not the essential. There are many stories in Wesley's journals that describe his preaching in town squares without people present at the beginning of the sermons. Today, we would not begin without an audience. Wesley trusted God to provide.

(4) Wesley's was almost purely a volunteer movement. This spirit was still alive in Methodism in the early part of the twentieth century. When Ernest W. Bysshe asked Missionary Secretary, Homer Stunz, for funds for Evangelists' salaries in 1913 he received this letter of response from the national Methodist leader: "The theory that you must hire men to propagate our work . . . is fundamentally erroneous. If Whatcoat and Asbury had landed in the United States prepared to hire preachers to propagate the Methodist doctrines among the Colonists, the work never would have spread as it did. It is upon the volunteer labor of men and women whose hearts are set on fire with the love of Christ that you must rely."[5]

CHAPTER 16
DISCIPLINES OF CHRISTIAN EDUCATION

Is it possible to academically teach the message of Christ? It cannot be accidental that the church school did not exist for the first seventeen centuries of Christianity or that it is so ineffective today. Wesley was under no illusions. His pragmatic judgment predicted the failure of "Sunday School": "If you would see the fruit of your labor, you must teach them not only early and plainly, but frequently too. It would be of little or no service to do it only once or twice a week. How often do you feed their bodies? Not less than three times a day. And is the soul of less value than the body? Will you not then feed this as often?"[1]

Wesley recognized that no single approach could accomplish the task of Christian education. He structured an elaborate and diverse system to meet an overall need. This system included family Bible study, a catechism for children, prayer meetings, class meetings, weekly and daily church schools, daily opportunity for congregational worship and private education, field evangelism, prayer fellowship, and individual, tutorial instruction. He combined these different services into the most inclusive and effectual educational system the church had yet seen. Wesley insisted on unified goals, motivated leadership, and personal, individualized instruction.

The Bible was the center for all instruction at every level. He insisted that each effort "pursue the whole of Scriptural Christianity." His conviction, that "Scripture interprets Scripture, one part fixing the sense of another," was the foundation of all his methodology.[2]

Only those who have "a zeal for God" can be entrusted with any part of the task.[3] A person who is lukewarm will be unable to teach others. Every preacher, teacher, class leader, and parent had to have personal experience with the Savior and commitment to the Kingdom, or, in Wesley's opinion, teaching would be ineffective regardless of technique or material. Every individual, adult or child, received an incredible amount of personal attention in Wesley's system. Everyone of his methods depended upon shared experience and dialogue. This program of Christian education, learned from Susanna, pointed first to personal conversion. It was followed by the construction of individual roads toward sanctification and perfection.

Insisting that his society follow his example, Wesley used every possible tool himself. He became a publisher, book salesman, hymn writer, small group teacher, school master, preacher, disciplinarian —in fact he was constantly experimenting in order to more effectively communicate scriptural holiness. He did not casually accept the materials or the methods of others, preferring to devise his own. "Of his pupils," we are told in Coke and Moore's LIFE OF WESLEY, published in 1793, "he took greatest care, accounting himself not only responsible for them to their parents and the community, but to God. He laboured not only to make them scholars but Christians also."[4]

Despite Wesley's unified goals and his insistence on committed teachers, an attitude of openness was part of all instruction. Critical attitudes and doubt, honestly expressed, were permitted since integrity is the first step toward growth. Wesley tried class attendance and achievement awards. High standards of achievement, coupled with a willingness to forgive and grant new beginnings, helped make his system dynamic. He recognized achievement, insisted that work not assimilated be repeated, and that each test his progress through assignments of Christian service in the secular world. Every student had responsibility for other students. In each setting education was an experience in mutual discovery.

Methodism consistently pioneered new programs in Christian education. As early as 1769 Hannah Ball, a Methodist laywoman of High Wycombe, set up a regular Sunday School. This was eleven years before the Anglican newspaperman, Robert Raikes, established his school in Gloucester. The first church school in America, if not the one started by Wesley himself in Georgia, was established by William Elliot, a Methodist layman, at Burton-Oak Church in Virginia in 1785. He also taught slaves and servants in a radical departure from the social custom of that time. Abel Stevens asserts in his HISTORY OF METHODISM that Francis Asbury began a Sunday School in 1786 at the home of Thomas Crenshaw in Hanover County, Virginia. It may be that the true roots of the church school are much earlier, for on the wall of Christ Episcopal Church in Savannah, Georgia, there is a plaque which reads: "To the glory of God in the memory of John Wesley, priest of the Church of England, Minister of Savannah, 1736–1737, Founder of the Sunday School of the Church, erected by the Diocese of Georgia."[5]

Wesley went on to establish full-time schools in England with Christian education as their primary purpose. The harsh standards of these schools were formulated by Wesley himself: "First, no child is admitted under six years of age. Secondly, all the children are to be present at the five a.m. morning sermon. Thirdly, they are at school from six to twelve, and from one to five. Fourthly, they have no play days. Fifthly, no child is to speak in school, but to the masters. Sixthly, the child who misses two days in one week, without leave, is excluded from the school."[6]

Right or wrong, Wesley based his methods on his mother's insistence on the subjection of the will. He faced severe criticism when he tried to educate the poor. He was condemned for "educating children above their station" and for "unfitting them for their God-appointed tasks." Robert Lucas spoke for a minority when he defended the new idea: "The general mass of the people still remain overwhelmed in a sort of hereditary ignorance and sloth. The lamp of reason is scarcely live in them. While the sun sheds its benign influence with equal kindness upon the cottages of the poor and the mansions of the affluent, the latter uncharitably would deny the former any part in that better radiance by which their own lives are illuminated."[7]

We have records of these early church schools which outline their courses of study and their methodology. An evaluation of our contemporary practice by their standards is illuminating:

(1) They were Christocentric. One's relationship with Christ was of primary importance. The Biblical word was always fundamental. Instruction was often catechetical (this question and answer method is the forerunner of modern programmed instruction used by computers), emphasizing the student's personal involvement with scriptural content. Wesley gave the following rules for studying scripture: "Take the literal sense, if not contrary to other texts in which case interpret the obscure text by the plain. Have a constant eye to the analogy of faith, the connection and harmony that is between (the) grand fundamental doctrine and the text." Wesley lists as "grand fundamentals": original sin, justification by faith, the new birth, inward and outward holiness. He instructed his students to deal with the scriptures as a whole. (II Timothy 2:15) "Use the scriptures with prayer, since 'scripture' can only be understood through the same Spirit whereby it was given."[8]

(2) They concentrated on fundamentals which found succinct statement in Wesley's Twenty-five Articles of Religion. Their early catechisms were far more realistic concerning life than many modern materials for they reflected its pain and struggle. Often twentieth century Christian education fails because it blandly ignores agony, pain, failure, depression, suffering, immorality, and social evils. It is often uninteresting and unrealistic because its goal appears to be a middle-class version of the American Way of Life.

(3) They taught the moral responsibilities of a life of love and service as the only proper response to God's love. Surprisingly non-legalistic and non-judgmental in all his teaching, Wesley organized his class meetings so that stewardship of time, person, and possessions were constantly evaluated. All in the class took personal interest in the others so that the blessings of Christ might be shared. When Captain Fox, a layman, suggested that members of the society should meet in groups under a leader, he formed not only the class meeting, but the most effective system of adult education yet initiated.[9]

(4) Their teaching was applied and personally followed up. Wesley's direction was explicit and instructive: "In meeting classes let them diligently inquire how every soul prospers; not only how each person observes the outward rules, but how they grow in the knowledge and love of God." He also stated that "the classes should be made lively and profitable to those who meet."[10] Beyond this he had strict requirements for continuing in various classes. Demanding both homework and progress, he recorded his attitude many times in the JOURNAL: "I met the classes, and found no increase in the society. No wonder, for discipline had been quite neglected; and, without this, little good can be done among Methodists."[11] Ever realistic, Wesley knew there was no substitute for hard work and personal involvement.

(5) They gave a significant amount of time to worship and prayer. The children began their day (at 5 a.m.) at worship; and had a regular schedule of prayer. Private prayer was taught both by example and precept. A child prayed until it became a habit and then until it became a personality trait. For Wesley life was filled with adventure and joy, bringing together elements of joyous expression: music, exhuberance, and exhortation.

Dependence on the Bible and Biblical studies, on devotional prayerbooks and doctrinal tracts made Wesley a publisher. He was impatient with the contemporary concern that kindergarten and primary children find God in nature. For him, God was found first in scripture: "Do not parents feed the Atheism of their children further, by ascribing the works of creation to nature? Does not the common way of talking about nature, leave God quite out of the question?"[12]

In January 1782 Wesley founded the first Tract Society ever formed. One of the first publications was A PLAN OF THE SOCIETY TO DISTRIBUTE RELIGIOUS TRACTS TO THE POOR. Wesley was always ready to try new educational methods: "I cannot but earnestly recommend this to all those who desire to see true Scriptural Christianity spread throughout these nations. Men wholly awakened will not take pains to read the Bible. They have no relish for it. But a small tract may engage their attention for half an hour; and may, by the blessing of God, prepare them for going forward."[13] For forty-two years Wesley wrote tracts in order "to furnish poor people with cheaper, shorter and plainer books than any I had seen."[14]

To aid in adult education he published the fifty volume CHRISTIAN LIBRARY from 1749 through 1755. He called it "extracts from the abridgments of the choicest pieces of practical divinity."[15]

The Foundery, his headquarters, contained a bookroom and a library for the poor. Each one of his traveling preachers sold religious books and tracts to further Christian education. This tradition continued in both England and in the United States until after 1870.[16]

Perhaps every church should become a center of distribution for Christian literature today. There are few books on Biblical and Christian themes for young children and teenagers available in secular book stores. Wesley demanded that his people be a "reading" and "praying" people.

The Wesleys' best known contribution to Christian education was their music. They took the popular tunes of the time, even the beer hall melodies, and educated through the joy of singing. Limiting themselves almost exclusively to scriptural versification, John and Charles started Christians singing. As early as 1742 a collection of tunes was published.[17]

Wesley based his own teaching on the best scholarship then available, changing his own thought in the light of new evidence many times during his lifetime. He was eclectic in the best sense of the word—tolerant of any teaching or position which furthered the Kingdom. He was anything but a narrow theologian, self-limited by fundamentalism. He was "fully catholic," absorbing all the fruits of the spirit, wherever he found them. His one criterion was the scriptures—everything he taught was correlated and judged by the content of revelation. But, to call him a fundamentalist, a nineteenth century concept, would be anachronistic. His sermons give abundant evidence of literary and cultural depth. In the fifty-three standard sermons alone, there are twenty different citations from the classical authors: Horace, Virgil, Juvenal, Ovid, Quintilian, Homer, Cicero, Seneca, Terence, and Plato. In the same sermons he makes twenty-eight references to the English poets: Milton, Shakespeare, Davies,

Young, Pope, Cowley, and Addison. In addition, these sermons contain eight references to European poets and twenty-six quotations from the hymns of his brother.

Wesley warned against individualism in religion. Only in a corporate community could the Christian life be complete. "The New Testament," he declared, "knows nothing of a solitary religion," and "there is no holiness except social holiness. The perfection which is God's purpose for us is perfect love, and perfect love involves someone other than ourselves. It is love of God and love of man, and these are not distinct and separate things, but two aspects of the same thing."[18]

Wesley mastered ten languages: Arabic, Hebrew, Greek, Latin, French, Italian, Spanish, German, Dutch, and English. In whatever field he studied he applied all his effort. John Dillenberger records in PROTESTANT THOUGHT AND NATURAL SCIENCE: "Whatever his attitude toward theoretical science, Wesley did popularize scientific results. His first concern was to make practical and useful information available. Two of his books belong in this category: one on medicine entitled PRIMITIVE PHYSIC and a book on electricity called, DESIDERATION: OR ELECTRICITY MADE PLAIN AND USEFUL. The former is full of helpful remedies for illnesses of the time, and it even suggests that psychological states have a bearing on bodily health."[19]

As the contemporary church struggles with the extraordinarily difficult task of renewing Christian education, the experience of Wesley is especially helpful . He realistically defined the dimensions of the task, setting no limits to methodology and experimentation as long as the whole was based on a broad and deep understanding of scripture. Here are some further implications of Wesley's thought for Christian education today:

(1) His emphasis on diligence and homework. Every weekly Christian education program faces a critical fact—that what goes on in glass underlines what is happening during the rest of the week. Families need many aids to help them nurture Christian education in the home. Every contemporary church should provide an extensive variety of computer software, supplying programmed instruction in every area of Christian education to meet the needs of every age group. Practical applications from confirmation classes to parental preparation for Infant Baptism could be combined with subjects of content: Bible study, theology, Church history, Christian ethics and morals, denominational emphases, doctrine and beliefs, including attention to helps with prayer, worship, stewardship, lifestyle, ethics, marriage, sex, social and mission issues, etc. Such software programs would be a direct extension of Wesley's use of different catechisms, a question and answer method directly comparable to programmed instruction for a computer. Computer software, television discs and tapes, and paperbacks are the direct descendents of Wesley's tracts, pamphlets, books, and newspapers.

(2) His emphasis on using new media of communication. Tracts and economical paperbacks were never used before Wesley invented them. He looked for new ways in which to communicate the Gospel, from new music to new forms of class meetings. If he was involved in Christian education today, he would be concentrating on the computer. He also would have been open to the possibilities of other new technologies, making creative use of videodiscs and tapes. These new ways to communicate will give national church leaders (seminary professors, bishops, various program boards and agencies) opportunities to communicate directly in an effective way with each local church organization. Aids in worship, missions, social concerns, teacher training, etc. can be channeled directly to the local committee or persons interested.

National boards and agencies should produce video tapes relating to the work of the local church. These could be played at meetings of the comparable local church service group. The best preachers, teachers and enablers could be shared. Program emphases could be addressed by each local governing body. The techniques of major leaders (male and female, lay and ordained) could be shared, and many elements of faith could be dramatically communicated.

(3) His emphasis on the education of his preachers, teachers and leadership. As late as 1790 Wesley wrote to a lay preacher: "It cannot be that the people should grow in grace unless they give themselves to reading. A reading people will always be a knowing people."[20] In today's world the Church must educate its members about the realities of their world if it is to communicate concerning justice and righteousness. Perhaps the need today is to form an educational program focused on issues of economic justice, social concerns, and the fabric of society. Amid the complexity and the sheer massiveness of modern civilization, many people have no idea how the Christian ethic or personal morality might apply. We have to develop programs to train laity and clergy so they can effectively minister in this complex and confusing world. We need to develop educational programs which speak to the needs of people and society and not simply to academic or intellectual curiosity.

In addition, we have to do a better job in seminary instruction and continuing education. In recent decades some Protestant churches have lowered the standards of academic training for ordained ministers. They are no longer required to study the Biblical languages. Many churches do not have a rigorous intern program to assure competence in pastoral care, other practical disciplines, or even a minimum of first-hand experience.

Furthermore, requirements for continuing education, in contrast to other graduate disciplines, are slight or nonexistent. There should be renewal programs every five years and concentrated programs for retraining every fifteen years of an ordained minister's career. Churches must insist that pastors, who are certain to speak out on issues of economics and politics, have at least a fundamental knowledge of these field. Church seminaries should develop programs on videotapes, providing a series of lectures and seminars in every discipline from outstanding professors. These could be viewed with study aids by ministers in clusters, meeting together in a local setting each week or month in an ongoing form of continuing education. A cable network would allow instantaneous feedback and dialogue.

(4) His emphasis on excellence in the teaching of local classes and societies. Seminaries should be challenged to connect the best of the new technologies of communication and the best teachers and scholarship. Professors in each academic discipline, working with colleagues in other disciplines, could produce material that would lead to a revolution in adult and youth Christian education. This would enable the church to have thousands of well-trained lay ministers. Imagine an advanced curriculum taught by outstanding seminary professors on video-cassettes for study in church and home and on audio-cassettes for automobiles and joggers, or a cable system connecting each local church or each home with a central source of Christian education. Consider the advantages of a computer network, allowing instantaneous feedback and communication between teacher and pupil. Computers provide a knowledge bank for each home that is literally unlimited. The possibilities for excellence and creativity are unlimited. Each local church could offer an array of educational opportunities that were unavailable anywhere just a few years ago. Each home can have available learning tools that can be used according to the speed and inclination of the student. Communications are the evangelistic outreach arm of the future.

(5) His emphasis on connecting education and human need. It would be exciting if churches could develop widespread educational programs that might be free, concentrating on equipping the poor and the unemployed. Few things the church could do would have as many positive effects on a vast, long-range problem.

I have tried to apply Wesley's teachings in many different fields in local churches with a mixed record of success. The following plan was implemented successfully in a suburban church and is offered as an example. The high educational level and general abilty of the laity helped with this program. Several class groups of adults, after outlining mission and educational values, developed a year-by-year syllabus of content and goals for every age level in the local church. Objectives were clearly listed for each of the first eighteen years of life, and then by subject groupings for adults. Denominational material proved helpful, serving as general guides for the preparation of the syllabus and as resources for the students in the program. However, they were not sufficient in themselves for they were of necessity graded to a general level, while local churches differ widely in size and are made up of people with diverse levels of education, experience, sophistication, and faith. (A class of seventh graders in a church which had provided excellent Christian education, leading to an early, first hand commitment for Christ, would need different materials and teaching than a class of the same grade in a mobile community composed of children who had experienced only episodic and spasmodic religious education, and had not yet made any real spiritual commitment.)

Wesley insisted that every class of Christians develop its own plan (syllabus) based on the content of God's revelation and the spiritual needs, health, and experience of the class. Wesleyan class meetings found content in Bible study specifically applied to the lives of the class members. In our three year experiment several adult classes had the continuing responsibility for the development of curriculum and a syllabus for all church school classes, as well as caring for the personal needs of class members and the spiritual guidance of the wider church community. The Wesley pattern for the early class meetings included not only Bible study and prayer, but the development of ethical standards, lifestyle patterns, and community goals. Class meetings were responsible for all aspects of mission. One class made its continuing project the constant re-evaluation and revision of the curriculum. Another developed and formulated a catechism for kindergarten and nursery classes. Two people worked at developing a software presentation of the catechism on a computer. Plans for evangelism and general mission were under Biblical study by other ongoing adult classes. Introductory classes in Bible, church history, social concerns, and mission were also available for adults and teenagers. All had specific, ongoing homework assignments.

Wesley taught that without day-by-day instruction there could be no real Christian Education. Therefore, the involvement of parents or other adults or teenagers in the home was an important task. From the nursery years, each class had a personalized, take-home assignment sheet each week which enabled parents and other adults to work together with the children. (This system is effective as a continuing adult education program because parents and other adults were naturally motivated.) The take-home sheets included: a clear and concise statement of the lesson covered in the class period just completed, including the Scripture and secular references, along with related prayers, worship, and devotional suggestions. It assigned purposeful activities related to the lesson and specific homework projects (many of which were personalized in the handwriting of the teacher). Often the homework assignment tried to involve the entire family group. The separate sheet for each class allowed the teacher to personally assign individual questions and projects which had arisen in class. The sheet also stated briefly the subject matter of the next week's lesson, the related scriptures, and homework based on age level and competence. A pattern for family home worship and directed family Bible study was also included. This was all placed on both sides of one sheet of 8" X 14" paper with the teacher's phone number and suggestions to the parents.

As this was a suburban church made up almost entirely of family units, all lessons were family-centered, allowing study at home to be corporate (after Wesley class meetings) with one member of the family as leader. When a family unit did not exist (or failed to participate), students were included in other church families or given a tutor. The work done at home was always reviewed and discussed, but never done again in class. At the elementary level, there was a heavy concentration on Biblical studies, allowing high school studies to be project and witness-centered—often involving youth in specific Christian service and witness projects within the wider community. Following Wesley's pattern, evangelism and Christian service became the focus of Christian education.

This system automatically made for more efficiently prepared teachers. They had to plan at least a week ahead (so the church office could have the material to be printed) and each teacher had to make a real effort to cover the announced subject matter. Each teacher could tell at a glance what other classes were doing, and every teacher knew with precision what her class had been exposed to the year before. In addition, a majority of the teachers felt the need to participate in a mid-week class for teachers.

Recognizing the difficulty class structure gives some high school students, the mobility of society, and the demands business travel places on many adults, class teaching was supplemented with units of instruction programmed on small, portable, teaching machines. Study took place wherever a person happened to be—in a plane, on the beach, or on a coffee break. Such programmed instruction equipped adults (parents) for the teaching task, for evangelism, and for life. Class meetings were more likely to be times of sharing since all (at least theoretically) covered the material given for homework. Many adults had first hand experience with computers in their work and far more ability than their ordained ministers to be effective teachers. Many subjects—Bible study, church history, teaching methods, family worship, ethics, stewardship, various social concerns, etc.—were handled well by programmed instruction. This method reclaimed the value of catechetical instruction with a modern technique. Homework took on a corporate form as each class was able to correlate the insights of all. Every member of the group was involved in feed-back. Some adult classes spent an entire year devising catechisms for younger children. Programmed instruction, teaching machines, and taped instruction were found to be particularly effective with teenagers.

This method was used experimentally for three years and continued with effective results for a five year period. Many more adults were involved in the educational process: devising the syllabus and curriculum, teaching, planning the weekly family assignments, teaching equipping sessions, and in family groups. The vast majority of parents fully cooperated, involving 80% of the families. Single adults enjoyed working with children whose parents could not help. It was a process of adult education focused primarily on responsibility for one's own children (the factor of highest motivation). The program was the major reason for the spectacular growth of the church and the church school (ten times as many people within a six year period).

CHAPTER 17
DISCIPLINES OF PASTORAL CARE

At first glance, Wesley's experience in pastoral care seems quite dated and commonplace. However, whenever his methods were applied, the society prospered, and the Spirit was given a channel through which effective ministry could be done. Whenever his methods were ignored, the evidence showed a decline in membership and spiritual fruits.

Anglican practice in the eighteenth century was remarkably like that of the larger denominations in the United States today. Clergymen were counselors who let people come to them. They were administrators who decided with a few advisors what was good for the parish. In many cases, they were strangers who connected with their parishioners only after emergencies occurred.

For Wesley, pastoral care was a natural outgrowth of New Testament preaching. People who live in a community formed in love deeply care for one another. The good news of God's love and care makes hypocrisy unavoidable unless a preacher is a caring and loving person. Of course, there are many times in every life when feelings of love and caring are lost. Yet within a Christian community there is a love relationship which patiently nurtures the trust which allows a person to reclaim the best of God's gifts. There is joy in being together. In Wesley's words, it "implies happiness as well as holiness."[1]

Some have mistakenly used Wesley's suggestion, "You have nothing to do but save souls" as an argument for a narrow, specialized ministry. Instead, the entire range of ministry is enclosed within this phrase. He was so impressed by the section on ministry in the Constitution of the Church of the Moravian Brethren at Herrnhut that he printed it in his JOURNAL for the edification of his society: The pastor, or teacher, is to be an overseer of the whole flock and every person therein; to baptise the children; diligently to form their minds, and bring them up "in the nurture and admonition of the Lord; when he finds in them a sincere love of the Cross, then to receive them into the Church; to administer the Supper of the Lord; to join in marriage those who are already married to Christ; to reprove, admonish, quicken, comfort, as need required; to declare the whole counsel of God-taking heed, at all times, to speak as the oracles of God and agreeably to the faith; to bury those who have died in the Lord, and to keep that safe which is committed to his charge, even the pure doctrine and apostolic discipline which we have received from our forefathers."[2]

He called those in Methodist connection to live "sober, virtuous and religious" lives, "based on a constant ruling habit of soul" and a "renewal of our minds in the image of God."[3] Wesley compares his followers to doctors, who, if they practice, must heal. He often pointed to the root of the word "minister" which means "servant" of others. The structure of the class meeting and of the itinerant ministry is founded on the New Testament claim that every person is a priest, responsible to God for other people.

The ministry of pastoral care was founded in prayer and Bible study. Wesley's plan of ministry was dependent on his belief that none in the community could stand alone. Growth and service did not depend on the great skill or the personality of the class leader, but on the spiritual strength of the entire group. Wesley found that most people who were ineffective in pastoral care had so much talent and personal power that they failed to make room for the Spirit. The phrase "we immediately began praying for him" is found many times in his records, for this was the source of pastoral power. Each class meeting was charged with finding God's will for the lives of each member and for corporately working out that purpose.[4]

In Wesley's system the preacher had explicit responsibility to equip the class members so they could meet their responsibilities as Christians. Visitation was the practice of all Methodists whether in pulpit or pew. A great historian has described the evolution of the class meeting: "At one time the class meeting was of somewhat rigid character, and personal testimony or experience was almost enforced. In these days personal testimony is, perhaps, the exception, but the open fellowship of believers in prayer, meditation, and praise is of none the less vale both for building up the Church and for the maintenance of the more public worship. Over every class, the numbers in which vary, there is a leader, generally a layman, who, though not ordained for this office is yet solemnly and deliberately chosen. Each leader is held responsible for the oversight of the members of his class, and for reporting to the minister cases of sickness, of indifference, and the like, while regular meetings of the ministers and leaders give full opportunity for systematic oversight of the whole society and church."[5]

The JOURNAL is literally full of examples of society decline due to lack of visitation: "Upon examination, I found the society at Newcastle also smaller than it was two years since. This I can impute to nothing but the want of visiting from house to house; without which the people will hardly increase, either in number or grace."[6]

Wesley had many personal failures in pastoral care, describing himself at one time as "utterly unwilling to speak close to any of my flock."[7] Nevertheless, he decided to follow his father's effective example. Samuel visited "all his parishioners, sick or well, from house to house, to talk with each of them on the things of God and observe severally the state of their souls. What he then observed he minuted down in a book kept for that purpose."[8]

So often does Wesley mention visiting the sick in his JOURNAL that one might think it was the major occupation of his ministry. When his preachers complained that he was asking them to visit too much, he answered, "By the sick I do not mean only those that keep their bed, or that are sick in the strictest sense. Rather I would include all such as are in a state of affliction, whether they fear God or not. But is there need of visiting them in person? Does it not answer the same purpose if we send them help, as if we carry it ourselves? The word that we render visit, in its literal acceptation, means to look upon . . . And this you well know, cannot be done unless you are present with them. To send them assistance is, therefore entirely a different thing from visiting them. The former then, ought to be done, but the latter not left undone."[9]

When they still complained, he pointed to the Biblical imperative. " 'Come unto me, all ye that are weary and heavy laden.' If, then, you say he calls those that cannot come; those whom he knows to be unable to come; those whom he can make able to come, but will not; how is it possible to describe greater insincerity? You represent him as mocking his helpless creatures, by offering what he never intends to give. You describe him as saying one thing, and meaning another; as pretending the love which he had not."[10]

Having personally visited individuals many times without any obvious result, Wesley speaks of the need for patience with those who do not immediately respond. It is especially helpful to know that Wesley admitted his mistakes and exposed himself and his weaknesses, recognizing that he was God's agent rather than a paragon of virtue holding all answers within himself. To Elizabeth Hardy he wrote: "Without doubt it seems to you that yours is a peculiar case. You think there is none like you in the world. Indeed there are. It may be ten thousand persons are now in the same state of mind as you. I myself was so a few years ago. I felt the wrath of God abiding on me. I was afraid every hour of dropping in hell. I knew myself to be the chief of sinners. Though I had been very innocent in the account of others, I saw my heart to be all sin and corruption. I was without the knowledge and the love of God."[11]

His system of pastoral care depended on the itinerant system of ministry. It was the laity who, as the long term residents, gave care to those in need. Wesley forced every congregation to accept its responsibility to minister as a priesthood of all believers—because here was no paid professional on hand who could be expected to do the job for them. By allowing the congregation to be the church, Wesley formed it into a loving community where Christ could exist. The breakdown of the itinerant system quickly caused problems of pastoral care. In his JOURNAL he reports receiving "but a melancholy account of the state of things here. The congregations were nearly as usual; but the society which, when I was here before, consisted of about a hundred and sixty members, was now shrunk to about fifty. Such is the fruit of a single preacher's staying a whole year in one place."[12]

Wesley's practical methodology grew out of his theology. Sanctification (the cardinal doctrine for pastoral care) may be implemented only through the pastoral concern of the entire community. Too often Christians have been ashamed of enthusiasm and embarrassed in any conversation concerning either the Spirit or faith. They have left pastoral care to sect groups and then wondered about their astonishing success at evangelism. Too often we put people off at just the point of their greatest need—when they want to talk of their fear of death, of their hatred of a wife, of their frustration as a parent, or of their moral ambivalence. Sometimes we have been unwilling to trust the work of the Holy Spirit. R. D. Lang cynically paints the worst case of pastoral care: "If they go to a Christian priest, the priest will probably refer them to a psychiatrist, and the psychiatrist will refer them to a mental hospital, and the mental hospital will refer them to the electric shock machine. And if this is not our contemporary mode of crucifying Christ, what is?"[13] Can we return to a curing of souls which looks into the frightened and frustrated individual to find the Holy Spirit at work.

SECTION V
DISCIPLINES OF SOCIAL CONCERN

From the beginning John Wesley had a wholistic view of life. He made no separation of its spiritual and moral aspects. The fruits of conversion were displayed by meeting the ethical and moral standards of Christ. Discipleship was the acting out of one's faith according to the model of Christ.

Those in the Wesleyan tradition justly celebrate the remarkable record of achievement his followers have had in the disciplines of social concern. Probably no religious group in history has been so active over a long period of time in a corporate attempt to shape the world according to Biblical principles. Certainly few ecclesiastical traditions have been as preoccupied with ethics and Christian service. Within the pages of this book we have noted how much Wesley was involved in all the social issues of his time. His ministry emphasized service to the poor and the oppressed. During his lifetime most religious institutions, with the conspicuous exception of Quakers and Puritans, avoided involvement in social concerns beyond narrowly defined "spiritual" matters and the personal concerns of their own membership. In contrast, Wesley felt that anyone who followed Christ was thrust by His word into the midst of life.

Wesley's movement took the lead in the abolition of slavery and in improving the conditions of life for the poor and the oppressed. On the mission field, literally millions of people have been helped: the hungry have been fed; the sick have been given hospitals, clinics, medical care, and love; the poor have been accepted and given the benefits of literacy, education, and a new hope; women have been freed from tragic practices of exploitation and taken on a new self-image; children have been protected as persons of great value in the sight of God; and ethnic people have found their gifts appreciated after centuries of persecution and neglect.

Unless we limit our celebration to intentions rather than results, however, we have little left to celebrate. The needs of people in the world and the social health of contemporary society are vivid reminders of how relatively insignificant and ineffective the enormous Wesleyan effort has been. The case could be made that in every area of social concern, conditions are now worse than they were two hundred years ago. Nuclear energy has added dimensions to war previously unthinkable. Economic injustice and the population explosion have compounded the agonies of hunger and poverty. Modern media of communication have geometrically raised the expectations and hopes of millions of people, far faster and far higher than possibilities for their fulfillment. The proliferation of "nation-states," combined with a "world economy" (mandated by revolutions in travel, speed, and instantaneous communication) complicates many problems of economic justice and political oppression to the point that they seem unsolvable.

Amid such pressures it might be best for every institutional church to adopt the old Hebraic principle of the "Year of Jubilee" where all slaves were emancipated, all alienated lands restored to their former owners, and everything begun afresh for another fifty years. Probably the first large institutional church to give away all its wealth to the poor and oppressed, and group its remnant around the gospel would find an amazing rebirth. In fact, such a church would have the opportunity of learning a great deal from Wesley, who acted very much in this way in the 19th century. He was forced to use radical techniques when he discovered that the social problems of his time could not be met by traditional institutional methods. He was led by scripture away from the preoccupations of an Oxford Don into the pressures of a world in need. As he became involved with hundreds of people trying to work out the results of a conversion experience, he discovered it was impossible to separate one's spiritual concerns from the rest of life.

Arminian theology, with its stress on the importance of good works following conversion and on the wholeness of human life, concentrated on issues of righteousness and justice. Wesley's special emphasis on sanctification and perfection made inevitable his concentration on moral and ethical ministries which applied the gospel to the life of the eighteenth century.

This effort was remarkably effective because of:

(1) The variety of his concerns. He was no "one issue" Christian. The reality of human need, not any theoretical construction, triggered his response. He fell into social concerns as he lived his life. As he ministered to those who surrounded him, their needs combined with the Biblical witness to command his involvement. His theology and spiritual commitment controlled his politics and his social action. With the possible exception of his stand on the Revolutionary War and other involvements with Tory politics, there is no record that his own needs ever controlled his social action.

(2) His openness to the opinion and advice of laity. His eight thick volumes of correspondence hold many letters of response to concerns of his lay members. He often changed his point of view after consultation with them. His entire system (with weekly accountability and self-examination of the members and regular reports of the activity of class and cell groups sent back to Wesley) assured that he was informed of the thoughts and needs of his followers. Such a structure for feed-back and input from laity is mandatory if a church group is to be effective, either in changing the minds of its own membership or in influencing the greater political community. He realized that the real work of the social gospel has to be done by lay persons.

(3) His primary dependence on spiritual disciplines to convert people to the Christian ethic of caring, loving, service and open them to the human needs of people in society. Wesley never expected to convert people to social consciousness by means of political arguments. Such involvement was a direct response to spiritual conversion based on new values. He emphasized the crucial importance of continuing Bible study, group self-examination, and a daily prayer life.

The Kingdom of God was not, for Wesley, an abstraction pointing to some far-off tomorrow, but a reality which God's grace allows today. He preached that "the Gospel of Christ knows no religion but social; no holiness but social holiness."[1] The Gospel forced him to take an interest in the structures and institutions of society.

Activity in politics and social life is the defined consequence of the process of sanctification, as illustrated by Wesley's own methodology. Only corporate action accomplishes regeneration in either church or society. The admission card to his societies had to be renewed quarterly and that renewal was contingent on performance in both mission and witness.[2] One of the greatest standard sermons begins: "I shall endeavor to show, first, that Christianity is essentially a social religion; and that to turn it into a solitary one is to destroy it. Secondly, that to conceal this religion is impossible, as well as utterly contrary to the design of its Author."[3]

We turn now to a brief examination of Wesley's thought in three specific social areas:

(1) Issues of Politics and Peace
(2) Issues of Racial Prejudice and Economic Justice
(3) Issues of Sexism and Agism

In each of these areas of social concern it was the model of Christ which was determinitive for Wesley. In each area Psalm 72:2-4 could have been his guideline: "He shall defend the afflicted . . . save the children of the poor, and crush the oppressor."

CHAPTER 18
ISSUES OF POLITICS AND PEACE
Politics

In his study of William Law, Wesley learned that "our life on earth is a mere journey to eternity" and that people are sent into this world "to prepare themselves to live with God in everlasting happiness." While not denying such an emphasis, Wesley went far beyond it, recognizing the importance of Christian activity in all areas of life. He speculated theologically on the Christian hope of the resurrection of the body, yet he accepted few of the idealistic notions which made the mystical pietists of his time so ineffective.[1]

Although a conservative, a partisan Tory, and an outspoken anti-revolutionary, Wesley was far ahead of his time on almost every issue affecting masses of people. Long before others, he considered slavery as "that execrable sum of all villanies" and proclaimed the equality of the races before God. He fought the effects of absentee-ism in Ireland and the disasters of colonial exploitation. Personally involved with the outcasts of his society, with those most oppressed, and those doing the most dangerous work, Wesley spoke to and, eventually, for the poor. Miners, soldiers, laborers, prisoners, and the weak were all his friends and followers. In his support for education and equal opportunity for the lower economic classes when all others denied them, Wesley threatened the established order. By demanding higher standards of law and justice for the poor and attacking the traffic in alcohol, drugs, and gambling (all activities which debilitate the lower classes), Wesley challenged the vested interests of the powerful.

Through all, he loyally, and quite blindly, supported the monarchy, believing it divinely ordained and directed. Francis Asbury explained away Wesley's violent denunciation of the Revolution as an act of patriotism, saying that if John Wesley were an American, he would have been among the Revolutionary leaders because he was, first of all, committed to the needs of his flock.

This general conservativism was a direct result of his belief in the providential activity of God in human affairs. H. B. Workman wrote, "that the importance of Wesley's political influence cannot be exaggerated."[2] One of the first to insist on the wholeness of ethical concerns, he taught that a Christian was irresponsible if he or she did not become involved in politics, recognizing that behind politics are the personal needs of human beings. He felt that preachers who did not attempt to guide their parishes toward righteousness did not know the range of God's word. Facing the matter directly he wrote the tract, HOW FAR IS IT THE DUTY OF A CHRISTIAN MINISTER TO PREACH POLITICS?: "Now, when a clergyman comes into a place where this and many more stories, equally false, have been diligently propagated against the King, and are generally believed, if he guards the people against this evil-speaking, by refuting those slanders, many cry out, 'O, he is preaching politics.' If you mean this by the term, it is the bounden duty of every Christian minister to preach politics. It is our bounden duty to refute these vile aspersions, in public as well as in private. But this can be done only now and then, when it comes naturally in our way. For it is our main and constant business to preach Jesus Christ and him crucified."[3]

Wesley went even further. He actively supported and urged other Methodists to support candidates for public office. From Bristol, October 1, 1789, he wrote to John Mason: "My dear brother, If, as I am informed, Mr. Gregor is a lover of King George and the present Administration, I wish you would advise all our brethren that have votes to assist him in the ensuing election."[4]

However, showing his humanity when political action was suggested that was contrary to his inclinations, Wesley felt it imprudent for his American preachers to engage in political affairs: "It is your part to be peacemakers; to be loving and tender to all, but to addict yourselves to no party. In spite of all solicitations, of rough or smooth words, say not one word against one or the other side; keep yourselves pure; do all you can to help and soften all."[5] Not always able to practice what he preached, he was anything but a peacemaker in his CALM ADDRESS.

Although we can easily disagree with Wesley on many subjects, his claim that Christians should be involved directly in politics and government is beyond criticism. There is no escaping responsibility, even if one makes dreadful mistakes as a result. In a political democracy one is involved and pays consequences whether active or not. Human error should not limit activity, rather it should temper the tendency to be judgmental concerning others. Proper witness comes when Christians are militantly involved in issues while humble in regard to persons.

Wesley was a born Tory, believing that the citizens were not fit to govern themselves for "the majority of people are not the wisest or best part." He probably was right in those days of illiteracy, before public education and any effective method of mass communication. Rather than resting upon his presuppositions, Wesley spent his life improving public education for the poor and developing ways of communication for all classes of people. In those days before either the French or American Revolutions, this was liberal activity. Mr. A. E. Dobbs in his scholarly book, EDUCATION AND SOCIAL MOVEMENTS, writes: "The part which the Evangelical Revival played in the political education of the masses has been often misrepresented or ignored. An exceptional degree of intelligence and attainment was not uncommon among the Methodists of humble station and those who had been raised in Methodist homes. The class meeting was the starting of serious friendships, and often contained an inner circle of companions, more intelligent than the rest, who would meet to converse on religion and matters of general interest, and who occasionally entered on a course of reading . . . a circle of labourers or mechanics led in worship or conference by one of their own rank, was a great step for democracy."[6]

The eighteenth century was similar to the twentieth in many ways: life was relatively cheap and unprotected over much of the world, wars were common and constant, governments were often corrupt and representative only of a powerful few, depressions and economic crises were frequent, change was constant, and only a relatively small number of people were concerned about the plight of the masses. Economic injustice and political oppression were frequently unrecognized, ignored, or denied.

Justice was unexpected and infrequent for the poor and powerless. Beginning in Georgia when he found the magistrates perpetuating injustice in the intervals between Oglethorpe's visits, and for the rest of his long life, Wesley consistently placed himself alongside the beleagued, demanding their rights.[7] Secular scholars of the period witnessed to both the effectiveness and the uniqueness of Wesley's social mission. H. D. Trail wrote in SOCIAL ENGLAND: "In the nation at large, the Methodist Revival brought about a new moral enthusiasm which, rigid and pedantic as it often seemed, was healthy in its social tone, and whose power was seen in the decrease of the profligacy which had disgraced the upper classes, and the foulness which had infested literature ever since the Restoration. A passionate impulse of human sympathy with the wronged and afflicted was the special glory of religion at the end of the eighteenth century, and it has the right to claim the honour of training and inspiring those uncanonized yet true saints—Wilberforce, Clarkson, and John Howard."[8]

Most intellectuals thought that poor delinquents had received their just rewards. One of the first to teach that poverty was not the result of some defect in character, in 1753, Wesley "told of visiting many poor, in garrets and cellars, who were half starved both with cold and hunger, added to weakness and pain. So wickedly, devilishly false is that common objection, 'They are poor only because they are idle.' "[9]

The State's interest in the welfare of the citizens, now taken for granted in many countries, was neither assured nor implemented in those years. Wesley not only stood for better conditions, but organized one of the first corporate programs of community action: "But I had for some years observed many who, although not sick, were not able to provide for themselves, and had none who took care to provide for them; These were chiefly feeble, aged widows. I consulted with the Stewards, how they might be relieved . . . So we took a lease of two little houses near; we fitted them up, so as to be warm and clean. We took in as many widows as we had room for, and provided them with things needful for the body; toward the expense of which I set aside."[10]

Renewed churches open themselves to the needs of all in the community. When his followers could find no funds, Wesley organized a savings and loan bank. When they were without jobs, he formed an unemployment bureau. When educational opportunities were systematically denied the poor, he built charity schools and initiated the fight which eventually led to public education for all. When medical care was denied the oppressed, he organized a free dispensary and started the great Methodist tradition of church related hospitals. Confronted with massive numbers of widows and orphans, he built homes for their care and personally took responsibility for raising funds to erect "the House of Poor Widows." Confronted with thousands of indigent strangers in the major cities, he founded the first "Stranger's Friend Society" which still serves the needs of transients.

War And Peace

In this area, as in so many others, Wesley followed the practice of the early church. In the first two centuries after Christ, a Christian "was altogether forbidden to become a soldier" because "the power of the sword" was inconsistent with the teachings of Christ. If a person already a soldier was converted he had "to undertake not to kill and not to swear oaths" in the future, "a dubious thing from a military point of view."[11]

Wesley was no pacifist, but he did speak often against war: "Man in general can never be allowed to be reasonable creatures, till they know not war any more. So long as this monster stalks uncontrolled, where is reason, virtue, humanity? They are utterly excluded; they have no place: they are a name and nothing more."[12]

Although his advice was often simiplistic, he placed the activities of the state under the judgment of the Gospel and insisted on the viability of prophesy. Galatians 5:6 ("Faith worketh by love") was crucial to Wesley. In all endeavor, love was the only acceptable New Testament relationship between human beings and human institutions: "Love, precisely because it is, in the same passage, called 'the end of the commandment,' is never a second factor of salvation added to faith; it is the whole of Christian life, viewed from a different angle. St. John's 'abiding in love' is identical with the Pauline 'walking by faith.' "[13]

This love ethic did not prevent Wesley from making the same mistakes as Luther before him, giving blind loyalty to King and country. Nevertheless, he analyzed war by looking to the roots of human aggression: the fact of class and poverty, the abuse of power and the exercise of ambition, the greed of business, the dangers of trade, the practice of slavery, and the absence of justice. He moved beyond the immediate event of war between nations to a world community embraced by the love of Christ. In making the world his parish he eliminated the very divisions which make for war and aggression. He offered an inclusive and serving faith that could bind people to higher loyalties and greater possibilities. In the century that followed his ministry, the world moved in the opposite direction toward an economically motivated colonialism and nationalism. The alternative of one world might seem utopian, but it is surely Biblical.

In his famous American letter he advised his followers in the colonies "to be peacemakers; to be loving and tender toward all" and this was the general stance of Methodists in America during the Revolution. Many paid a significant price because they did not display "patriotic zeal." Jesse Lee, the Methodist apostle to New England was drafted into the Continental Army in 1780. His account is revealing: "My mind was settled; as a Christian and as a preacher of the Gospel, I could not fight. I could not reconcile it to myself to bear arms or to kill one of my fellow-creatures." When he arrived to take his place in a regiment he refused to touch his musket and was placed under guard. "Before sunrise," he reported, "I was up and began to sing; some hundreds soon assembled and joined with me, and we made the plantation ring with the songs of Zion." He proceeded to preach and convert many in the camp.[14]

This experience began a long and unbroken pattern of United Methodist support for those who are conscientious objectors. General Conferences have always supported the right of United Methodists who are conscientious objectors to be exempt from military service.

Many United Methodists, with the support of their Church, have been pacifists. The Episcopal Address to the General Conference of 1912 gives an overview of United Methodist feeling in the twentieth century: "It is for mammon, not for righteousness, that thrones and parliaments are crowding the oceans with leviathans of battle, even while the people are praying for an end of war and pleading for international arbitration; for they have balanced the ledgers of the centuries and they have found that the honors and spoils of war have never been equitably divided. Save in the wars of the people for freedom, the thrones and the honors have gone to the few, and thorns and horrors to the many."[15]

The statement of the 1980 DISCIPLINE is reflective of the Wesleyan position as we come to a new century: "We believe war is incompatible with the teachings and example of Christ. We therefore reject war as an instrument of national foreign policy and insist that the first moral duty of all nations is to resolve by peaceful means every dispute that arises between or among them; that human values must outweigh military claims as governments determine their priorities; that the militarization of society must be challenged and stopped; that the manufacture, sale, and deployment of armaments must be reduced and controlled; and that the production, possession, or use of nuclear weapons be condemned."[16]

Disciplines of social concern are more extensively treated with modern day examples in my recent book CHRISTIANITY WITHOUT MORALS. It has partcularly detailed sections on issues of war and peace, racial prejudice and economic justice.

CHAPTER 19
ISSUES OF RACIAL PREJUDICE
AND ECONOMIC JUSTICE

Racial Justice

The Bible proclaims that all persons are equal in the sight of God despite obvious differences in physical power, intellect, and character. Wesley took this theory out of the realm of spiritual speculation by means of practical application. When slavery was justified in Parliament as legal, Wesley was furious: "The grand plea is, 'They are authorized by law.' But can law, human law, change the nature of things? Can it turn darkness into light, or evil into good? By no means. Not withstanding ten thousand laws, right is right, and wrong is wrong still. There must still remain an essential difference between justice and injustice, cruelty and mercy. So that I still ask, Who can reconcile this treatment of Negroes, first and last, with either mercy or justice? Where is the justice of inflicting the evils on those that have done us no wrong? of depriving those that never injured us in word or deed, of every comfort of life? of tearing them from their native country, and depriving them of liberty itself?"[1]

The Conference of April 24, 1780, declared that "slave keeping was contrary to the laws of God, man and nature, and hurtful to society; contrary to the dictates of conscience and pure religion, and doing that which we would not want others to do to us or ours." The Conference passed "its disapprobation on all our friends who keep slaves" and "advised their freedom."[2] Such stands seem obvious now, but Wesley was among the first of national leaders to publically express such a position and the most militant in his opposition to such travesty.

Eighteenth century life provided an incredible chronicle of human insensitivity. During Wesley's lifetime the British Parliament passed twenty-three specific acts legalizing and regulating the slave trade. In the Treaty of Utrecht of 1713, England agreed by contract to supply 5,000 slaves annually to South America for thirty years. This contract was renewed as official policy in 1748. Even the State Church was indifferent to what Wesley called "the execrable villany," and a bishop breathing the rarefied atmosphere of the episcopal bench, declared that "Christianity and the embracing of the Gospel does not make the least alteration in civil property, even when the property consists of human flesh and blood."[3]

Wesley not only insisted that Methodists have no part in such traffic, but that they actively witness against it. He insisted upon its legal abolition and taught the equality of all peoples. It was with Wesley's encouragement that Dr. Thomas Coke made witness in America of "his unequivocable conviction as to the evil of the slave trade." This stand got many a Methodist in trouble "in the colonies", and those under attack were always backed by Wesley.[4]

Wesley encouraged Wilberforce again and again to speak out because he believed that the time had come for Christians to act. At the very end of his life he wrote Wilberforce: "Unless God has raised you up for this very thing, you will be torn out by the opposition of men and devils . . . O be not weary in well-doing. Go on, in the name of God and the power of His might, till even American slavery (the vilest that ever saw the sun) shall vanish before it."[5]

Wesley was not afraid to bring God's judgment to the powerful: "But if the most natural act of running away from intolerable tyranny, deserves such relentless severity, what punishment have these lawmakers to expect hereafter, on account of their own enormous offences? This is the plain, unaggravated matter of fact. Such is the manner wherein our African slaves are procured, such is the manner wherein they are treated in our plantations. I would not inquire, whether these things can be defended, on the principles of even heathen honesty; whether they can be reconciled (setting the Bible out of the[6] question) with any degree of either justice or mercy."[6] It was Alfred North Whitehead's judgment that "the Methodists produced the final wave of popular feeling which drove the anti-slavery movement to success."[7]

Although there were many discordant notes struck during the period approaching the American Civil War and during the Period of Reconstruction and many examples of overt prejudice and racism within the United Methodist church from the time of Richard Allen to the present, there has not been a time when a strong and vital Black influence has not been present within United Methodism. The record shows that Black Methodists have often been much truer to their Wesleyan heritage and much more conscious than others of Methodist spiritual roots. Harry Richardson has traced the story of the Black experience in United Methodism in his fine book, DARK SALVATION. That dramatic history records the initially firm stands which American Methodists took against slavery, and the long period of erosion of such moral positions under the temptation of economic and political expediency over the next one hundred and fifty years. He is careful to trace both the positive and the tragic in this record. While applauding the record in education (by 1916 the

176

Methodist Episcopal Church had established 12 colleges, 20 academies, a theological and a medical school for blacks), he understood that this method, while benefiting individuals, assured segregation and was based on paternalistic attitudes.[8] He recorded the pathos Black leadership felt at the time of church union in 1939 when the church looked away from moral responsibility as it asked blacks to pay the price of union. "Of the 47 black delegates to the uniting conference, 36 voted against the plan and eleven abstained. When the plan was later presented to the 19 black annual conferences, they voted seven against, two for, and nine abstaining." It is reported that when the General Conference delegates arose, after the voting, to sing, "We are marching upward to Zion," the black delegates remained seated and some of them wept."[9]

In the years following the merger almost all the fears of the Black delegates were realized. Institutional racism, often with subtle implications, became a way of life in the Church. The rigid lines of separation brought artificial comfort to the white membership.

An event of major significance took place in February of 1968 when two hundred Black Methodists met in Cincinnati issuing a "Black Paper" which said, in part: "We, as black Methodists, must first respond in a state of confession because it is only as we confront ourselves that we are able to deal with the evils and forces which seek to deny our humanity. We confess our failure to be reconciled with ourselves as black men. We have too often denied our blackness (hair, texture, color and other God given physical characteristics) rather than embrace it in all its black beauty. We confess that we have not always been relevant in service and ministry to our black brothers, and in so doing we have alienated ourselves from many of them. We confess that we have not always been honest with ourselves and with our white brothers. We have not encounted them with truth but often with deception. We have not said in bold language and forceful action that, 'You have used "White power" in and outside of the church to keep us in a subordinate position.' We have failed to tell our white brothers 'like it is.' Instead, we have told our white brothers what we thought they would like to hear. We confess that we have not become significantly involved in the Black Revolution because, for the most part, white men have defined it as 'bad'; for the other part, we have been too comfortable in our 'little world' and too pleased with our lot as second class citizens and as second class members of the Methodist Church. We confess that we have accepted too long the philosophy of racism. This has created a relationship in which white people have always devined the 'terms' and defined when and how black people would exist."[10]

This statement resulted in the formation of "Black Methodists for Church Renewal" which has been a positive force for the entire church ever since. At the General Conference of 1968, when the United Methodist Church was born, a new spiritual intentionality to combat racism and racial prejudice began to emerge in the church. The Fund for Reconciliation was formed as an initial commitment to attack the cancers within the body of the church which had been so persuasively identified by BMCR. That organization was formally recognized and partially funded. A process began that would result in an active and effective Commission on Religion and Race, the gradual entrance into positions of power by Black lay and clergy members, and the formation of a single national misional priority for the entire church: The Ethnic Minority Local Church priority.

In the 1970's and 80's, the United Methodist Church was sensitized in many ways and greatly enriched as it threw off its blinders to rediscover portions of its heritage. Soon the great contributions of the diversity of peoples who together make up United Methodism began to be apparent to all. New creative leaders were found among Spanish-speaking members, Native American members, members with an Asian heritage, members from the Pacific Islands, and Black Americans.

In many ways this discovery led to a new church, far more Wesleyan than before, since ethnic United Methodists retained their Wesleyan heritage more completely than most other United Methodists. In every area of church life (worship, organization, mission, evangelism, social concerns, education, prayer groups and Bible study, community witness, etc.) the ethnic minority contribution has been creative and substantial. While former church leaders were, for the most part, full of good intentions, several generations had looked upon ethnic minority church members as people needing help rather than as people who shared a common faith and a common ministry who could enrich, teach, and minister to all other United Methodists.

In recent years, at the national level at least, many of the most effective and innovative and powerful United Methodist leaders have come from the ethnic minority membership. The definition of the theological task by theologian James Cone has been generally embraced by all ethnics from the perspective of their own heritage: "The task of Black Theology is to analyze the black man's condition in the light of God's revelation in Jesus Christ with the purpose of creating a new understanding of black dignity among black people, and providing the necessary soul in that people, to destroy white racism. . . . It is not possible to want God without Blackness, Christ without obedience, love without death."[11]

Despite the advances which have been obvious in the history of the last quarter century, there is still much to be done. Many Americans, both within and outside the church, seem exhausted by the revolution initiated by Dr. Martin Luther King Jr. in the cause of racial justice. Many leaders seem to be turning away from positions commonly agreed upon during the past decade. Within the church there seems less commitment to both racial and economic justice. The leadership of the national church has not adequately led the members of local churches. Often the national statements are not reflected in local programs and attitudes.

John Wesley judged the authenticity of conversion by the fruits offered in the life of the person converted. When he saw that the powerful forces of society got in the way of Christian love and justice, he committed himself to changing these forces. Any renewal of the church will be judged by its fruits. Wesley would be in agreement with Dr. Martin Luther King Jr. who said that "a person is either a molder of society or is molded by society." King was disturbed to find that "Christians in particular, are thermometers that record, or register the temperature of majority opinion, not thermostats that transform and regulate the temperature of society."[12] As long as this remains true, no renewal in the tradition of Wesley is possible. He never doubted that for a church to be renewed, it had to be shaped first by the spiritual power of Christ.

Issues of Economic Justice

At one time the personal ethics of the Ten Commandments was all that seemed necessary. Now even the New Testament standards of Christian ethics seem difficult to apply amid the urban complexity, nationalistic competition, the terrifying rate of change, and the incredible variety of social problems in the twentieth century. Problems of ecology and stewardship, wealth and taxation, labor conditions and market competition, oppression and revolution, advertising and foreign trade, poverty and injustice demand more than good intentions and an individualistic ethic. Worldwide images of success and failure need a less materialistic definition. Modern complexity in economics and business was just beginning in Wesley's time—at the birth of the industrial revolution, yet his principle of the total involvement of the church in the life of its people and the wider community remains valid.

Soon after his own "conversion," Wesley developed an "Employment Bureau" and gave his attention to the urban poor (two obvious actions which no one had thought of before). His "lending society" was one of the first labor cooperatives. In the JOURNAL of 1760 we read: "How much better is it to carry relief to the poor than to send it, and that both for our own sake and theirs. For theirs as it is so much more comfortable to them, and as we may then assist them in spirituals as well as temporals and for our own, as it is far more apt to soften our heart, and to make us naturally care for each other."[13]

Because so many of the poor became members of the society, Methodism could not escape the economic injustice of its time and became, almost unwillingly, a power for social change. Many United Methodist churches have identified themselves with a middle-class, moralistic "American Way of Life" ethic. Wesley, on the other hand, had extensive personal relationships with the poor of his society. The Gentleman's magazine of June, 1741, describes a meeting at the Foundry: "Most of those persons, who frequent them, are the poorest and meanest sort of people, who have families to provide for, and hardly bread to put in their mouths." Maldwyn Edwards says that Wesley deeply cared about the poor: "His life was one long crusade in the cause of the poor, and he encouraged others to follow his example." Wesley himself wrote: "I have found some of the uneducated poor, who have the most exquisite taste and sentiment, and many, very many of the rich who have scarcely any at all. In most genteel religious persons there is such a mixture that I scarcely ever have confidence in them; but I love the poor, and in many of them find pure genuine grace unmixed with folly and affectation . . . If I might choose, I should still preach the gospel to the poor."[14]

Although Wesley fed hundreds of the unemployed at a time, formed many associations for the relief of poverty (such as the Friendly Union Benefit Society and the Poorman's Guardian Society), he addressed himself primarily to the symptoms of economic injustice, rather than addressing economic injustice itself. This fundamental criticism is well stated by Dean Walter G. Muelder: "John Wesley never made a direct attack on the general pattern of economic and political injustice. He denounced specific social evils, but he did not attack the principles underlying the commercial revolution or the incipient Industrial Revolution. . . . Because Methodism was led and guided by men of the middle class in large part, its ethic was one of humanitarianism born out of love rather than one of flaming social justice with respect to property control. Thus, while its enthusiasm and passion caught the interest of the poorer classes, its ethic was capable of acceptance by the more well to do."[15]

This situation, important as it is in criticism of Wesley, is even more vital in analysis of contemporary life, where social ills involve not simple, one-dimensional activity, but a never ending chain of causes and circumstances in which personal guilt or innocence is impossible to access. Hindsight is often unfair. Wesley had as clear a vision of social change as any leader of his time, and much more influence on social change than any contemporary religious leader.

There were facets in Wesley's teaching which dealt creatively with the structures of society and provoked real change. One of the few who dared to speak against the practice of enclosure, Wesley attacked all practices which could not be defended by scripture. "Great Landowners had fenced in the traditional free land upon which poor Englishmen had farmed strips of cultivable ground, each strip in three remaining fallow each third year. From this 'waste land' the poor had traditionally the privilege of cutting firewood and pasturing livestock. In the hundred years before Wesley the rich enclosed this common land for their own use—as sheep runs, great pastures, or centers for recreation, with the resulting ruin of thousands of small farmers. Wesley, at great personal cost, stood against the new system of enclosure and attacked the powerful."[16]

Unafraid to give pastoral care to the wealthy, Wesley's doctrine of stewardship was so strong that he believed the very possession of riches was dangerous: "I have not known three score rich persons, perhaps not half the number, during three score years, who, as far as I can judge, were not less holy than they would have been had they been poor . . . O that God would enable me once more, before I go hence and am no more seen, to lift up my voice like a trumpet to those who gain and save all they can, but do not give all they can . . . The Methodists grow more and more self-indulgent, because they grow rich. And it is an observation which admits of few exceptions, that nine in ten of these decreased in grace in the same proportion as they increased in wealth."[17] He wrote in his JOURNAL: "Religion must necessarily produce both industry and frugality, and these cannot but produce riches. But as riches increase so will pride, anger and love of the world in all its branches . . . So although the form of religion remains, the spirit is swiftly vanishing away." His first organization of stewards was for the relief of the poor. Whenever he found a wealthy man who would listen, he gave the injunction: "Put yourself in the place of every poor man; and deal with him as you would with God."[18]

Among those few who spoke about conditions of employment, Wesley was a chaplain for miners and mill workers. He urged those workers to leave any employment which was "unhealthy" and insisted that employers give better protection to their laborers. He categorically attacked the conditions of employees who dealt with arsenic, who handled "harmful minerals" or had "to breathe an air tainted with streams of melting lead." He spoke against long workdays and working conditions which demanded hours in the same position or an "uneasy posture."[19]

Many agree with United Methodist scholar Jose Miguez Bonino that Wesley provided a beginning point for those seeking to correct economic injustice. Wesley himself was unable to fully see the structural nature of the social problems with which he grappled. In THOUGHTS ON THE PRESENT SCARCITY OF PROVISIONS, Wesley made an attempt to identify and relate the causes of the economic crisis that gripped England in the early 1770's. His vivid portrayal of the miserable conditions of the poor reminds us of Engle's systematic description, less than a century later, of "the condition of the working class in England in 1844." Wesley's prophetic tone of denunciation was at times arresting. His attempt to work with hard data-statistics, prices, and market conditions was extraordinary for a religious leader. But, when he attempted to find causes and remedies, he remained totally within the premises of the merchant system and completely unaware of the structural causes of the crises. He could not see in it the birthpangs of a new mode of production and organization of society, and consequently he could not see that the poverty he described and denounced as the "selling of flesh and blood" was the inevitable sacrifice that the gods of the new order demand. Those of us who still have confidence in a capitalist economy have to fight to rid it of economic injustice and open its blessings to all peoples through political and legal means. Anything less is contrary to the gospel of love.

CHAPTER 20
ISSUES OF SEXISM AND AGISM

When learning to ride a bicycle, Frances Willard found a parallel to her experience as a reformer. She would occasionally lose her forward impetus and fall into the gutter. This, she felt, was similar to her experience as a worker for renewal in the church. Unless she could provide constant renewal impetus and momentum, her efforts at reform lagged and fell backward.[1]

Within almost every Christian church all women, and men over the age of sixty-five, share a common condition:

• Studies show that although they make up seventy percent of the majority of the active membership, and are the most dedicated workers, they have only rarely participated in the leadership of the Church or held any substantial power. Often church legislation has explicitly excluded them from such roles.

• They are given "busy-work" and often not treated as individuals who have special talents, gifts and graces needed by the entire community. Their particular interests and preferences are often not even considered.

• They are subject to a great deal of prejudice in the general society which consequently effects their relationships within the church as well.

• They are subject to negative image-building within the language itself and by the media.

Women have faced such restrictions for centuries. However, people over sixty-five have experienced restrictive conditions for only two of three generations because so few people lived to be older than sixty-five years of age before 1900. It is our contention that this is a crucial area of concern for those interested in church renewal since far more than half the strength, talent, and ability of the community which is the Church is represented by these two groups of people. Unless they take a leadership role in a church which is responsive to their needs and their ideas, the chance for a truly Wesleyan revival will be gone. Wesley was deeply dependent on both women and older members for his own renewal experience.

Issues of Sexism

The history of the Christian church parallels that of the general society in the use and abuse of women. Far more than most people care to admit, women have been systematically denied not only equal status with men, but also the opportunity to experience in their lives many pursuits and privileges taken for granted by men.

Wesley was far from perfect as his language and his record of initially rejecting proposals for the participation of women reflect. Yet he had an important vision of what women could do in ministry.

(1) Wesley was one of the first church leaders to listen seriously to women as advisors. In both his JOURNAL and correspondence there are incidents of women making a difference in Wesley's own ministry. Everyone knows how often and how profoundly Susanna influenced his theology. She was not alone. He was also influenced by Mary Bosanquet Fletcher, Margaret Davidson, Hester Ann Roe, Sarah Crosby, Sarah Mallet, Grace Walton, Grace Murray, Hannah Ball, Elizabeth Richie, Elizabeth Harrell, and many others, to the extent that he listened to their problems and suggestions, answered their questions, took a continuing interest in their ministries, and was willing to become their advisor and to listen to their advice. Even such followers as Ann "Praying Nannie" Cutler were able to involve Wesley in ongoing theological dialogue. These women brought many men into the itinerant ministry and the effectiveness of their work compares very well with that of any other of the early saints of United Methodism.

(2) Wesley gave women more power in his societies than they had ever had before in any church. He defended himself from those that attacked his practice by an appeal to the early church, writing: "It is well known, that, in the primitive Church, there were women particularly appointed for this work. Indeed there was one or more such in every Christian congregation under heaven. They were then called Deaconesses, that is, servants; servants of the church, and of its great Master."[2]

The experience of his early societies was, in truth, no different from that of most other churches. They were all, and always had been, from apostolic times, institutions that had been substantially supported in ministry and in mission by women. The difference was that of perception. Wesley was one of the first men to give close attention to what was going on in the pastoral work of a parish and realize how much of the ministry was under the leadership of women.

Howard Snyder writes: "By the time Methodism had reached 100,000 members at the end of the century, the movement must have had over 10,000 class and band leaders with perhaps an equal or larger total of other leaders. Many of these, as well as some of Wesley's preachers, were women with opportunities for leadership available nowhere else."[3]

Wesley encouraged women preachers and evangelists. In a fine article, Dr. Earl Kent Brown lists the various kinds of witnessing that women did: "Casual conversation, talks or prayers in band and class meetings, prayer in society or other public meetings, testimony exhortation, expounding, Biblical exegesis and application."[4] He goes on to point out that several undertook the kind of Biblical exegesis and application considered 'preaching' within the narrow definition."[5] In addition, several traveled as evangelists and preachers. Almost all were very effective evangelists.[6] It was common for women to be leaders at every level of society and to lead Bible study, prayer meetings, and provide pastoral care.

Wesley wrote to Mary Bosanquet, before she became Mary Fletcher: "I think the strength of the cause rests there—in your having an extraordinary call. So I am persuaded as every one of our lay preachers; otherwise I would not countenance his preaching at all. It is plain to me that the whole work of God termed Methodism is an extraordinary dispensation of His providence. Therefore, I do not wonder if several things occur therein which do not fall under ordinary rules of discipline."[7]

Rosemary Skinner Keller writes in her introduction to the two volume series WOMEN IN NEW WORLDS: "We labor under the false assumption, states Earl Kent Brown . . . that females simply were present but silent in the early class meetings of the Wesleyan movement in England. In practice, however, they prayed and spoke freely of religious experience, 'not loud, yet fervent,' exhorted others to respond and expounded on Scripture. The effectiveness of their witness led Wesley to conclude that God was owning the ministry of these women with a harvest of souls."[8]

Dorothy McConnell concluded her study of the women of early Methodism with the observation that Wesley seemed to be "more at ease on paper with women than he was with men" and noted that "a great proportion of Wesley's extant correspondence is with women."[9]

(3) His theology is remarkably free of sexism when considered from the point of view of eighteenth century standards. Not only did Wesley fail to paint an image of women in his writings as dependent, subordinant adjuncts of the male life, but through his societies he, quite unintentionally, gave them a new image. For one of the first times in history women were given status in a public sphere. Previously, they had been seen as "mate," "mother," "servant," "chattel," or even as the "object of love." Rarely had women been allowed to be leaders, preachers, evangelists, counselors, organizers, or teachers. Before Wesley the teaching profession, at every level, was as much a male preserve as any other profession in society.

In his EXPLANATORY NOTES UPON THE NEW TESTAMENT, Wesley gives more than usual prominance to women in his commentary. He highlights their witness to the incarnation and the resurrection. He suggests in his commentary that Christ gives a special promise to Mary Magdalene on the Day of Resurrection: "You will have other opportunities of conversing with Me."[10]

Since Wesley's doctrine of sanctification emphasized fruits, women won their way into leadership because they produced so much spiritual abundance. They demonstrated through acts of converting love that the Spirit was working through them, and Wesley respected them because he saw their discipleship.

(4) The Wesleyan tradition, with many mistakes and backward steps, has been more open to women in leadership and in both ordained and lay ministry than any other major church tradition. Once the door was opened, women accomplished remarkable feats of ministry, often while having to overcome the subtle or outright opposition of other Christians. Several books have been written of their witness, and many more will be. In this brief section five ways women have been involved in ministry are highlighted: (a) as ordained ministers; (b) as preachers and evangelists; (c) as missionaries; (d) as ministers of social reform; and (e) as lay ministers.

(a) As ordained ministers

Frances Willard, who spent a lifetime of effective ministry, was constantly fighting for ordination and a chance to do parish ministry. She developed many arguments for the ordination of women, most taken from Methodist tradition. She quoted Wesley's decision to ordain Thomas Coke when the Bishop of London refused to ordain missionaries for America as a key act of his ministry: "That decision of the intrepid founder of Methodism cost the Episcopal Church its future in the New World as time has proved. . . . We stand once more at the parting of the roads; shall the bold, resolute men among our clergy win the day and give ordination to women, or shall women take this matter into their own hands."[11]

From 1869 to 1956 the various branches of United Methodism fought over the status of women in the Church and their ordination. The issue of sexist language was faced for the first time in the General Conference of 1880 of the Methodist Episcopal Church.[12]

Women were allowed to work where they were desperately needed—in local churches, on foreign mission fields, and in home missions among the poor and in the cities. But, they were denied roles of significant leadership as lay persons and denied ordination as well. The first compromise was to lift again the office of Deaconess as a consecrated ministry of service taken from Scripture, specifically from Romans 16:2 "In which Phoebe, a wealthy and cultured woman known for her beneficence, is reported to have served in the primitive Christian church . . . freely and lovingly . . . (she) challenged hunger and disease on the doorstep of the perishing and, in Christ's name, made them retire." The tradition of Phoebe's diakonia—her ability to see "the world's pain" and her desire to overcome it through personal service was the ministry offered to women.[13] Many thousands were willing to make the enormous sacrifices such ministry required.

From 1880 to 1956 battles were fought at every level of United Methodism to obtain ordination for women. In 1876 a church licensed Anna Oliver as a local preacher. In 1880 she was recommended for ordination as Deacon by the New England Conference. The Bishop refused to allow the conference to vote because he believed that church law did not allow the ordination of women. His decision was appealed to the General Conference. The New England Conference by a very large majority instructed its delegates "to work and vote for the removal of all sex distinctions pertaining to ministry."[14]

In answer to her critics, Anna Oliver wrote: "The (woman) evangelist arrives and is thrust before another crowd of strangers. Women are said to be timid and shrinking, and yet will our good mother Church take these shrinking, delicate, modest, sensitive, home-loving, nestling, timid little things, and toss them about from Maine to California, or send them as missionaries to wild and naked barbarians, at the same time forbidding them to engage in the motherly work of the pastorate.

"Pastoral work is adapted to women, for it is motherly work. The mother has her little group, the pastor the flock. As the mother spreads her table with food suited to the individual needs of her family, so the pastor feeds the flock. Each knows the sick ones, the weak ones, those that must be carried in the arms, and those strong enough to help others. I recognize this field as suited to my natural qualifications.

"My interest begins with conversions. Then an evangelist leaves. And I always felt as though a whole nursery full of my own little ones were being turned over to the care of strangers. The experience was, in a word, fearful."[15]

After her rejection, her response was even more poignant: "God sanctions my pastoral work. In proof of this I appeal to the record in Passaic, N.J. and Brooklyn, N.Y. But it may be said, notwithstanding the reasons given, that I am mistaken in my call. Then it is a very great pity for myself that I cannot be convinced that I am mistaken—a pity that I lived in this delusion all these years. I have made almost every conceivable sacrifice to do what I believe God willed. Brought up in a conservative circle in New York City, that held it a disgrace for a woman to work, surrounded with the comforts and advantages of ample means and trained in the Episcopal Church. I gave up home, friends and support, went counter to the prejudices that had become second nature to me, worked for several years to constant exhaustion, and suffered cold, hunger, and loneliness. The things hardest for me to bear were laid upon me. For two months my own mother did not speak to me. When I entered the house she turned and walked away. When I sat at the table she did not recognize me. I have passed through tortures to which the flames of martyrdom would be nothing, for they would end in a day. And through all this time and today, I could turn off to positions of comparative ease and profit. However, I take no credit to myself for enduring these trials, because at every step it was plain to me, that I had no alternative but to go forward or renounce my Lord."[16]

It would be seventy-six years of pain and struggle for women before the rights of equality in ordained ministry were fully granted.

Frances Willard, who learned the importance of momentum and new impetus as she learned to ride her bicycle, was the outstanding spokesperson for the cause of ordination for women in the nineteenth century, as Georgia Harkness was in the twentieth. Both carried out ministries for God which were at least equal to that of any of their male contemporaries. But, they had the additional burden of rejection and artificial limitations placed upon them. "The deepest thought and desire of my life would have been met," wrote Frances Willard, "if my dear old Mother church had permitted me to be a minister. The wandering life of an evangelist or a reformer comes nearest to, but cannot fill, the ideal which I early cherished, but did not expect ever publicly to confess." In WOMEN IN THE PULPIT, she wrote: "I was too timid to go without a call; and so it came about that while my unconstrained preference would long ago have led me to the pastorate, I have failed of it."[17]

(b) As preachers and evangelists

Wesley came to realize how effective women were as preachers and evangelists. As a child he saw the great power of his mother's witness. It was this woman who converted, trained and shaped him for his own ministry. She continued to be his close advisor through much of his adult ministry. Her influence liberalized his views concerning both women and the laity.

Wesley soon recognized many gifts and graces in the women who entered his societies. This was not surprising since these women were far more likely than the men among his followers to have had the benefits of education. They possessed the tools of literacy by which they could study the Bible, Wesley's own works, and the collections which he edited. Using their gifts they became leaders of classes and bands as well as of Bible study and prayer groups. Soon some became preachers and evangelists.

Almost immediately after Wesley's death, women began to lose their positions of leadership in his society and were soon denied the right to preach and evangelize. It would be after the middle of the twentieth century before they would reclaim that which had been their prerogative during Wesley's lifetime.

(c) As missionaries and social workers

When denied the right of ordained ministry and positions of leadership in the Church, women turned wherever they could to serve Christ. The institutional church was perfectly willing to "use" them in ministry where no one else wanted to serve. They were sent to the poor, the sick, the homeless, and the neglected. They went to the slums of the cities and to isolated rural communities. They went to difficult mission fields in other countries.

In the first hundred years of United Methodist missions more than sixty percent of all those sent to serve in the rest of the world were women. These women inherited the work few others wanted to do. They learned other languages so they could teach children and youth living in poverty and oppression. They learned medicine so they could serve people afflicted with dread and contagious diseases. They learned to be social workers so they could help the poor, the forgotten, and the weak.[18]

Walter Lacy's book A HUNDRED YEARS OF CHINA METHODISM presents an endless line of missionary sacrifice by

189

women who had to overcome the patronizing attitudes of their "superiors," thousands of customs negating women, and incredible poverty. Two of the first three persons to join the Methodist Church in China, were women. They later brought their families and others to be baptised.[19] In the official history of United Methodist Missions this summary statement is made: "On the mission field it should be said that our laymen are nearly all women."[20]

In 1869, the year the first Local Preacher's License was granted to a woman, the Woman's Foreign Missionary Society was formed. This began a century of accomplishment in missions and reform by women. Their organization which eventually grew to become The United Methodist Women, the largest organization for women in the world, eventually developed a program of social action, missionary work, and political reform unprecedented in history. The United Methodist Women have been constantly at work sensitizing the Church and working out the implications of the Gospel in the world. Far from limiting themselves to "women's issues," there has not been an area of human need, from world peace to racism, in which the United Methodist Women have not given both prophetic leadership and sacrificial service. Many times they have been the source of renewal in the Church, the nation and the world.

(d) As lay ministers and lay leaders

Although women were denied a place of leadership in worship, finance, and church government in the years following Wesley's death, they turned to the ministries of education, compassion, and social concern. This involvement was nothing new. From the time when Hannah Ball organized the first church school, approved by Wesley after the fact, United Methodist women have always been active in all outreach ministries of compassion and mission. Wherever the needs, women got involved and Wesley supported them.

However, when pushed out of church leadership positions, they turned outward. The next century and a half found them to be progressively more active in mission, social work, and reform movements within the wider society. Wherever people were in poverty, hungry, ill, or abandoned, laywomen were there offering help. They got involved in reform movements for fair labor legislation, women's suffrage, child labor laws, and more honest government. They fought against prostitution, slavery, alcohol, and drugs. No group has been more effective in promoting welfare and social security legislation, public health care, better education, and fair employment practices. They have fought racism, agism, and sexism in many forms and worked for better penal facilities and cleaner, safer cities. Women led in building support for the United Nations and have been most active in ministries for world peace, disarmament, and social justice.[21]

In 1878, not a single laywoman served on any general board or agency of any church in the Wesleyan family. Less than a hundred years ago, in 1892, the first four women were elected as voting members of a General Conference. One was a fully ordained clergywoman of the Methodist Protestant Church. The other three were laywomen.[22]

The challenges of contemporary society require further action:

(1) Care must be taken that we are not unintentionally forming another sexist generation. Language is important, especially language used in worship and in the community by church members, because language shapes people's images of themselves and others. An earlier reference has been made in this book to the excellent materials of Sharon and Thomas Neufer Enswiler, WOMEN & WORSHIP, A GUIDE TO NON-SEXIST HYMNS, PRAYERS AND LITURGIES, and WHOLENESS IN WORSHIP.

(2) As Letty Russell reminds us, women "are frequently invisible," not only in today's society but in history."[23] A renewed church must reclaim that history. The two volumes on women in ministry in the Wesleyan tradition, WOMEN IN NEW WORLDS, make a wonderful beginning, but much more has to be done. Children's books, television programs, software for computers, tapes and disks for home TV, and programs for cable television must be developed to show history as it really was. Church history is not accurate unless it tells the stories of all church people.

Issues Of Agism

Since I have recently completed two books on this subject, NO GOLDEN AGERS HERE and "GEE, YOU LOOK GOOD!," this will be a brief section on a very important topic. The two books tell the story of thousands of people over sixty-five in ministries of active, caring, serving love.[24]

John Wesley, in addition to his personal example, had a great deal of insight concerning those we call senior citizens. He recorded: "The rush of numerous years have occasioned me little suffering, it is true that I am not as agile as I was in times past. I do not run or walk so fast as I did; my sight is a little decayed; my left eye is grown dim, and hardly serves me to read; I have daily some pain in my right shoulder and arm, which I impute partly to a sprain, and partly to the rheumatism. I find likewise some decay in my memory, with regard to names and things lately passed, but not at all with regard to what I have read or heard twenty, forty, or sixty years ago; neither do I find any decay in my hearing, smell, taste, or appetite; (although I want but a third of the food I did once); nor do I feel any such things as weariness, either in traveling or preaching; and I am not conscious of any decay in writing sermons, which I do as readily, and, I believe, as correctly as ever.

"To what cause can I impute this, that I am as I am? First, doubtless, to the power of God, fitting me for the work to which I am called, as long as He pleases to continue me therein; and, next, subordinately to this, to the prayers of his children.

"May we not impute it, as inferior means. 1. To my constant exercise and change of air? 2. To my never having lost a night's sleep, sick or well, at land or at sea, since I was born? 3. To my having sleep at command, so that whenever I feel myself almost worn out, I call it, and it comes day or night? 4. To my having constantly, for above sixty years, risen at four in the morning? 5. To my constant preaching at five in the morning for above fifty years? 6. To my having so little pain in my life, and so little sorrow or anxious care? Even now, though I find pain daily in my eye or temple, or arm; yet it is never violent, and seldom lasts many minutes at a time.

"Whether or not this is sent to give me warning that I am shortly to quit this tabernacle, I do not know, but, be it one way or another, I have only to say:

> My remnant of days
> I spend to his praise
> Who died the whole world to redeem:
> Be they many or few,
> My days are his due,
> And they are devoted to Him."[25]

This man, who so completely experienced all stages of life himself, developed a remarkable place in ministry for those over sixty-five. Such people were rare in those days when an average life span was under thirty-five. Wesley's own experience, considering his life of discipline and extraordinary hard work, was almost unique. His insights are especially helpful in this area for church renewal. Any renewal of the Church must vitally involve those over sixty-five for they make up almost one-fourth of the active members in all Christian churches in the United States. Wesley's thought is helpful in three areas:

(1) His unique contribution to Christian theology, the doctrines of sanctification and perfection, has important implications for those over sixty-five. As the members with spiritual experience, many of them have spent a lifetime reaching for the perfection Wesley preached. Like the patriarchs of the Old Testament, they are those in the Church most likely to be full of the Spirit and free from the spiritual limitations of self. Many possess the qualities the church needs for leadership.

(2) Wesley's concept of everyone in ministry, built on the Protestant principle of the priesthood of all believers, had no artificial limits. Everyone was called "to serve all they could for as long as they could." He would not have understood any arbitrary retirement age for either clergy or laity.

(3) Some of his most effective helpers were over sixty-five. They furnished leadership in the societies, bands, classes, and conferences. The apprentice system was possible because those with experience helped those new in the faith. Today, many of the most faithful and able ministers, lay and clergy, are over sixty-five. Those experienced in the faith have the patience and the time to give to those who are newcomers.

(4) In the 18th century those who survived beyond the age sixty-five were often, in a day without any pensions or social security, among the poorest of the poor. Their human needs drew them to Wesley who welcomed them and gave them significant work to do for Christ.

As the pastor of a large city church with three thousand people in the congregation over sixty-five I learned how important that group was for church renewal. We found that those over sixty-five were much more responsive to new ideas and to risk-taking than any other age group. They were willing to question any action and any value in the name of truth. I discovered a pattern of behavior that surprised me. A large majority of those over sixty-five supported our efforts to open up the church, to risk using the building, to serve the poor and the young, to take chances in serving the neighborhood, and to be more active in mission. Many supported the protest against the Viet Nam War and worked hard for peace, often in confrontation with their sons and daughters. They worked for equal opportunity for all people, especially for women and ethnics. I rarely found an active person over sixty-five displaying overt racism. In the life of our church they constantly supported spending our substance for work in the community, in the prisons, among the transients, on the mission field, and with our young people.

Those over sixty-five had lived long enough to experience life as it is. They were free to be honest. Most had escaped the restraints which force a person to conform. Even most of those who had not retired did not have to compromise their integrity to keep their jobs. Their values were authentic because they had worked them out.

They had discovered how relatively unimportant possessions were. All of them had lived through the Great Depression when many families had nothing. These were often recalled as among the finest years of their lives. They found out early in life that possessions often brought additional worry and labor. Possesions had to be cared for, repaired, insured, transported, and protected. Often they caused jealousy and bitterness within the family. Older people learned that any success or value system that revolved solely around matters of wealth or possessions was empty. My contemporaries were often afraid to take risks because they felt they had too much to lose.

Another equally freeing discovery made by those over sixty-five involved their friends. True friends cared about them, not their possessions. Their experience had taught them that pretense did not pay in personal relationships. People were generally unconcerned with the victories and material success of others. Our society may shout loudly of the crucial importance of being Number One, but in a day or two the shouting stops and no one cares. I heard story after story about how quickly yesterday's accomplishments fade. A person works to get to the top of his or her business and is then retired. Repeated experience teaches how unimportant it is to be first in competition. The quality that is most respected and remembered is not winning but loving. Because those over sixty-five are free from the competitive struggle, they can concentrate on life itself—on being the best persons they can be. They are free to enter into relationships without ulterior motives. They can love and be open without suspicion. They are free to enjoy today, without worrying about the possibility of future success. As the ego factors fade, the happiness that comes from pure and honest choices comes clearly into focus.

Because they were free, the spirit of those over sixty-five renewed our church and shaped our ministry. Their freedom liberated our entire church from the bondage that contained it. They brought a commanding spirit because:

(1) Most were free to be honest. If I wanted candid advice, I went to a member over the age of sixty-five. The over sixty-five persons were the best evaluators I had because they had few vested interests.

(2) Most were free to take chances. They weren't as interested in what "others were thinking" and were a lot more interested in what was "right" and what Christ would expect of them. They also had many of the best new ideas because they were not chained by the threat of being wrong.

(3) Most were free to serve. The traditional binds of time and family pressures were not as absolute. Those over sixty-five were free to make their decisions according to who they really were. Their questions were real questions: Is the job worthwhile? Can I do it? Should I do it? Not only did those over sixty-five claim freedom for themselves but they shared that freedom with their church. Because of their powerful place in the decision-making process of the church, many of the congregation's decisions were made more honestly. We did far fewer things for show and did many more things for service.

(4) Most were free to love. Since so many of their ego needs had been quieted in the experience of living, they were able to give of themselves selflessly as no other group. In countless instances I saw them risk the act of love in the most difficult circumstances.

(5) Most were free to be themselves. I had been around smooth, successful people before. They knew every strength of style, etiquette and success, but often one wondered who they really were. Most of those over sixty-five in my new parish had taken over their own lives and no longer spent much time pretending. They didn't care about impressing me or anyone else. Instead they looked on each opportunity and challenge on the basis of human need.

(6) Most were free to be socially concerned. Many had lived through years of personal struggle in the quest of individual success. Both those who had "made it" and those who fell short had discovered that the quest was hollow. Many wanted to wrap themselves in a cause that really was important. They were willing to be used by Jesus Christ as helpers in our community and in mission around the world.

(7) Most were free from strong ego needs. Their pleasures now came from real accomplishment not from recognition. They had already accomplished what they felt they had to do.

These are the reasons I have so much trust in those over sixty-five. They are able to apply spiritual disciplines in their own lives. Through them churches can come alive!

SECTION VI
WESLEYAN THEOLOGY:
AGENT OF CHURCH RENEWAL

This chapter is not an attempt to summarize Wesleyan theology or to structure a theology upon which renewal depends. Wesley made no claim to be a systematic theologian. He found that theoretical considerations often divide Christians while dissipating energy needed for Christian service. He considered himself to be both orthodox and reformed in outlook.

Renewal became possible for him because he made the great breadth of the Christian experience his own inheritance. Before the world knew the word "ecumenical," Wesley defined Christian truth in its essence, in such a way that few would be excluded, and those few by their own choice. He saw the gospel as God's free gift to all. He resisted any attempt to narrow that constituency either by judgmentalism or theological complexity. Everyone was welcome. Only when a person retreated from commitments freely made, would Wesley approve separation. Those who withdrew were always welcomed back if they sought readmission and demonstrated a contrite spirit.

The distinct theological doctrines usually attributed to Wesley—Arminianism, Sanctification, and Perfection—are a theological working out of the meaning of renewal and rebirth. The foundation of his ministry was the saving love of God in Christ.

In the preface to the first edition of his SERMONS, the standard of faith during the first century of Methodism, Wesley presented scripture as the only authority. On all questions "which do not strike at the root of Christianity, Christians should think and let think."[1]

Although he studied diligently, Wesley did not believe that philosophy or metaphysics could furnish a path to any essential truth. He was unhappy that William Law philosophized in his religious writings and even found Luther too influenced by abstract, intellectual conceptions.[2]

The Church had moved away from the patristic Biblical tradition after Constantine's so-called conversion. Thus Wesley, in his defense of New Testament Christianity, anticipated what today's scholars call the "Constantine Tradition." Wesley felt that the church was much better off under persecution. He wrote in a sermon: "Persecution never did, never could, give any lasting wound to genuine Christianity. But the greatest it ever received, the grand blow which was struck at the very root of that humble, gentle, patient love, which is the fulfilling of the Christian law, the whole essence of true religion, was struck in the fourth century by Constantine the Great, when he called himself Christian, and poured in a flood of riches, honours, and power, upon the Christians; more especially upon the clergy . . . Just so, when the fear of persecution was removed, and wealth and honour attended the Christian profession, the Christians did not gradually sink, but rushed headlong into all manner of vices. Then 'the mystery of iniquity' was no more hid, but stalked abroad in the face of the sun. Then, not the golden age but the iron age of the church commenced."[3]

Wesley is highly critical of some parts of Augustine, defending not only Montanus, but also Pelagius! (OF THE CHURCH), anticipating today's historians, who recognize that the only accounts we have of Pelagius come from Augustine's quotations. Finally, Wesley felt the Reformation did not go far enough in its application of the New Testament to the Church. He tried to push all traditions back to the source of truth. (The same process is leading to ecumenical understanding in the twentieth century.) Scripture became the unifying foundation: "The Scripture, therefore, of the Old and New Testament is a most solid and precious system of divine truth."[4]

Because salvation has a "NOW" aspect for Wesley, his theological investigations accentuate the present and not the future. For this reason he could combine both Catholic and Protestant tradition and be able to view Calvin and Luther as complimentary theologians. It explains why all his distinctive theological emphases (Arminianism, Sanctification, and Perfection) have to do with the here and now and not the hereafter, and why Christology is the key to his theology.

Catholics And Protestants

In the heritage of the other great reformers, Wesley studied scripture first and then the experience of the early church. He also took his place as an Anglican priest within the wider Catholic tradition. While a zealous advocate of the major tenents of the Reformation, he found much in Catholicism worthy of preservation. More than most Protestants he saw the significance of tradition and the place of reason in the church: "It is a fundamental principle with us (the Methodists) that to renounce reason is to renounce religion, that religion and reason go hand in hand, and that all irrational religion is false religion."[5]

Many, including both major Roman Catholic Wesley scholars, Piette and Todd, find that he was remarkably close to the Catholic tradition when he spoke of good works as a necessary adjunct to salvation. In one of his letters Wesley wrote: "Is not this salvation by works? Not by the merits of works, but by works as a condition. By salvation I here mean final salvation. And who can deny that both inward works (keeping the commandments) are a condition of this? What is this more or less than 'without holiness no man shall see the Lord?' "[6]

Wesley could not fully combine the Catholic ethic of holiness with the Protestant view of grace. He urged and expected good works; but they were, in his view, simply the inevitable response in love to the free gift of God. Purgatory seems irrelevant because man's salvation is in no way earned by what he or others do. Assurance may be ascertained only by the evidence of the future.

When George Croft Cell wrote that Wesley's theology was a "necessary synthesis of the Protestant ethic of grace with the Catholic ethic of holiness,"[7] he provided the ecumenical context for understanding Wesley on sanctification and perfection. As we shall see, contemporary scholarship is progressing toward a meeting of traditions by means of a more complete understanding of grace, with Wesley's emphasis becoming the meeting ground for Protestants and Catholics. In Wesley's view most Protestants did not give enough attention to the Catholic teaching on what Christ has done nor on the wholistic response required of converts. Most Roman Catholics, in his opinion, did not recognize the uniqueness of the once-for-all sacrifice nor the extent of the power of grace. Wesley came, on many occasions, close to embracing the Catholic position of "double justification" (once by faith alone and another final justification coming only when the believer merits his salvation by works). In his sermon, "On The Wedding Garment," Wesley speaks of "Sanctification being a condition of the final (not the present) justification." This is in line with his interpretation of the text: "Without holiness no man shall see the Lord."[8]

Unlike Calvin, Wesley fought for the universe availability of salvation. Unlike orthodox Roman Catholic dogma, Wesley proclaimed the unconditional power of God's grace. In such a way he was able to combine the possibilities of grace with the potentialities in creation.[9]

Wesley's major debate with Roman Catholics was at the crucial point of tradition. With his love for the devotional classics and the work of the fathers, he respected that tradition as no Protestant of his time. Yet, he did not move from the conviction that the final authority in all matters of theology must be with Christ alone, and that all facts of tradition and experience must conform to the Biblical witness. "The Scriptures are the touchstone whereby Christians examine all, real or supposed revelations. In all cases they appeal 'to the law and testimony' to try every spirit thereby."[10] It was on this same basic appeal to scriptures alone that he tried to walk a path between Luther and Calvin.

Luther And Calvin

While criticizing both reformers with candor, Wesley maintained and valued his place within their tradition and affirmed their fundamental unity. This very openness to all differing traditions and his appreciation of both Calvin and Luther forced the contemporary church back to scripture and the apostolic period to evaluate the fruits of the reformation.

Wesley's two great criticisms of Luther are based on Scripture. He found Luther's criticism of the value of reason and his negation of parts of the law and the Old Testament unjustified. He offered this evaluation when reading Luther's COMMENTARY ON THE EPISTLE TO THE GALATIANS: "How does he decry reason, right or wrong, as an irreconcilable enemy to the gospel of Christ? . . . Whereas what is reason but the power of apprehending, judging and discoursing? Which power is no more to be condemned in gross than seeing, hearing, or feeling."[11]

The Thirty-Nine Anglican Articles which Wesley inherited and modified were originally composed during a period of pervasive Calvinistic influence. They set forth the doctrines of the Reformation in a Calvinistic perspective. Wesley was especially strong in his endorsement of the fundamental doctrine of the Reformation: Justification by grace through faith. "I think of justification," Wesley taught, "just as Mr. Calvin does. In this respect I do not differ from him a hair's breath."[12]

However, on the crucial doctrines of predestination and universal salvation, Wesley opposed that which he understood to be Calvin's position. He found Calvin's denial of universal salvation "flatly contrary to Scripture," particularly those texts which give "a clear proof that Christ died, not only for those that are saved, but also for them that perish." "He is the Savior of the World." (John 4:42) He is "the Lamb of God that taketh away the sins of the world." (1:29) "He is the propitiation, not for our sins only, but also for the sins of the whole world." (I John 2:2) "He is the living God, the Saviour of all men." (I Timothy 4:10) "He gave himself a ransom for all." (2:6) "He tasted death for every man." (Hebrews 2:9) He found no adequate doctrine of prevenient grace in Calvinism. Therefore, Wesley saw predestination as fatalism with Christ's work going for naught.[13]

Wesley escaped Pelagianism in his doctrine of Creation and Fall (which presented men and women as totally depraved because of the fall), without any power to resist temptation or the ability to turn to God. His doctrine of prevenient grace (that the Holy Spirit freely gives light to every person providing power for ethical duty and motivation to appeal to God for salvation and help) makes him reject Calvinism with equal firmness. Unfortunately, his understanding of Calvin was second hand, based on presentations by Whitefield, Berridge, Toplady, and Rowland Hill which were almost cariacatures of Calvin's theology.

Wesley's great attack on antinomianism was based on the certainty that Christians stood corporately before God, sharing the blessings of the new birth with one another. It is because Christ has done all, that all may be saved. Wesley, in the steps of both Calvin and Luther, combined a reverance for the authority of scripture with an awareness of the living witness of the Holy Spirit in Christian experience. For Wesley the assurance that Christ has done all that is necessary for salvation frees Christians to live triumphantly, taking risks for love and spiritual fulfillment. Luther allowed whatever scripture does not condemn. Calvin allowed only what scripture commands, Wesley stands as a Calvinist on "essentials" and relegates the rest to "opinion." But, he would not exclude a person (such as a Catholic) due to unscriptural opinions or practices.

The Arminian

For Wesley "the cornerstone of the whole Christian building" was justification by faith. Here "the atonement of Christ is actually applied to the soul of the sinner."[14] What happened when this took place? Is atonement available to every sinner? Does experience lead to an assurance of salvation? Can an individual rise from a fallen state and enter a path to perfection? Does God intend for persons to be sanctified?

Wesley's answers to all these questions mark him as a Arminian. He chose the name of Arminius for his house organ, at a time when this would insure both misunderstanding and controversy, because he thought he had found the truth. Arminianism is often attacked as a mongrel theology of semi-Pelagianism without the attacked ever studying Arminius' theology. Wesley did not accept all that had become known as Arminianism, but he agreed with Arminius' own position as "a lover of free grace." Wesley wrote: "The errors charged upon these (usually termed Arminians) by their opponents, are five: (1) That they deny original sin; (2) That they deny justification by faith; (3) That they deny absolute predestination; (4) That they deny the grace of God to be irresistible; and, (5) That they affirm a believer may fall from grace.

"With regard to the first of these charges, they plead: Not Guilty. They are entirely false. No man that ever lived, not John Calvin himself, ever asserted either original sin, or justification by faith, in more strong, more clear and express terms, than Arminius has done. . . .

"But there is an undeniable difference between the Calvinist and Arminians, with regard to the three other questions. Here they divide; the former believe absolute the latter only conditional, predestination. The Calvinist hold, first that God has absolutely decreed, from all eternity, to save such and such persons, and no others; and that Christ died for these, and none else. The Arminians hold, God has decreed, from all eternity, touching all that have the written word, 'He that believeth shall be saved; he that believeth not, shall be condemned.' . . . .

"The Calvinists hold, secondly, that the saving grace of God is absolutely irresistible; that no man is any more able to resist it, than to resist the stroke of lightning. The Arminians hold, that although there may be some moments wherein the grace of God acts irresistibly, yet in general, any man may resist, and that to him eternal ruin, the grace whereby it was the will of God he would have been eternally saved.

"The Calvinists hold, thirdly, that a true believer in Christ cannot possibly fall from grace. The Arminians hold, that a true believer may 'make shipwreck of faith and a good conscience; that he may fall, not only fouly, but finally, so as to perish for ever.' "[15]

In each case Wesley clearly and consistently held that Arminian principles pointed to the truth. Of course, he could not know that the Calvinists he attacked so virogously did not accurately present the theology of Calvin. In many ways Wesley goes beyond Arminius in his demand for "natural free will" but he refuses to place any limits on God's grace. Wesley finds predestination contrary to both Scripture and experience. It makes preaching needless, missionary work irrelevant, and the good life accidental. The whole of Christian revelation (all of the scriptures and the work of the Holy Spirit become irrelevant because "unchangeable decrees must be affected.")

These words of Wesley are clear and consistent with his work. Both Arminius and Wesley believed in election, but in an election which does not compromise either the character or the power of God. Wesley denied absolute predestination and irresistible grace. His own experience demonstrated that a believer can fall from grace. He had discovered God's amazing love and he refused to place limits upon it. The sermon on "Free Grace," preached in Bristol in 1740, proved to be the breaking point with Whitefield and all Calvinists: "The grace of the love of God . . . is free in all to whom it is given. It does not depend on any power or merit in man; no, not in any degree, neither in whole nor in part. It does not in anywise depend either on the good works or righteousness of the receiver; not on anything he had done, or anything he is."[16]

This stand is crucial for the renewal of the Church because it eliminates the judgmentalism which has often set Christian against Christian, and Christians against the rest of the world. Any theological excuses for ignoring the world and its people must be overcome if the Gospel is to be shared. Nevertheless, Wesley scholars should admit that this is a major theological and hermeneutical problem. Much of Scripture clearly does teach at least some form of predestination. Yet Wesley, having no better alternative, rejected it altogether.

Sanctification

Just as justification is the continuous work of atonement, so sanctification becomes the continuous process of salvation. Sanctification is a description of regeneration and renewal. What happens in the process of sanctification? The saving act of Christ is apprehended by faith as justification and new birth. Suddenly all the power of that act is available for use by the person who has found the assurance of his own salvation. Wesley paints the picture: "The new birth is here described . . . The Spirit of God is the sole author of it. He does not help a man to regenerate himself, but takes the work into his own hands. A child of God. . . . is not renewed by the power of his own carnal will; . . . 'But of God,' by the sole power of his Spirit. In regeneration, the Holy Spirit modifies the old man, corrupt nature, and breathes a principle of life into the soul; a principle of faith, of sincere love, and willing obedience to God. He who was 'dead in sin,' is 'alive to God through Jesus Christ.' "[17]

Wesley claimed that Christians can have assurance of this process in their lives. The assurance gives no confidence in self, rather it is based on supreme confidence in God. This confidence trusts God as Savior. It proclaims that one can know that reality of personal salvation, not as a possession, but as the gift of grace, freely offered and freely claimed. This does not mean that any person ceases to be a sinner in this life, but that the force of prevenient grace can enter life and allow the hope of perfection.

The Doctrine Of Perfection

In 1764 Wesley wrote his summary statement which is valid today:

(1)"There is such a thing as perfection; for it is again and again mentioned in Scripture.

(2) It is not so early as justification; for justified persons are to 'go on unto perfection,' (Hebrews 6:1)

(3) It is not so late as death; for St. Paul speaks of living men that were perfect. (Philip. 3:15)

(4) It is not absolute. Absolute perfection belongs not to man, nor to angels, but to God alone.

(5) It does not make a man infallible: None is infallible, while he remains in the body.

(6) Is it sinless? It is not worthwhile to contend for a term. It is 'salvation from sin.'

(7) It is 'perfect love' (I John 4:18). This is the essence of it; its properties or inseparable fruits, are, rejoicing evermore, praying without ceasing, and in everything giving thanks. (I Thess. 5:16).

(8) It is improvable. It is so far from lying in an indivisible point, from being incapable of increase, that one perfected in love may grow in grace far swifter than he did before.

(9) It is amissible, capable of being lost; of which we have numerous instances. But we were not thoroughly convinced of this, till five or six years ago.

(10) It is constantly both preceded and followed by a gradual work.[18]

This gradual work is the practice of holiness, the lifelong quest to be 'in Christ.' Christian perfection, therefore, does not imply (as some seem to have imagined) an exemption either from ignorance, or mistake, or infirmities, or temptations. Indeed, it is only another term for holiness. They are two names for the same thing. Thus, every one that is holy is, in the scriptural sense, perfect. "Yet we may, lastly, observe, that neither in this respect is there any absolute perfection on earth. There is no perfection of degrees, as it is termed; none which does not admit of continual increase. So that how much so ever any man has attained, or how high a degree so ever he is perfect, he hath still need to 'grow in grace,' and daily to advance the knowledge and love of God his Savior."[19]

Aware of the dangers inherent in such a doctrine, Wesley feared that the voice of imagination would be accepted as the Spirit of God or that assurance might bring arrogance instead of humility. He warns again and again of the dangers of "enthusiasm" and of self-deception.[20]

For most people in the twentieth century perfection is a lost goal. D. H. Lawrence wrote: "The perfectability of man! Ah, heaven, what a dreary theme." To have individuals attain a level of perfection which would make them inhuman in this world not only implies a defective doctrine of sin, but also eliminates the very anxious, discontented and passionate qualities which make for benevolent change in the world. To keep from being laughable folly, perfection must be a gift and a goal for Christians—never an attainment or a possession.

If repentance is the porch of religion, faith the door, then it is perfect holiness which is religion itself. This evergrowing experience is completely dependent on the fusion of grace and faith. This process is the business of the church, the community in which Christ is forming and shaping his people. One has assurance, not of perfection (as Wesley sometimes taught), but of justification by grace. Perfection is never assured in this life (as Wesley often admits), but it is the goal of the dynamic process of sanctification which ends finally in the perfection planned for and provided by God.

Wesley was not a theologian, nor is a local church a meeting house for professional theologians. Yet Wesley resolved to become a "Bible Christian, and that, by the grace of God, not in some but in all points."[21] The emphasis of Wesley was on complete loyalty to word and spirit, without the fetters of doctrinal confessions. He found a full heritage, Catholic and Reformed. While able to criticize Rome, Luther and Calvin, he affirmed far more than he denied because he protested by affirmation. It is not a coincidence that his distinctive emphases: Arminianism, Sanctification, and Perfection, form the foundation for a practical ministry and a renewed church. He wanted to release the possibilities for a new birth in the Holy Spirit while freeing Christians for the possibility of a lifetime "in Christ."

Conclusion

Church renewal will come to every community of believers faithful enough to the New Testament to be formed and shaped by Jesus Christ. This was the experience of the societies of John Wesley. Facing a revolutionary, secular age, he put his trust in Christ and led an evangelical awakening. Not all of his methods are still applicable, but is is my conviction that Wesley's spiritual power can bring vitality to today's church, a vitality not limited to any denominational or theological posture.

His commitment to the Gospel led Wesley to form a social movement with the expressed purpose of transforming the whole of life through its organization. Amid the complexities of the twentieth century only such a corporate approach can bring success. Keeping fast to the whole Gospel and depending on the Savior for power, Wesley brought together the pious enthusiasm of the sects and a witness of social change. He made Christian ethics and a social gospel part of a life of spiritual devotion. His faithfulness abolished the artificial division between the secular and the sacred.

President Woodrow Wilson summarized Wesley's genius in his brochure JOHN WESLEY'S PLACE IN HISTORY: "The church was dead and Wesley awakened it; the poor were neglected and Wesley sought them out; the gospel was shrunken into formulas and Wesley flung it fresh upon the air once more in the speech of common men; the air was stagnant and fetid; he cleared and purified it by speaking always and everywhere the word of God; and men's spirits responded, leaped at the message, and were made wholesome as they comprehended it."[1]

It is my conviction that the same possibilities are with us, for Wesley's movement was not built upon a man's genius. Wesley himself considered it "a vessel unto honor, sanctified, meet for the master's use." (II Timothy 2:21)

John Wesley was a cautious revolutionary. He rarely acted impulsively, but once convinced that he was following the will of God, nothing could stop him. That would be his criteria today. Perhaps he would be cautiously symapthetic with the Manifesto of the Young Church at Chile, which was nailed to the door of Santiago Cathedral on August 11, 1968: "We want once again to become the church of the people, as in the Gospel, living with the same poverty, simplicity and struggle. That is why we say: No to a church that is enslaved to the structures of social compromise, Yes to a church that is free to serve all people, . . . No to a church which compromises with power and wealth. Yes to a church which is prepared to be poor in the name of its faith. . . . In Jesus Christ . . . Yes to the struggle for a new society which will give human beings back their dignity and make love a possibility."[2]

We continue to have a charge to keep. They sing:

TO SERVE THE PRESENT AGE
MY CALLING TO FULFILL:
OH, MAY IT ALL MY POWERS ENGAGE
TO DO MY MASTER'S WILL.

NOTES

PREFACE

1. Joseph Yeakel, "Our Identity and Purpose as a People of God," *Research Bulletin*, No. 19, (May 1982), p. 3.
2. James Pilkinton, *The Methodist Publishing House*, Vol. I, pp. 496–497.
3. Frederick A. Norwood, *The Story of American Methodism*, p. 259.
4. John Fletcher Hurst, *The History of Methodism*, Vol. VI, p. 1052.
5. Frederick Ayres, *The Ministry of the Laity*, p. 117.

INTRODUCTION

1. Frank Baker, "Unfolding John Wesley," *Quarterly Review*, (Fall, 1980), p. 45.
2. *Ibid.*, p. 54.
3. John Wesley, "Original Sin," *Sermon XLIV*, Vol. VI, p. 59.
4. John Fletcher Hurst, *The History of Methodism*, Vol. II, p. 955.
5. William Warren Sweet, *Methodism in American History*, p. 15.
6. Elmer T. Clark, *An Album of Methodism in American History*, p. 15.
7. John Wesley, *Letters*, Vol. IV, p. 189.
8. *Ibid.*, Vol. III, p. 191.
9. Francis J. McConnell, *John Wesley*, p. 9.
10. Harold Lindstrom, *Wesley and Sanctification*, p. 1.
11. McConnell, *op. cit.*, pp. 30–31.
12. Franz Hildebrandt, *Christianity According to the Wesley*, p. 10.
13. Thomas C. Oden, "Methodist Theology: Its Need and Promise," *New Christian Advocate*, (13 April 1961), p. 7.

SECTION I DISCIPLINES OF SPIRITUAL FORMATION

1. *Wesley's Works*, Vol. X, p. 119f.
2. Tr. Louis J. Puhl, *The Spriitual Exercises of Saint Ignatius;* Aloysius Ambruzzi, *A Companion to the Spiritual Exercises.*
3. Kenneth Leech, *Soul Friend*, p. 110.
4. *Ibid.*, p. 21.
5. *Ibid.*, p. 79.
6. Jon Sobrino, *Christology at the Crossroads*, p. 9.
7. *Ibid.*, p. 10.
8. Juan Luis Segundo, *The Liberation of Theology*, p. 31.
9. Martin Schmidt, *John Wesley: A Theological Biography*, Vol. II, pp. 25–26.
10. Robert Funk, *Language, Hermeneutic, and the Word of God*, pp. 11–12.

CHAPTER 1 SPIRITUAL DISCIPLINES FOR INDIVIDUALS

1. Howard Snyder, *The Radical Wesley*, p. 13; Journal, Vol. I, p. 467.

2. John Fletcher Hurst, *The History of Methodism*, Vol. I, p. 312.

3. *Ibid.*, p. 256.

4. Bruce Beheney and Paul Eller, *History of the Evangelical United Brethren Church*, p. 39; Frederick A. Norwood, *The Story of American Methodism*, pp. 105–107.

5. Hurst, *op. cit.*, Vol. IV, p. 329; Norwood, *op. cit.*, pp. 51–52.

6. William R. Cannon, *The Theology of John Wesley*, p. 63.

7. *Wesley's Sermons*, Vol. I, p. 153.

8. Albert Outler, *Theology in the Wesleyan Spirit*, pp. 81–82.

9. Gerald R. Craig, ed., "Introduction," *Works of John Wesley*, Vol. XI, p. 11.

10. Meister Eckhart, *The Fragments*, p. 239; Gustavo Guteriez, *A Theology of Liberation*, p. 308.

11. *Sermons*, "Justification by Faith," Vol. I, p. 112f.

12. *Works*, Vol. XI, p. 403.

13. *Sermonds*, Vol. II, p. 250.

14. *Letters*, Vol. IV, p. 90.

15. James Hastings, *Christian Doctrine of Prayer*, p. 414; *Works*, Vol. VIII, p. 343.

16. John C. Bowmer, *The Sacrament of the Lord's Supper in Early Methodism*, p. 25.

17. *Journal*, Vol. VI, p. 412; John Deschner, *Wesley's Christology*, p. 170.

18. *Works*, Vol. XI, p. 207.

19. Frances H. Tees, *Methodist Origins*, p. 114.

20. Leslie F. Church, *The Early Methodist People*, p. 163.

21. *Works*, Vol. VI, p. 81.

22. Frederick C. Gill, *John Wesley's Prayers*, p. 15; *Works*, "Forms of Prayer," Vol. XI, p. 216.

23. John Wesley, Matthew 6:11, *Notes on the New Testament*, p. 38.

24. *Works*, "Prayers for Families," Vol. XI, p. 250; *Ibid.*, "Forms of Prayer," p. 234; *Journal*, Vol., V, p. 461.

25. *Ibid.*, Vol. II, p. 464.

26. *Journal*, Vol. VII, p. 503.

27. Church, *op. cit.*, pp. 268–269.

28. Thomas Keppler, ed., *The Evelyn Underhill Reader*, p. 107.

29. *Letters*, Vol. IV, p. 230.

CHAPTER 2   SPIRITUAL DISCIPLINES FOR SMALL GROUPS

1. *Twelve Steps and Twelve Traditions, Alcoholics Anonymous World Services*, pp. 5–8.

2. Robert Tuttle, Jr., *John Wesley*, p. 278.

3. Howard Snyder, *The Radical Wesley*, pp. 61–62.

CHAPTER 3   SPIRITUAL DISCIPLINES FOR CHURCHES

1. Wade Crawford Barclay, *Early American Methodism*, Vol. II, p. 1.
2. *Works*, Vol. VIII, p. 300.
3. Eduard Thurneysen, *A Theology of Pastoral Care*, p. 37.
4. *Journal*, Vol. VII, pp. 426–429.
5. Herbert Asbury, *A Methodist Saint*, pp. 77–78.
6. John Fletcher Hurst, *The History of Methodism*, Vol. II, pp. 579–581.
7. *Works*, Vol. V, p. 296; *Letters*, Vol. II, p. 293.
8. *Sermons*, Vol. II, p. 430.
9. *Ibid.*, Vol. I, pp. 284–285.
10. *Ibid.*, Vol. II, p. 445–446.
11. Leslie Church, *The Early Methodist People*, p. 21.
12. *Letters*, Vol. I, pp. 218–219.
13. *Journal*, Vol. V, p. 230.
14. *Works*, Vol. VII, p. 63.
15. *Journal*, Vol. I, p. 340; *Ibid.*, Vol. V, pp. 171–172.
16. *Sermons*, Vol. I, p. 519.
17. Church, *op. cit.*, p. 149; *Works*, Sermon CVIII, Vol. VII, p. 217; John S. Simon, *John Wesley and the Advance of Methodism*, p. 21.
18. Church, *op. cit.*, p. 151.
19. *Journal*, Vol. I, pp. 231–232, Notes by Curnock.
20. *Journal*, Vol. III, p. 338.
21. Francis J. McConnell, *John Wesley*, p. 340.
22. *Journal*, Vol. VI, p. 188; Simon, *op. cit.*, pp. 289–290; *Journal*, Vol. V, pp. 360–361.
23. *Letters*, Vol. I, p. 3.
24. Robert Southey, *The Life of John Wesley*, Vol. II, p. 95; *Letters*, Vol. VII, p. 150.
25. J. Ernest Rattenbury, *Wesley's Legacy to the World*, p. 167.
26. *Works*, Vol. X, pp. 159–160.
27. *Ibid.*, p. 351.
28. *Sermons*, Vol. II, p. 132.
29. *Ibid.*, pp. 126, 142–143.
30. John Lawson, *Notes on Wesley's Sermons*, p. 206; *Sermons*, Vol. I, p. 206.
31. *Sermons*, Vol. II, pp. 135–136.
32. John Parris, *John Wesley's Doctrine of the Sacraments*, p. 21; Luke Tyerman, *John Wesley*, Vol. I, p. 147; *Works*, Vol. X, p. 145ff.
33. *Ibid.*, Vol. VII, pp. 15–16.
34. John Wesley, "A Letter to a Roman Catholic," *Great Voices of the Reformation*, ed. Harry Emerson Fosdick, p. 523.
35. *Ibid.*, pp. 528–529.
36. *Ibid.*, p. 522.
37. John Wesley, *Explanatory Notes Upon the New Testament*, p. 8.

SECTION II DISCIPLINES OF LAY MINISTRY

1. Howard Snyder, *The Radical Wesley*, p. 156; Paul Mickey, *Essentials of Wesleyan Theology*, p. 143; Bruce Behney and Paul Eller, *History of the Evangelical United Brethren Church*, p. 41; Wade Crawford Barclay, *Early American Methodism*, Vol. II, pp. 4, 76; *Journal*, Vol. IV, p. 199; J. Manning Potts, ed., *The Letters of Francis Asbury; Works*, Vol. VIII, p. 343.

2. *The Journal of Charles Wesley*, p. 7.

CHAPTER 4 THE UNITED METHODIST HISTORY OF LAY MINISTRY

1. Frank Baker, *From Wesley to Asbury*, p. 201.
2. *Ibid.*, p. 29.
3. John Fletcher Hurst, *The History of Methodism*, Vol. II, p. 562.
4. Emory Bucke, ed., *History of American Methodism*, Vol. I, p. 550.
5. Maldyn Edwards, "Laymen and Methodist Beginnings," *History of American Methodism*, ed. Emory Bucke, p. 57.
6. Baker, *op. cit.*, pp. 199–200; Frederick A. Norwood, *The Story of American Methodism*, pp. 66–67.
7. Herbert Asbury, *A Methodist Saint*, p. 115.
8. Hurst, *op. cit.*, Vol. II, p. 523.
9. Baker, *op. cit.*, pp. 58–59.
10. Norwood, *op. cit.*, pp. 68–69, 76; Winthrop Hudson, *Religion in America*, p. 120.
11. Wade Crawford Barclay, *Early American Methodism*, Vol. II, pp. 435–436.
12. William R. Cannon, "Education, Publication, Benevolent Work, and Missions," *History of American Methodism*, ed. Emory Bucke, Vol. I, p. 566.
13. William Warren Sweet, *Methodism in American History*, p. 168.
14. Hurst, *op. cit.*, Vol. VII, pp. 994–995.
15. Frank Ballard, "Psalma, Psalm 108," *Interpreter's Bible*, pp. 578–579.

CHAPTER 5 A PRACTICAL PROGRAM OF LAY MINISTRY TODAY

1. John Fletcher Hurst, *The History of Methodism*, Vol. IV, p. 328.
2. Kenneth Leech, *Soul Friend*, p. 176.
3. Saint Augustine, *De Baptismo*, 3.16.21.
4. Blaine Taylor, *Gee, You Look Good!*; Blaine Taylor, *No Golden Agers Here.*
5. George Lawton, *The Shropshire Saint*, p. 31.
6. *Letters*, Vol. V, p. 187; Maximin Piette, *John Wesley in the Evolution of Protestantism*, p. 390–391; Hurst, *op. cit.*, Vol. V, pp. 485–486.
7. *Ibid.*, Vol. II, pp. 900–901.
8. James H. Cone, "Sanctification and Liberation in Black Religious Tradition," *Sanctification and Liberation*, ed. Runyon, p. 181.

9. William Warren Sweet, *Methodism in American History*, p. 159.
10. Stephen Charles Mott, *Biblical Ethics and Social Change*, p. 45.
11. Frank Baker, *From Wesley to Asbury*, pp. 72–73.
12. Wade Crawford Barclay, *Early American Methodism*, Vol. II, p. 26.
13. Hurst, *op. cit.*, Vol. II, p. 534.
14. *Ibid.*, p. 535.
15. John K. Fairbank and William R. Hutchinson, eds., *The Missionary Experience in China and America*, p. 395.
16. Lambertus Jacobus van Hollk, "From Arminius to Arminianism in Dutch Theology," *Man's Faith and Freedom*, ed. Gerald McCulloh, p. 34.
17. Mina and Arthur Klein, *Kathe Kollwitz*, p. 1.
18. Gilbert Highet, "An Iconography of Heavenly Beings," *Horizon*, (Nov. 1960), pp. 28–29.
19. Charles J. Connick, "Windows of Old France," *International Stuio*, (Jan. 1924), pp. 327–328; Johan Huizinga, *The Waning of the Middle Ages*, p. 269; G. G. Coulton, *Five Centuries of Religion*, Vol. II, p. 138ff.
20. E. H. Gombrich, *The Story of Art*, p. 115.
21. William Ayrshire, "The Crucifix and Western Art," *The International Studio*, (Oct. 1927), pp. 30–32.
22. Huizinga, *op. cit.*, p. 267.
23. Clement Greenberg, *Art and Culture*, pp. 16–17; G. G. Coulton, *Art and the Reformation*, p. 73.
24. Jacques Maritain, *Modern Sacred Art and the Church at Assy*, p. 26.
25. Jurg Spiller, *Klee*, pp. 12–13.

SECTION III   THE DISCIPLINES OF ORDAINED MINISTRY
CHAPTER 6   THE RENEWAL OF THE CLERGY

1. *Works*, "Predestination Calmly Considered," Vol., X, p. 210; *Letters*, Vol. V, p. 193.
2. Henry Carter, *The Methodist Heritage*, p. 14.
3. Robert Southey, *The Life of Wesley*, Vol. II, p. 84.
4. *Works*, Vol. VII, p. 185.
5. *Letters*, Vol. V, p. 4.
6. Colin Williams, *John Wesley's Theology Today*, p. 234.
7. *Sermons*, Vol. II, p. 120.
8. Francis J. McConnell, *John Wesley*, pp. 170–171.
9. Richard Cameron, *Methodism and Society in Historical Perspective*, p. 42.
10. Henry Wheeler, *One Thousand Questions and Answers Concerning the Methodist Episcopal Church*, p. 37.
11. *Sermons*, Vol. II, p. 121.
12. Carter, op. cit., p. 215.
13. *Sermons*, Vol. II, p. 121.
14. John S. Simon, *John Wesley, The Last Phase*, p. 182.
15. John Wesley, *Notes on the New Testament*, p. 641.

16. John S. Simon, *John Wesley and the Advance of Methodism*, p. 85.
17. *Works*, "Address to the Clergy," Vol. X, p. 484.
18. *Ibid.*, Vol. VII, p. 208.
19. Simon, *op. cit.*, p. 85.
20. Francis H. Tees, *Methodist Origins*, p. 91.
21. *Works*, "A Plain Account of Christian Perfection," Vol. XI, p. 437.
22. Robert Southey, *op. cit.*, p. 317; *Sermons*, Vol. II, p. 317.
23. *Ibid.*, pp. 511–516; Martin Schmidt, John Wesley, *A Theological Biography*, Vol. II, Part 2, pp. 204–206.
24. *Works*, Vol. VII, p. 29.
25. Simon, *op. cit.*, p. 210; *Letters*, Vol. VII, p. 222; *Works*, Vol. VII, p. 459.
26. *Ibid.*, Vol. VIII, p. 315.
27. *Letters*, Vol. III, p. 40; John Deschner, *Wesley's Christology*, pp. 74–75.
28. *Works*, "Thoughts Concerning Gospel Ministers," Vol. X, p. 456.
29. *Letters*, Vol. VII, p. 38.
30. *Ibid.*, p. 302.
31. Charles Ferrell, "Conversation with Francis Asbury," *New Christian Advocate*, (24 Dec. 1959), p. 9.

CHAPTER 7   THE PREACHING OFFICE

1. William R. Cannon, *The Theology of John Wesley*, p. 19; J. Wesley Bready, *England Before and After Wesley*, pp. 90–91.
2. *Letters*, Vol. II, p. 264.
3. *Journal*, Vol. I, p. 60, Introduction by Curnock.
4. Richard Watson, *The Life of the Rev. John Wesley*, p. 294.
5. *Sermons*, Vol. I, pp. 17–18.
6. *Journal*, October 14, 1738, Vol. II, p. 125.
7. *Letters*, Vol. V, p. 121.
8. John Lawson, *Notes on Wesley's Sermons*, p. 1.
9. *Sermons*, Vol. I, p. 30.
10. *Works*, Vol. VIII, p. 317.
11. *Letters*, Vol. IV, p. 122.
12. Robert Southey, *The Life of Wesley*, Vol. I, pp. 294–295.
13. Wade Crawford Barclay, *Early American Methodism*, Vol. I, p. xvi.
14. Horton Davies, *Worship and Theology in England*, p. 160.
15. *Journal*, April 22, 1772, Vol. V, p. 455; *Letters*, "To Ebenezer Blackwell," Vol. III, p. 79.
16. *Ibid.*, "To Mrs. Bennis," Vol. V, p. 291; Franz Hildebrandt, *Christianity According to the Wesleys*, pp. 59–60.
17. David C. Steinmetz, *Reformers in the Wings*, p. 49.
18. Hildebrandt, *op. cit.*, p. 11–12.

CHAPTER 8   THE SACRAMENTAL OFFICE

1. Ole Borgen, *John Wesley on the Sacraments: A Theological Study*, p. 47.

2. *Ibid.*, pp. 217–221.
3. *Works*, "Treatise on Baptism," Vol. X, p. 193.
4. Henry Wheeler, *One Thousand Questions and Answers Concerning the Methodist Episcopal Church*, p. 144; *Ibid.*, p. 28.
5. Ernst Troeltsch, *The Social Teaching of the Christian Church*, Vol. II, pp. 722–723.
6. *Works*, Vol. XXVI, p. 269; Henry E. Jacobs, Introduction to Luther's "A Treatise on the Holy Sacrament of Baptism," Vol. I, (1519), pp. 54–55.
7. John Wesley, Matthew 3:6, *Notes on the New Testament*, p. 22; Carl Michalson, "Why Methodists Baptize," *New Christian Advocate*, (June 1958), pp. 19–20.
8. John R. Parris, *John Wesley's Doctrine of the Sacraments*, p. 62.
9. H. B. Workman, *Methodism*, pp. 108–109.
10. *Works*, Vol. VII, p. 147.
11. John C. Bowmer, *The Sacrament of the Lord's Supper in Early Methodism*, p. 173; Wesley, Luke 22:17, *Notes of the New Testament*, p. 286; *Letters*, Vol. II, p. 282; Bowmer, *op. cit.*, p. 111; Franz Hildebrandt, *I Offered Christ*, pp. 180–181.
12. *Wesley Hymnal*, No. 125; Bowmer, *op. cit.*, pp. 106–107.
13. John S. Simon, *John Wesley and the Religious Societies*, p. 166; Wheeler, *op. cit.*, p. 339; Bowmer, *op. cit.*, pp. 170–171; Bowmer, *op. cit.*, p. 95, John Bishop, *Methodist Worship*, pp. 137–138.
14. *Letters*, Vol. IV, p. 272.
15. *Ibid.*, p. 66.
16. *Journal*, Vol. V, p. 40; Horton Davies, *Worship and Theology in England*, p. 206.
17. Rattenbury, *op. cit.*, p. 197; Bishop, *op. cit.*, p. 70.

CHAPTER 9 A CONTEMPORARY VIEW OF ORDAINED MINISTRY

1. Dennis Campbell, "The Ordained Ministry as a Profession," Quarterly Review, (Summer 1983), pp. 2124.
2. Frederick Norwood, ed., "The Itineracy, The Episcopal Address," *Sourcebook of American Methodism*, (1912), p. 562.
3. *The Book of Discipline*, (1980), pp. 107–109.
4. William Willimon, "The Spiritual Formation of the Pastor," *Quarterly Review*, (Summer 1983), p. 38; John Fletcher Hurst, *The History of Methodism*, Vol. I, p. 54.
5. *The Journal of Francis Asbury*, Vol. I, p. 76.
6. *Ibid.*, pp. 114, 122, 131.
7. Edward Eggleston, *The Circuit Rider*, pp. 206–207.
8. George Lawton, *A Shropshire Saint*, pp. 26–27.
9. Francis J. McConnell, *John Wesley*, p. 113.
10. Lawton, *op. cit.*, p. 27.
11. Hurst, *op. cit.*, p. 404.
12. Frederick Maser, *John Wesley's New Testament*, p. 6–7.

13. Wade Crawford Barclay, *Early American Methodism*, Vol. II, p. 296.
14. Gustavo Gutierrez, *A Theology of Liberation*, p. 118.
15. Hurst, *op. cit.*, p. 261.
16. *The Journal of Francis Asbury*, Vol. I, p. 10.
17. Henri Nouwen, *Intimacy*, p. 83.
18. Kenneth Leech, *Soul Friend*, p. 41.
19. *Ibid.*, pp. 41–42.
20. Hurst, *op. cit.*, p. 186.

**SECTION IV   CHAPTER 10   DISCIPLINES OF THE CHRISTIAN
CHURCH: THE MISSION OF THE CHURCH**

1. *Sermons*, Vol. II, p. 96.
2. *Works*, Vol. VI, p. 23; *Ibid.*, Vol. VIII, p. 299.
3. *Letters*, Vol. V, p. 7.
4. Henry Wheeler, *History and Exposition of the Twenty-Five Articles of
Religion of the Methodist Episcopal Church*, p. 19.
5. Leslie F. Church, *The Early Methodist People*, p. 100; *Works*,
"Predestination Calmly Considered," Vol. X, p. 254.
6. *Sermons*, Vol. I, p. 444–445.
7. *Letters*, Vol. I, p. 353; *Sermons*, Vol. II, pp. 25–26; Colin Williams, *John
Wesley's Theology Today*, p. 17; *Works*, Vol. VIII, p. 339.
8. *Journal*, Vol. I, p. 418.
9. *Works*, Vol. VII, p. 366.
10. *Works*, "Predestination Calmly Considered," Vol. X, pp. 226–227; *Ibid.*,
Vol. VIII, p. 300; *Works*, Vol. VI, p. 206; *Letters*, Vol. II, p. 118; *Ibid.*, Vol.
VI, p. 214.
11. Henry Carter, *The Methodist Heritage*, p. 72.

CHAPTER 11   MEMBERSHIP IN THE CHURCH

1. John Lawson, *Notes on Wesley's Sermons*, pp. 210–211.
2. Norman W. Spellmann, "The Formation of the Methodist Episcopal
Church," *History of American Methodism*, Vol. I, p. 221.
3. John S. Simon, *John Wesley and the Religious Societies*, p. 331.
4. Umphrey Lee, "Freedom from Rigid Creed," *Methodism*, p. 128.
5. *Journal*, Vol. III, p. 284–285.
6. John L. Peters, *Christian Perfection and American Methodism*, p. 53.
7. Millar Burrows, *Dead Sea Scrolls*, p. 24.
8. A. Skevington Wood, *The Inextinguishable Blaze*, p. 168.
9. *Journal*, Vol. V, p. 116.
10. *Works*, Vol. VII, p. 64.
11. *Journal*, Vol. V, pp. 404–405.
12. *Works*, Vol. VIII, p. 258.
13. Robert G. McCutchan, "A Singing Church," *Methodism*, p. 162.
14. *Sermons*, Vol. II, pp. 502–503.

CHAPTER 12 DISCIPLINES OF RENEWAL IN WORSHIP

1. *Sermons*, Vol. II, pp. 139–140.
2. Thomas C. Oden, "Methodist Theology: It's Need and Promise," *New Christian Advocate*, (13 April 1961), p. 8.
3. Nolan B. Harmon, "Methodist Worship: Practices and Ideals," *Methodism*, p. 233.
4. Richard Watson, *Theological Institutes*, Vol. III, pp. 239–240.
5. S. G. Dimond, *The Psychology of the Methodist Revival*, p. 122.
6. John Bishop, *Methodist Worship*, pp. 17–18.
7. *Journal*, Vol. VII, p. 18.
8. John S. Simon, *John Wesley and the Methodist Societies*, p. 124.
9. *Journal*, Vol. V, pp. 80–81.
10. Simon, *op. cit.*, p. 66; *Journal*, Vol. IV, p. 482; *Ibid.*, December 31, 1779, Vol. VI, pp. 266–267.
11. Horton Davies, *Worship and Theology in England*, p. 200.
12. John C. Bowmer, *The Sacrament of the Lord's Supper in Early Methodism*, p. 96.
13. James Armstrong, *Mission, Middle America*, p. 32.

CHAPTER 13 DISCIPLINES OF STEWARDSHIP

1. *Works*, Vol. VI, p. 138.
2. *Sermons*, Vol. II, p. 479.
3. *Ibid.*, pp. 463–464.
4. *Works*, Vol. VII, p. 20.
5. J. Wesley Bready, *England Before and After Wesley*, p. 238.
6. *Letters*, January 11, 1779, Vol. VI, p. 334.
7. *Works*, Vol. VII, p. 1.
8. John S. Simon, *John Wesley and the Advance of Methodism*, pp. 78–79.
9. Francis J. McConnell, *John Wesley*, p. 247; *Works*, Vol. VII, p. 286; John S. Simon, *John Wesley and the Methodist Societies*, p. 65.

CHAPTER 14 DISCIPLINES OF CHRISTIAN MISSIONS

1. Luke Tyerman, *The Biography of Samuel Wesley*, p. 431.
2. *Ibid.*, pp. 295–296.
3. James Stoughton, *History of Methodism*, Vol. VI, p. 13; John Todd, *John Wesley and the Catholic Church*, p. 55.
4. John Vickers, *Thomas Coke, Apostle of Methodism*, p. 326ff; John Fletcher Hurst, *The History of Methodism*, Vol. III, p. 1215.
5. *The Journal of Francis Asbury*, Vol. II, p. 751.
6. Wade Crawford Barclay, *Early American Methodism*, Vol. II, p.v.
7. William Warren Sweet, *Methodism in American History*, p. 204.
8. Wade Crawford Barclay, *History of Methodist Missions*, Vol. III, p. 377.
9. *Journal*, Vol. III, p. 24.
10. Luccock & Hutchinson, *The Story of Methodism*, p. 411.

11. Walter Lacy, *A Hundred Years of China Methodism*, p. 226.
12. John K. Fairbank, ed., *The Missionary Enterprise in China and America*, p. 358.
13. John K. Fairbank, *China Bound*, p. 87.
14. *The United Methodist Reporter*, (5 August 1983), p. 1.

CHAPTER 15 THE DISCIPLINES OF EVANGELISM AND WITNESS

1. Robert Funk, *Language, Hermeneutic and the Word of God*, p. 11.
2. *Journal*, Vol. II, p. 67; John S. Simon, *John Wesley and the Methodist Societies*, p. 33; *Works*, Vol. VII, p. 317.
3. *Sermons*, Vol. II, pp. 119–120; *Works*, Vol. VII, p. 21.
4. *Sermons*, Vol. II, p. 231–232; *Journal*, Vol. I, pp. 475–476; *Letters*, Vol. IV, p. 90; *Works*, Vol. VIII, pp. 269–270; Thomas C. Oden, "Methodist Theology: Its Needs and Promise," *New Christian Advocate*, (13 April 1961), p. 8.
5. J. Tremayne Copplestone, *Twentieth Century Perspectives*, p. 349.

CHAPTER 16 DISCIPLINES OF CHRISTIAN EDUCATION

1. *Works*, Vol. VII, p. 82.
2. *Letters*, "to Christopher Hopper," Vol. III, p. 148; *Works*, Vol. X, p. 482.
3. *Sermons*, Vol. I, pp. 133–134.
4. Frederick G. Gill, *John Wesley's Prayers*, p. 7.
5. J. Manning Potts, "The First Sunday School in America," *New Christian Advocate*, (16 Feb. 1961), p. 14; Paul B. Kern, *Methodism has a Message*, p. 127; David C. Shipley, "The European Heritage," *History of American Methodism*, Vol. I, pp. 26–27; John Fletcher Hurst, *The History of Methodism*, Vol. III, p. 994; Wade Crawford Barclay, *Early American Methodism*, Vol. II, p. 15.
6. *Works*, Vol. VIII, p. 266.
7. J. Wesley Bready, *England Before and After Wesley*, p. 83.
8. *Works*, Vol. XIV, p. 253.
9. Frederick C. Gill, *In the Steps of John Wesley*, pp. 72–73.
10. John S. Simon, *John Wesley and the Advance of Methodism*, p. 87.
11. *Journal*, Vol. VII, p. 21.
12. *Works*, "On the Education of Children," *Sermon XCV*, Vol. VII, p. 91.
13. Simon, *op. cit.*, p. 87.
14. *Works*, Vol. VII, p. 9; *Letters*, Vol. VIII, p. 247.
15. Thomas Langford, *Practical Divinity*, pp. 20–21.
16. William R. Cannon, "Education, Publication, Benevolent Work, and Missions," *History of American Methodism*, Vol. I, p. 574.
17. John S. Simon, *John Wesley and the Methodist Societies*, p. 293.
18. Eric Backer, *The Faith of a Methodist*, p. 103.
19. John Dillenberger, *Protestant Thought and Natural Science*, p. 157.
20. *Letters*, "To George Holden," Vol. VIII, p. 247.

CHAPTER 17 DISCIPLINES OF PASTORAL CARE

1. *Sermons*, Vol. I, p. 153.
2. *Journal*, Vol. II, p. 52; Francis J. McConnell, *John Wesley*, p. 113.
3. *Letters*, Vol. I, p. 152.
4. *Letters*, Vol. II, p. 304.
5. H. E. Workman, *Methodism*, pp. 120–121.
6. *Journal*, Vol. V, p. 472.
7. *Ibid.*, Vol. I, p. 414; *Ibid.*, Vol. VI, p. 9.
8. *Letters*, Vol. II, p. 11.
9. *Works*, Vol. VII, p. 118.
10. *Ibid.*, p. 382; Leslie Weatherhead, *Psychology in the Service of the Soul*, pp. 26–27.
11. *Letters*, Vol. IV, p. 20.
12. *Journal*, Vol. V, p. 366.
13. R. D. Laing, *The Role of Religion in Mental Health*, p. 57.

SECTION V DISCIPLINES OF SOCIAL CONCERN

1. Richard Cameron, *Methodism and Society in Historical Perspective*, p. 25.
2. Maximin Piette, *John Wesley in the Evolution of Protestantism*, p. 458.
3. *Sermons*, Vol. I, pp. 381–382.

CHAPTER 18 ISSUES OF POLITICS AND PEACE

1. Harold Lindstrom, *Wesley and Sanctification*, p. 162.
2. H. B. Workman, *Methodism*, p. 64.
3. *Works*, "How Far is It the Duty of A Christian to Preach Politics?" Vol. XI, p. 154.
4. *Letters*, Vol. VIII, p. 173.
5. Robert Southey, *The Life of Wesley*, Vol. II, pp. 243–244.
6. J. Wesley Bready, *England Before and After Wesley*, p. 265.
7. John S. Simon, *John Wesley and the Religious Societies*, p. 150.
8. H. D. Trail, *Social England*, Vol. V, p. 410f.
9. Richard Cameron, *Methodism and Society in Historical Perspective*, p. 58.
10. *Works*, Vol. VIII, p. 265.
11. Hans Leitzmann, *The Foundation of the Church Universal*, p. 152.
12. *Works*, "The Doctrine of Original Sin," Vol. IX, p. 221.
13. Franz Hildebrandt, *From Luther to Wesley*, pp. 126–127.
14. John Fletcher Hurst, *The History of Methodism*, Vol. IV, p. 187.
15. William Warren Sweet, *Methodism in American History*, pp. 370–371.
16. *1980 Discipline of the United Methodist Church*, pp. 102–103.

CHAPTER 19   ISSUES OF RACIAL PREJUDICE AND ECONOMIC JUSTICE

1. *Works*, "Thoughts on Slavery," Vol. XI, p. 70.
2. Francis H. Tees, *Methodist Origins*, pp. 64–65.
3. J. H. Whiteley, *Wesley's England*, p. 28.
4. Luccock & Hutchinson, *The Story of Methodism*, p. 327.
5. *Letters*, Vol. VIII, p. 265.
6. *Works*, Vol. XI, p. 69.
7. Alfred North Whitehead, *Adventures of Ideas*, p. 31.
8. Harry Richardson, *Dark Salvation*, pp. 248–249.
9. *Ibid.*, p. 275.
10. James Cox, *Black Theology and Black Power*, pp. 109–110.
11. Kweei H. Dickson, "The Methodist Witness and the African Tradition," *Sanctification and Liberation*, ed. Runyon, p. 202.
12. James H. Cone, "Sanctification and Liberation in Black Religious Tradition," *Sanctification and Liberation*, ed. Runyon, p. 45; Martin Luther King, Jr., *Strength to Love*, p. 10.
13. Leslie F. Church, *More About Early Methodist People*, pp. 179–180.
14. Howard Snyder, *The Radical Wesley*, pp. 48–49.
15. Walter G. Muelder, "Methodism's Contribution to Social Reform," *Methodism*, p. 193.
16. Francis J. McConnell, *John Wesley*, p. 251.
17. *Sermons*, Vol. I, p. 310, Notes by Sugden.
18. *Works*, Vol. II, pp. 58–59; Henry Carter, *The Methodist Heritage*, p. 99; Reinhold Niebuhr, Does Civilization Need Religion?, pp. 104–105; *Works*, Vol. VII, p. 315.
19. *Sermons*, Vol. II, p. 315.

CHAPTER 20   ISSUES OF SEX AND AGISM

1. Frederick Norwood Ed., *Sourcebook of American Methodism*, p. 470.
2. *Works*, Vol. VII, p. 126.
3. Howard Snyder, *The Radical Wesley*, p. 126.
4. Earl Kent Brown, *Women In New Worlds*, p. 71; *Arminian Magazine*, Vol. III, (1790), pp. 329–330.
5. *Ibid.*, p. 74.
6. *Ibid.*, p. 78.
7. *Letters*, Vol. V, p. 257.
8. Rosemary Skinner Keller, *Women In New Worlds*, p. 18.
9. Dorothy McConnell, *Forever Beginning*, pp. 179–180.
10. John Wesley, *Explanatory Notes Upon the New Testament.*, p. 386.
11. Frances Willard, *Women in the Pulpit*, p. 56–57.
12. Mary Frederickson, "Shaping a New Society," *Women In New Worlds*, pp. 246–247.

13. Mary Agnes Dougherty, "The Social Gospel According to Phebe," *Women In New Worlds*, p. 204.
14. Norwood, *op. cit.*, p. 446.
15. Anna Oliver, "On Ordination of Women," *Soucebook of American Methodism*, ed. Frederick Norwood, p. 450.
16. *Ibid.*, p. 451.
17. Nancy Hardesty, "Minister as Prophet or as Mother," *Women In New Worlds*, p. 89.
18. John K. Fairbank, ed., *The Missionary Enterprise in China and America*, pp. 136–137.
19. Walter Lacy, *A Hundred Years of China Methodism*, pp. 224–225.
20. Wade Crawford Barclay, *History of Methodist Missions*, Vol. II, p. 254.
21. Daniel Mathews, "Women's History/Everyone's History," *Women In New Worlds*, p. 46.
22. William T. Noll, "Laity Rights and Leadership," *Women In New Worlds*, p. 219.
23. Letty Russell, *Human Liberation in a Feminist Perspective*, p. 85.
24. Blaine Taylor, *Gee, You Look Good!*; Blaine Taylor, *No Golden Agers Here*.
25. Robert Tuttle Jr., *John Wesley*, pp. 26–27; *Works*, Vol. IV, p. 427f; Charles Wesley's Birthday Hymn, CXC, v. 14; Hymns and Sacred Poems, p. 402.

SECTION VI   WESLEYAN THEOLOGY: AGENT OF CHURCH RENEWAL

1. Paul Schilling, *Methodism and Society in Theological Perspective*, p. 32.
2. Maximin Piette, *John Wesley in the Evolution of Protestanism*, p. 416.
3. *Works*, Vol. VI, pp. 246–247.
4. John Wesley, *Notes on the New Testament*, p. 9.
5. *Letters*, Vol. V, p. 364.
6. *Ibid.*, p. 264.
7. George Croft Cell, *The Rediscovery of John Wesley*, p. 361.
8. *Works*, Vol. VII, p. 316.
9. Schilling, *op. cit.*, p. 67.
10. *Letters*, Vol. III, p. 117.
11. John M. Todd, *John Wesley and the Catholic Church*, p. 85.
12. *Letters*, Vol. IV, p. 298.
13. *Works*, Vol. VII, pp. 380–381.
14. John Deschner, *Wesley's Christology*, p. 172.
15. *Works*, Vol. 10, pp. 359–360.
16. *Sermons*, Vol. I, pp. 244–245.
17. *Works*, Vol. IX, pp. 404–405.
18. *Ibid.*, Vol. XI, p. 441.
19. *Ibid.*, Vol. VI, p. 5.

20. *Sermons*, Vol. I, pp. 202–203; *Letters*, Vol. V, p. 18.
21. *Letters*, Vol. V, p. 54.

CONCLUSION

1. Paul Kern, *Methodism has a Message*, p. 7.
2. Alain Gheerbrandt, *The Rebel Church in Latin America*, pp. 63–64.

Blaine Taylor

Blaine Taylor currently serves as district superintendent in the Southern New England Conference of the United Methodist Church. Before accepting appointment to that position, Blaine pastored a number of parishes in the New England area and has been a pioneer in ecumenical relationships. In 1963 Richard Cardinal Cushing became the first Roman Catholic Bishop in history to preach in the sanctuary of a Protestant Church; he came to the Sudbury United Methodist Church at the invitation of Blaine Taylor. While Blaine was president of the Council of Churches in Sudbury, that group became the first in Massachusetts to have Protestants, Catholics, and Jews as full participating members.

Blaine has spent many years studying John Wesley and his writings, and believes that many of Wesley's ideas and practices can have great impact on the church today. Blaine has traveled widely, including two cultural exchanges to Japan and the Soviet Union. He has studied with Karl Barth, Paul Tillich, Eberhard Betghe, Rudolf Bultmann, Reinhold Niebuhr, and Will Herberg. Blaine's previous books include **Black Power and White Racism, John Wesley's Theology Today, The Success Ethic and the Shattered American Dream,** and **Real Life, Real Faith.** His other C-4 Resources publications include **No Golden Agers Here** and **"Gee, You Look Good!"** (both of which deal with the church and those over sixty-five) and **Christianity Without Morals,** a look at the Moral Majority.

He is an active member of numerous denominational and ecumenical organizations at the regional, national, and world levels. He is deeply committed to ecumenical endeavors and to the strengthening of the local church.